DISCARD

THE CONFLICT SOCIETY

KALMAN H. SILVERT

THE
CONFLICT SOCIETY

Reaction and Revolution
in Latin America

Revised Edition

HARPER COLOPHON BOOKS
Harper & Row, Publishers
New York and Evanston

Chapter 2: "National Political Change in Latin America" by K. H. Silvert was published in *The United States and Latin America*, edited by Herbert L. Matthews. Reprinted with the permission of the publishers, Prentice-Hall, Inc., Englewood Cliffs, N.J. © 1963 by The American Assembly, Columbia University, New York, N.Y.

Chapter 6: "Political Leadership and Institutional Weakness in Argentina" draws on "The Costs of Anti-Nationalism: Argentina" by K. H. Silvert in *Expectant Peoples*, edited by K. H. Silvert. Reprinted with the permission of the publishers, Random House, New York. © 1963 by The American Universities Field Staff.

Chapter 7: "The Social Origins and Politics of University Students" appeared as "The University Student" by K. H. Silvert in *Continuity and Change in Latin America*, edited by John J. Johnson. Reprinted with the permission of the publishers, Stanford University Press. © 1964 by the Board of Trustees of the Leland Stanford Junior University.

Chapter 15: "Hemispheric Relations in the Light of Castro" was written for a forthcoming publication of The Brookings Institution and is given prior publication here with the permission of The Brookings Institution, Washington, D.C.

Chapter 16: "Peace, Freedom, and Stability in the Western Hemisphere" by K. H. Silvert was published in *Alliance for Progress*, edited by William Manger. Reprinted with the permission of the publishers, Public Affairs Press, Washington, D.C. © 1963 by Public Affairs Press.

THE CONFLICT SOCIETY: Reaction and Revolution in Latin America. © 1961 by The Hauser Press. © 1966 by American Universities Field Staff, Inc.

Printed in the United States of America.

This book was originally published in 1961 by The Hauser Press. The revised edition was published in 1966 by American Universities Field Staff, Incorporated, New York, and is here reprinted by arrangement.

First HARPER COLOPHON edition published 1968 by Harper & Row, Publishers, Incorporated, 49 East 33rd Street, New York, N.Y. 10016.

Library of Congress Catalog Card Number: 66-20311

To my Family
in all its extension

CONTENTS

PREFACE

As this book shows, Professor Silvert is a social scientist who has not only a strong sense of history but also a firm grasp of the history of Latin America. This helps to explain why he has a rare talent for writing about the current problems of that area in terms that do not need to be revised with every change in the headline news. A striking example was mentioned in my review of the original edition of the book. Noting that it was completed before the Alliance for Progress took shape, I said that, nevertheless, "Silvert's analysis of most of the Latin American problems and situations relevant to the Alliance is so penetrating and comprehensive that his book ought to be made required reading for anyone who wishes to express an opinion on the subject."

Since there are few Latin American problems and situations that are not relevant to the Alliance for Progress, that was a sweeping endorsement of Silvert's book. It still stands and the present revised edition only reinforces it. Hence I am happy to find that, except for the omission of a very few of the original chapters and the addition of a few new ones, the book remains virtually unaltered, even in the chapter of "Conclusions." And why not? Why change what was so good to begin with?

The new chapters do not alter the original lines of thought, but rather project them to different situations—for the most part, situations that have arisen since the first edition. Particularly notable in this group, to my taste, are those entitled "Hemispheric Relations in the Light of Castro" and "American Academic Ethics and Social Science Abroad." The former provides a refreshingly new analysis of this most important aspect of *castrismo*. The latter illustrates Silvert's skill in combining the particular with the general—in this case, the notorious "Camelot Project" with the ethics and scholarship of American social scientists. I hope the trumpet call of this chapter will reach the ears of leading American social scientists. For one thing, it shows that ignorance among them is a principal reason for the disesteem in which they hold their Latin Americanist colleagues. For another, the

whole book is a compound of soundness, sophistication, and originality that any political scientist could be proud of.

As a historian who hopes he appreciates the social sciences, I com-
mend this book most warmly to other members of my guild as an in-
valuable aid in the study of Latin American history in the national
period, and, for comparative purposes, in the study of other areas
as well. We historians cannot let the social scientists do our work for
us, but, as we should have learned by this time, neither can we do
it without their aid.

If I may conclude on a personal note, I first knew Kalman Silvert
as a student at the University of Pennsylvania, and although most of
his work was done in another department, I am proud to think that
I may have contributed even a little to the training of a man who has
become one of the leading Latin Americanists in the United States.

Arthur P. Whitaker

Princeton, New Jersey
April 10, 1966

FOREWORD

The United States has not proved itself well prepared for the recurrent crises of the past twenty years in hemispheric affairs. Nor is there a respite from difficulty in sight, for no Latin American republic has as yet passed through the storms of the tag end of traditionalism into the self-sustaining growth of modernism. Partial blame for the spreading inflammation of the hemisphere certainly rests with the United States. No extraordinary perceptiveness is needed to tick off the insufficiencies of government and business in their Latin American dealings, nor does it require great acumen to see the attempts to bring greater business skill, diplomatic subtlety, and fresh policy to bear on developing countries everywhere. However, the vagaries of American politics have made this deepening of wisdom a sporadic and at times uncertain process and, more subtly, what remains even more uncertain is whether improved techniques in themselves will produce more desirable ends or simply more intelligent mistakes.

For the American scholar to carp at the diplomat and the investor, though, is at the least ungracious in view of the shortcomings of academia itself. Aside from the fields of language and literature, anthropology, and history, scholarly work in Latin America has been erratic, uneven in quality, and inadequate to the needs of the country. It is only recently that the economist, political scientist, or sociologist devoting himself to Latin American problems has ceased to be a shady fellow to his disciplinary colleagues. And so social-science research in Latin America has not been traditionally attractive to the best of our scholars, nor are Latin American materials commonly used by non-specialists in the area. Now that the nation urgently needs information and analysis, there is little capital stock of mature, accumulated knowledge of Latin America's special circumstances upon which to draw. I do not mean to imply that there are not brilliant scholars in all disciplines devoting themselves to Latin America; my point is that the number and their experience are as yet short of what is needed to give us reasonably rounded and yet profound analyses of the array of social situations of the several Latin American republics.

Excuses are easy to find, of course. Foreign studies require a special set of skills and techniques in addition to the knowledge of theory and method normally to be expected of the scholar. The social scientist working overseas must learn another language so well that he can understand the subtle nuance; he must know the history of another country as intimately as that of his own in order to be able to feel the meaning of symbols and stereotypes, and he must recognize when his theory is alien and inadequate to what he is finding. Also, he must very often accomplish all of these intellectual feats in the absence of any antecedent studies or foreign colleagues of enough sophistication to permit him to hone his insights to satisfactory sharpness.

Another great difficulty—one inherent in the nature of the area itself—is that Latin America is not at all an easy theater of research but, on the contrary, is extraordinarily difficult to subdue intellectually. The twenty countries are disparate and growing more unlike each other every day. Worse, they are sufficiently European to look familiar and yet sufficiently special to defy their being forced into the standard categorical boxes of "Westernness" or "underdevelopment."

An inevitable result of this shortage of personnel, insufficiency of research, and difficulty of the material has been the development of what we may call the doctrine of misplaced excellence: the substitution of scarcity for quality as the criterion of value. Increased demand can be met with increased quality only after requisite training, the creation of a body of reliable literature, and the building of interpretative traditions. Now that the discomfiture caused by Guatemala, Cuba, the Nixon episodes, Venezuela, Panama, Brazil, and the Dominican Republic is fanning the interest of government, the private foundations, and hence of the universities, our specialists are experiencing the heady intoxication of being in demand and their resources are being stretched ever thinner.

In the social sciences we are not yet ready to proceed with confidence to shape complex comparative statements concerning the Latin American republics. We do not know enough as yet about such essential matters as, for example, class structure and political power, mobility patterns, and the educational establishment in relation to other social institutions. What knowledge we do have, particularly in the fields of politics and sociology, is of uneven quality and distributed almost at random among the twenty cases. Until such time as we have more data we must be cautious when speaking of the role of the Church, the functions of the military, the workings of the so-called "demonstration effect," and so forth. We are not prohibited from analyzing, of course; we simply must use more than ordinary restraint and make perfectly clear the paucity of our data and the tenuousness of our conclusions.

These limitations determine the manner in which Latin America is discussed in this book. My purpose has been to indicate what may be some of the critical variables that should be taken into account when one sets out to explain Latin American social behavior. I have not offered firm conclusions but rather have suggested some generalizations which may be useful to interested persons outside as well as within the scholarly world. I have tried, therefore, to raise theoretical questions of some complexity but to test those notions only against very specific and hence limited examples. Only in the first two and the last two chapters do I treat Latin America as a whole in order to present some idea of the entire cast of characters. Otherwise I have limited myself to writing about lands in each of which I have spent at least a year of research time. (Although length of time given to study is of course no substitute for competence, academic capacity is in its turn no substitute for field work, which is the only reason I mention the fact of familiarity with the cases chosen.)

My essential purpose here, then, is to mingle insights and intuitions with factual matter in order to help the professional to generate hypotheses and the lay reader to gain some conditioned understanding of an area certain to continue to command greater attention. I also hope that some of the intellectual excitement Latin America has inspired in me can be transmitted.

I have debated with myself at some length concerning what changes to make in this second edition. Some of my friends urged that I leave the book untouched, allowing it to serve as a necessarily dated record of fact, interpretations, and feelings exactly as they were initially recorded. Because some of my opinions have changed and because we now know more about some of the matters here touched on, other counselors urged a complete rewriting. I finally retreated into solitary contemplation and decided to come down on the side of those urging little or no change, but in a way which might satisfy the renovators. That is, the selections appearing in the first edition have been allowed to remain as they were except for a few editorial changes I could not stop myself from making. But I deleted four chapters to make room for five others which bring my attitudes somewhat up to date. In no case, however, did I permit myself substantive revision. The reader, then, will detect some contradictions—sometimes direct ones, sometimes differences in shading and tone. I have no apologies to make for these changes in opinion. As a matter of fact, I am rather proud of them.

Because the contents of this book involve research spread out over quite a bit of time and space, personal acknowledgments would be cumbersome and necessarily unjust to the many who would be perforce omitted. Let me merely extend a blanket appreciation to all those persons who contributed to my understanding and to the enrichment of my personal life. Because various American foundations cared for my economic welfare during my travels and have already been thanked many times in print, I once again express a general gratitude to them. I shall violate my rule against naming names only in the cases of Messrs. Phillips Talbot and Teg C. Grondahl of the American Universities Field Staff for having given me the confidence to extend myself into the essay form; they have been worthy colleagues and fine catalysts.

To my family goes my admiration for their being able and willing to survive the gypsy life which this book implies.

K. H. S.

Norwich, Vermont
January, 1966

PART ONE

AN OVERVIEW

One of the most usual of assertions to be made about the twenty republics of Latin America is that each must be treated separately, that they are all so dissimilar one from another that no generalizations are possible. Equally hackneyed is the assertion that there is an American "spirit," a quality of this hemisphere that makes all men walk alike and share the same idealistic notions of life and its purpose. Because this book carries the designation "Latin America" in its title, we must justify the implied presumption that there is utility of more than a geographical nature in the generalization. This first section, then, seeks to define in just what sense we can speak intelligently of a Latin America and in what senses we must distinguish among the twenty republics.

1

THE NATURE OF LATIN AMERICAN
UNDERDEVELOPMENT

Latin America is different from other underdeveloped areas. But economic statistics alone will not reveal the special nature of Latin
America's particular variety of underdevelopment. If one were to compare the vital statistics of Chile, for example, with those of Egypt, the
quite similar numbers obviously would not indicate the yawning cultural differences between the two countries.

More than in most other underdeveloped areas, Latin American
leaders accept a wide range of political and economic notions derived
from classical liberal thought. Because this process of acceptance and
amendment of European ideas has been occurring through many centuries, a Latin American style of analysis has developed not alien to
generic European thought, even if truncated and sometimes cheap-
ened. The style itself, however, is clearly recognizable.

These Latin American leaders do not act in class-bound isolation, for
social structures are usually sufficiently complicated to provide opportunity for the wide dissemination of beliefs across lines of social division. The subject of social structure will be explored at greater length
and complexity in several of the chapters which follow, but emphasis
must be given from the outset to the growing complication of Latin
American society if the special nature of the region is to be understood.
For the purposes of this introduction, however, no more is necessary
than to advance the proposition that in Latin America there are many
countries in which reasonably broad social consensuses are arrived at,
expressions of belief in popular sovereignty are common occurrences,

communications jump class lines, and elites speak for more than themselves. These phenomena are not usually associated with social retardation.

Because underdevelopment is essentially an economic term, to move across into the more general concept of "social underdevelopment" requires definition. This chapter, then, will concern itself with the derivation of an ideal type definition of social underdevelopment and an impressionistic setting of Latin America against this definition.

In establishing the following definition of social underdevelopment, I have specifically avoided questions of causation and even of temporal relationship of what may or may not come first. I have assumed a given slice of time and thus further assumed that these social characteristics coexist in absolute correlation *in the ideal or "pure" situation*. The specific choice of the characteristics themselves was made on the basis of social science convention, again in order to avoid questionable theoretical novelties. But they may be further justified by arguing that each of these hallmarks inhibits any wide range of those rational choices which may lead to capital accumulation in a narrowly economic sense or to maximization of individual potential in the widest social sense.

No real types will fit exactly into this ideal type statement, of course. There are, after all, degrees of economic underdevelopment and also degrees of difference in the social concomitants of such an economic situation. The very purpose of this type of analysis is to provide a scale along which the differences may be measured. If Burma, for example, should have the same per capita income, say, as Paraguay, it may fit more or fewer of these social characteristics than Paraguay, or it may answer to yet other ones.

Any given economic index can be in correlation with a spread of probabilities with respect to other social characteristics, but the spread is not infinite. In politics, for example, an underdeveloped country cannot have an individualistic democracy, nor can it support a modern totalitarianism. But underdeveloped nations can have a wide variety of elites, many differing ways of changing governors, and many varying traditions concerning political mobility or rigidity. If a country with a per capita income of $200.00 consistently leans toward one side of the array of probabilities, while another with the same income just as consistently leans toward the other, then their types of social underdevelopment are certainly substantively different.

A reasonable hypothesis concerning Latin America may be as follows: because this region is a part of the Western cultural continuum, its social underdevelopment is less pronounced than its economic underdevelopment; thus an exaggerated part of its value structure and its knowledge is gained as a kind of unearned income in greater degree than other extra-Western areas because of its historically higher receptive ability. As a corollary, when Latin American countries choose methods for modernizing their economies, there is less resistance to European norms than in most other parts of the underdeveloped world.

Following are some of the characteristics of "classical social underdevelopment" in societies intermediate between the village and the nation state:

1. Bi-class societies of a very rudimentary sort are usual in geographically extended underdeveloped areas. A small ruling group, native or superordinate European, makes the few decisions necessary at the so-called "national" or colonial levels. Sometimes a skeletal artisan and service occupational middle group will exist, but of course it will lack the social values of what we are accustomed to think of as a middle class. Where caste systems prevail, oligarchical rule also still pertains.

2. Consistent with this social structural pattern, politics tend to be crudely paternalistic, perhaps even gerontocratic. Economic, social, and political powers are grouped in the same hands at any level above the village.

3. Incipient or actual clash exists between native and European culture groups, whether the latter be represented by colonial administrators, business undertakings, or by an established or aspiring elite seeking to impose new modalities.

4. Again consistent with the above characteristics, extremes in the distribution of wealth are to be found; the poverty is of the usual rural variety while the wealth is Byzantine.

5. Occupational skills are few in number, in itself a factor very inhibiting to social mobility and economic development.

6. Population tends to be stable.

7. Population controls are "natural," ranging from high infant mortality to hunger cycles.

8. Where there are racial distinctions, caste or caste-like rankings emerge.

9. Social cohesion is based on loyalty to kin and class group, rather than on feelings of national identification.

10. Education is modeled on foreign example for the elite, who usually go to Europe or the United States for their university training, and is extremely rudimentary or nonexistent for the remainder.

Some Latin American regions fit all of these defined attributes; certainly Indian culture areas are closely apposite. But it must be emphasized that without exception these Indian regions are enclaves within political nations and that the process of Indian acculturation is accelerating, the speed determined by the ability of non-Indian parts of the population to absorb the autochthonous groups. If racially distinct regions on the one hand and such national exceptions as Haiti, on the other, are momentarily left out of consideration, certain valid generalizations about the remainder of Latin America may be made. Let us trace "European Latin America" as a whole through the foregoing criteria to see how it may conform.

1. *Class Structure.* The closest one gets to simple bi-class societies is in Honduras and Nicaragua, but even there one finds an active service and professional middle group. At the other end of the scale, in Argentina, Chile, Uruguay, and Costa Rica, there are middle classes in an occupational, attitudinal, and political sense which certainly rival those of even some western European countries. The transmutation of the Hispanic tradition of service urbanization into industrial urbanization has gone very far in Latin America. Obviously this process does not proceed independently of the creation of middle social sectors. The cultural importance of Mexico City, São Paulo, Lima, Santiago, Buenos Aires, Montevideo, Havana, Caracas, Bogotá, and others simply cannot be forgotten. Nor do these major centers exist in isolation, for the many other concentrations of 250,000 to 500,000 population copy the life styles and the attitudes of the larger metropolitan centers. This statement is true across national boundaries; San Salvador, for example, quite consciously imitates Mexico City.

2. *Politics.* The range of political phenomena in Latin America stretches from family dictatorship (Nicaragua), to rural middle-class democracy (Costa Rica), on to the possibilities for full-blown democracy or totalitarianism (Argentina). Since 1945 revolutions implying basic social change have occurred in the following countries: Guatemala, El Salvador, Honduras, Costa Rica, Panama, Venezuela, Colombia, Ecuador, Peru, Brazil, Bolivia, Argentina, the Dominican Republic, and Cuba. In most of the cases the long-run results have been to extend the possibilities for open and thus relatively more democratic politics. These revolutions are part of the process of social development and are not merely the confirmation of given pre-existing power balances.

3. *Native vs. European Cultures.* European culture values are dominant everywhere in Latin America, not any longer as a superimposition but as a phenomenon in integral relationship with the distribution of social power in the several countries. Where Indian elements still exist, the manner of acommodation varies from one place to another. But wherever cultural integration occurred, it has always been under the sign of nationalism as understood in the West. Culture clash in Latin America is not of the same family of events as in North Africa or in Asia. Latin America is, for all practical purposes, an offshoot of

late medieval Western culture in the process of making an adjustment to modernism.

4. *Distribution of Wealth.* In Latin America urban poverty co-exists with softer rural poverty, and wealth may be in television sets as well as concubines. Internal markets are strong enough in about one-half of the Latin American countries to support not only certain mass-production industries but a limited number of such modern commercial undertakings as Sears, Roebuck and Co. The widespread consumption aspirations to be seen in many Latin American countries are demonstrated by the fact that market analysis is no longer a stranger to local statisticians.

5. *Skills.* The complication of the social structure, the cosmopolitan nature of upper groups, and the availability of the printed word have combined for over a century in many countries to foment the development of service and luxury industries. The partial breakdown of the hacienda system and the development of modern industries provide mobility possibilities and incentives. There a wide range of skills does not exist, the active desire for such extension may nevertheless often be found.

6. *Population.* Rather than having a stable population, Latin America as a whole is expanding at one of the fastest rates in the world. Underpopulation and underdevelopment, but not unemployment, are general characteristics of all but the most inert of the republics. Everywhere cities are growing phenomenally, internal migration is speeding up, and birth rates are climbing dizzily. The present population of Latin America is estimated at around 200,000,000; by the end of the century, demographers predict that there will be some half billion Latin Americans.

7. *Natural Population Controls.* I know of no examples of hunger cycles in Latin America. Infant mortality and abortion rates vary extremely widely in incidence, not only from region to region, but also from country to country.

8. *Race Relations.* Practices differ widely among the Indian countries from the gentleness of the accommodation in Guatemala to the sharpness of the dividing line in Peru. Caste-like distinctions certainly exist in all countries having substantial Indian populations, including Mexico, but since the differences are almost invariably cultural and not physically racial, the resolution of tension never involves such disturbance as can be seen in Algeria or South Africa. Racial mixture has proceeded so far in certain areas that physical distinctions are no longer "seen," as in Chile. In other cases, such as Mexico, Venezuela, and Brazil, *mestizaje* is so much an accomplished fact that it has become popularly viewed as the ideal.

9. *Social Cohesion.* Extended families and strong feelings of loy-

alty to class and occupational peers are still very characteristic of Latin America. These buffers offer individuals one of their strongest protections against the vagaries of politics and constitute a major factor contributing to the inability of governments to be truly totalitarian in that area. But at the same time, sentiments of nationalism have been growing stronger, especially among the middle classes. The new expansion of the cities and restricted housing have also contributed to reducing the size of the socially recognized family. The patterns of relationship among the various levels of loyalty to nation, class, and family are of great social science interest in Latin America.

10. *Education.*   Significant strides have been made in extending literacy in many Latin American countries. The integrated population of Argentina has lent itself to U.S.-style aspirations, while the Mexicans have embarked on their own quite original manner of attacking illiteracy in Indian as well as mestizo villages with mixed success. At the top levels, even though foreign education is common, Latin American universities have an ancient and at times honorable tradition. Native educational institutions have a long history and exercise a profound effect on the molding of opinion and attitude.

What makes Latin America unique among underdeveloped areas is that it has shared many of the attitudes, aspirations, and ideals of the developed world on the basis of an economic situation which in greater isolation would almost certainly have led to other, more "standard" social concomitants of underdevelopment. The normal processes of reasoning concerning the usual paths of causation are thus of doubtful validity in Latin America. The common view is that an economic change gives rise to an occupational shift, which in turn affects the social hierarchy, the last reflection being in politics. This single-line chain is always questionable; in Latin America it is untenable. To the contrary, one of the manners in which social change has occurred in Latin America is along the following line: change of ideology in Europe, carry-over to Latin America and readaptation by local intellectuals, translation of the notions into political terms, change in the political institution, and then a political attempt to implement economic and social policies. I do not mean to imply that culture shift has not also resulted from technological change, or that the circle has not been broken into at the level even of warfare. There have been many processes at work, but the ability to import a notion and then use tutelary politics to implement it is a long-standing tradition of the area.

These habits of emulation are no longer confined to a small, oligarchical elite. The historic identification with the European world has already been transmitted to imposingly important middle classes and even, in a substantial number of cases (Argentina, Uruguay, Chile,

Costa Rica, Mexico, Cuba, Venezuela, Colombia, and Brazil,) is shared by members of the lower socioeconomic categories.

In this book we shall be dealing with opening societies, with transitional countries burdened with a long and arduous history of this very process of transition. Complexity and asymmetry—and not simplicity —are the reigning characteristics of Latin America's underdevelopment.

2

NATIONAL POLITICAL CHANGE IN

LATIN AMERICA

The United States and the Western world as a whole shower Latin America with a persistent stream of cultural stimuli. But even though the West's ideas of industrialization, expanded consumption, and political egalitarianism pour forth equally for all Latin American countries, what is absorbed varies widely from one to another. How and why and toward what immediate ends each nation moves is conditioned by its own traditions and appreciations as well as by the historical course of its particular set of involvements with the technology, ideologies, and cultures of the industrially advanced nations. The recurrent crises of most Latin American countries today are of a type symptomatic of a beginning maturity, a ripening understanding of what they want, and of what methods they will use. Thus the recently alerted awareness in the United States of the problems of Latin America is not a simple passage from unthinking Yankee neglect to fatherly notice. It is the direct product of a now purposively and rapidly reacting group of newly synthesizing societies gaining the power to force themselves on world attention.

That the internal dynamics of the Latin American countries are in part driven by the general cultural stance of the United States as well as by military aid, investments, and loans is obvious. Wittingly or not, then, the United States in the past has had much to do with the social changes which in turn are bringing Latin America new international notice. And indeed, with the inauguration of the Alliance for Progress, the United States has undertaken a cooperative relationship for the conscious social development of Latin America—that is, for the the rational attempt to complete the modernization of Latin American life without running any more of the risks of violence and totalitarianism than necessary. Whether planned or spontaneous, the growth of national Latin American societies is carrying that region closer to the problem areas and value systems of the European-type states, but what has been occurring is not mere slavish imitation. The many Latin variations on the general themes of underdevelopment and progress toward modernism may well eventually demonstrate to other parts of the world broad and varied possibilities in the decent and dignified adjustment of the individual to national social organization.

To lump the development process of Latin America carelessly in with that of other economically retarded areas is a mistake, as has been pointed out in the first chapter. Commonly available statistics force one immediate exception of consequence: Argentina, Uruguay, Venezuela, and significant social sectors of Brazil, Colombia, Mexico, Chile, and Cuba must be counted as intermediately developed. Even more important culturally, Latin America has had the longest history of European colonialism in the world. While it may not bear the stamp of Western industrialism, the area has a long and varied experience with a portion of European custom and thought not as a superimposition but as a deeply internalized aspect of society. Latin America's underdevelopment thus bears a direct lineal relation to idealized Iberian feudalism.

And, lastly, another unusual aspect of Latin America's position is its traditionally close identification with the United States. The intimate relationship has not always been of the most cordial, but it is there, and among the reasons for it are proximity, defense considerations, in certain measure shared ideology, and the leverage exerted by the great economic and cultural strength of the United States relative to the Latin American republics. Hemispheric readjustments from paternalism to fraternalism are a logical (although by no means certain) next step as political change in Latin America mingles with the other social shifts involved in the process of going from systems of necessary authoritarianism for most persons to those of possible democracy. These developments should be anticipated by diplomatic policy planners, for the period of one-man, one-family, and one-class government is just about over in a Latin America that is now doing much more than merely copying the standard recipes for democratic government.

THE COMMONWEALTH NOTION

The justification for writing about Latin America as a whole is that there are some universal concepts among the symbolic tools used by political leaders within and without the area. *Latin America, Hispano-*

America, Indo-America, and *Ibero-America* are more than terms of convenience, for the opinion leaders of the area themselves recognize an emotional commonwealth. They have hardened this awareness in unique international juridical principles, in a regional organization, in their voting in international bodies, in their preferential treatment of their neighbors' nationals, and in their constitutional theories. At this formally legal level, the United States, too, has expressed its recognition of a set of special circumstances through the Monroe Doctrine in its various interpretations, particularized recognition procedures, and participation in regional political and economic as well as jurisprudential arrangements. Special note should also be taken of the strikingly few cases of international warfare in this cartographically Balkanized region, a phenomenon which finds one of its better explanations in the notion of a certain commonwealth identification.

From the historical facts of politics there emerge other likenesses further serving to tie the republics together. If the common experience of colonialism stamped some similar hallmarks, whether the metropolitan power was France, Portugal, or Spain, so did the fact of independence, sweeping through all of Latin America, except for Cuba and Panama, in the same chronological period and under the same ideological banners borrowed from the United States and France. Every country underwent a "time of trouble" after independence, and every one has had at least one great integrating dictator, whether named Díaz, Portales, Rosas, or Carrera. These men are to Latin America as Louis XIV was to France or Ivan the Terrible to Russia: they broke the independent power of the local *caciques* and established centralized control over the territories of their nascent nation-states. Where the integrating centralists could not extend their effective sway to appreciable distances, city-states emerged, as in Central America.

This forced integration almost always was loaded with ideological freight. The *caudillo,* authoritarian leader of a geographically national arena, sought legitimacy in law and authority in party, while he used naked power to break the isolation of the local *caciques.* Although *caudillismo* naturally conduces to the personalistic political parties so widespread in Latin America, conflicting idealisms have also been present. The Conservative-Liberal divisions of the last century, and in some countries even of this century, have echoed true policy and interest clashes as well as mere personality differences. The *caudillo,* then, often has been the personification of ideological disagreement, manipulating the power of the idea as well as the sword.

In contemporary Latin America, the emergence of impersonal political institutions is everywhere clearly visible to one or another degree. Bound into a democratic bundle, economic development, nationalism, institutionalization, and modernism are widely generalized goals. These common aspirations and a common dependence on a common world buttress the fraternal feelings of the commonwealth notion.

HISTORICAL RANGE OF POLITICAL DIFFERENCE

A factor weakening feelings of hemispheric identification, however, is that these sentiments are restricted largely to élite leadership groups whose ideas are projected against much political divergence and large sectors of non-participant persons alienated for one or another reason from the mainstream of the nation. In addition, variation among the countries is becoming accentuated as individual national histories become an increasingly strong force pushing the Latin American republics ever further apart into differing political cultures and styles. They are all somewhere along the continuum to democratic nation-state status, but accident, history, and resources combine in differing ways to produce varying results.

Independence sometimes came easily, for example, as in the case of Central America, heir to the greater efforts in Mexico. But in Mexico itself, the independence movement was confounded with social revolution, and the process was painful and relatively protracted. The succeeding times of trouble also varied widely in intensity and duration, from the relatively easy transition of Argentina to the fifty years of convulsion in Mexico. Where the integrating dictatorship came early, as in Chile, national life subsequently has tended to develop with comparative ease; yet other countries, such as Venezuela, show a procession of *caudillos* persisting into yesterday's headlines. The Liberal-Conservative conflicts were usually fairly well resolved everywhere by the turn of the century, the Liberals almost invariably victorious either partially or completely. The major exception is Colombia, where the issue is still not settled. Colombia, in fact, remains the only important country in which the two major parties still bear the names *Liberal* and *Conservative*.

National revindication, social justice, economic independence, anti-imperialism, industrialization, and *nationalism* are the words of the current Latin political lexicon everywhere. But they do not have the same tone in every country, nor even within each set of national boundaries does this vocabulary permeate all the population strata. Although the generalized aspirations of the leadership elements may have ingredients in common, the development of an adequate American policy vis-à-vis the entire area must take into account not only the vast differences of the present but also the fascinatingly diverse manners in which further development is certain to manifest itself.

POLITICAL VALUES AND TYPES OF POLITIES

SOCIAL CLASS

A hobby of Latin Americanists, their hands forced by the variety of their area of study, is to develop sets of social categories within which to squeeze all twenty republics. One of the efficient ways in which to build a distribution is in accordance with social class, a most obvious feature of Latin societies manifested in clothing, speech, occupation, habitation, education, and of course, political power. The allied subjects of social class and social mobility tell us whether a society is open or closed and thus are essential to predictions concerning stability and the probabilities for democratic processes. Social structural analysis is also indispensable for an understanding of nationalism and potentialities for economic growth.

The simplest societies in Latin America are those popularly called semi-feudal, ruled by a small élite, the holders of major economic power, recipients of the highest social status and prestige, monopolists of the political organism. Under them can be found a shriveled administrative and professional group charged with the operation of the cities, the public service, and the discharge of the necessary professional functions, especially law and medicine. At the bottom are the peasants, migratory or tenant farmers, sometimes the owners of their own small plots; and in the cities, those persons necessary to the more menial functions. In some countries the lowest agricultural group is divided ethnically into Indians and other persons considered Europeanized, no matter what their physical race, by virtue of their speaking a European language, their wearing of non-Indian dress, and their feeling of being a part of the national life, even though most tenuously.

Guatemala is an excellent case of a structure only slightly more complicated than that described above. Of a total population of about three million, perhaps only 125,000 can be counted as effective actors in the reaching of political decisions at the national level. This figure is arrived at by subtracting the Indian population, those rural *mestizos* who are not truly national in their concepts, the illiterates, persons under eighteen, and a part of the female population.

At the other end of the scale is Argentina. Almost a third of the twenty million Argentines live in Greater Buenos Aires; and in the country as a whole, two-thirds live in towns and cities of over 2,000 population. About a third of the Argentines are in the middle and upper occupational levels. Except for scattered and isolated Indian and mixed rural groups, the population is European. Agricultural labor is not rooted to the soil as in Peruvian and Chilean haciendas; for example, farm workers and ranch hands may and in fact do make use of the channels of social mobility, forming one of the important mass groups supporting ex-dictator Juan Perón and contributing to the huge increase in the city populations of the past fifteen years.

Caste-like racial distinctions and a sharp cultural cut between the city and the country make popular sovereignty and the dispersion of political power at best a very limited possibility in such countries as Guatemala. The homogeneity of Argentina speeds communications, distributes aspirational goals almost universally, and promotes mass participation in politics for good or ill.

The velocity of Latin American social change—and it is in some fundamental respects the fastest moving part of the world—can create very complicated class systems. Mexico and Brazil, to take two examples among various, have what may be called double systems. There is an old and a new upper group, the former generally agrarian and clerical in orientation, the latter urban industrial and secularist. The old service middle class coexists with the new white-collar and professional elements, while the industrial blue-collar groups find little in common with depressed agrarian persons. Add the racial complication of the Indian populations of Mexico and this somewhat oversimplified picture is complete.

The most important class phenomenon from a political viewpoint is the rapid growth of middle groups. Rooted in the exploding cities and fomented by the complex skills demanded by the new industries, the expanding welfare functions of government, and the extension of the professions, the middle sectors are already the decisive voice in at least half of the Latin American countries. Their presence spells the doom of traditional *caudillismo,* but not necessarily the immediate and automatic stability and democracy which popular myth attributes to them.

NATIONALISM

An ordinary view of nationalism is that it is a negative sentiment, backward looking, exclusivist, anti-foreign, and at times even insane, as in Nazi Germany. A cooler reaction would be to think of nationalism as a social value elevating loyalty to a state and to the citizenry included therein to a supreme position. In the event of a clash involving, say, religious institutions or even the right of a parent to beat his child, a national society would assume ultimate adherence to the decisions of the state within a broadly prescribed realm rather than to the norms of any intervening, buffer institutions. Some of the usual historical manifestations of nationalism are citizens' armies, such symbols as flags and anthems, a public education system, reverence for the past as well as glorification of the future, and so on.

The creation of new middle (as well as upper and lower) economic positions, which occurs in developing countries, forces apart the traditional social structure, introducing the middle classes which are such a dynamic part of the new Latin America. These complications are at the same time rationalized by nationalism, a loyalty pattern to cover not only the geographical areas involved, but now also the new identifications across the class lines which build consistency and stability into the higher degree of interdependence that industrial urbanism always implies. Where there are middle groups, there is nationalism, the basic political organizing value of Westernism.

Despite a lack of reliable data, some informed guessing may be done as to the degree to which various Latin American countries have become truly national societies. In point for this subjective evaluation are such criteria as ethnic integration of the population, political history as it may indicate cohesiveness or disorganization, complexity of the city and the occupational range of the economic apparatus, degree of autonomy or dependency of the countryside and the political power of the peasantry, if any, mobility factors, and so on. Closest to nation-state standing in Latin America are Uruguay, Argentina, Cuba, Costa Rica, and Chile, and perhaps in that descending order, although to be so exact as to give rankings within the categories is to open the door to much wrangling. The next category might well include those countries moving rapidly toward nationhood with a solid social consensus approving the trend. Again in questionable descending order, these countries are Mexico, Colombia, Brazil, Venezuela, and recently the Dominican Republic. The third category includes those in which some upper groups are moving strongly toward nationalist objectives, but with sluggish response in the body social. They are Peru, Bolivia, Guatemala, Ecuador, El Salvador, and Panama, once again in dubious order. And lastly, slow rates of movement, with almost all social sectors stagnant, are to be found in Honduras, Paraguay, Nicaragua, and Haiti.

CLASS, NATIONALISM, AND DEMOCRACY

The social value of nationalism is a necessary condition for democracy but obviously not a sufficient one. Without it, however, the almost universal acceptance of the rules within which democracy works and the necessary belief in the reciprocating continuity of acquiescence and opposition cannot function.

> Democracy presupposes a toughminded and tenacious acceptance of the nation as deserving a continuing loyalty which transcends loyalty to class. Democracy assumes that the proper adjustments and accommodations among classes, probably accompanied by vigorous debate and pulling and hauling, will be made peacefully within the frame-

work provided. If loyalty to a class, whether a proletariat in the professional sense or an elite group, supersedes the common loyalty then democracy suffers accordingly.[1]

National loyalty identifications, however, are not sufficient to guarantee democracy, since the sentiment may also be employed for the implementation of totalitarian, as contrasted with authoritarian, rule. Totalitarianisms are so called precisely because they seek to destroy completely the institutional buffers between the individual and the state, to erase all non-state loyalties, and to void all doctrines propounding governmental self-restraint. When scientific techniques are not well developed, then the full weight of the dictator can fall directly only on the visible élite; others escape for negative reasons, saved by the sheer impossibility of the police task. With IBM machines, radio patrol cars, and modern propaganda techniques, the state gains the power to "finger" anyone, to minimize if not erase the cushioning effects of religious, kin, and class shock absorbers. If technological complication implies middle classes and middle classes imply nationalism, then nationalism in turn also implies possibilities for sterner autocracies as well as fuller democracies. In short, nationalism is a neutral factor, its color a reflection of other choices. It may be argued that full national integration so clearly demands widespread respect for the rule-of-law that all truly mature and self-sustaining nations must be libertarian. However, immature nations sometimes use the power of the almost-national state for anti-democratic purposes.

What we may call "political culture," notions of civic goodness and badness, the attitudes of innovating groups, and the pressures from the international world all contribute to throwing the choice toward more or less freedom. In Latin America, even the harshest dictators customarily attempt to clothe themselves in legal legitimacy and to talk in the name of democracy. This pose is not mere farce; it influences future action most importantly.

Latin American constitutions are an excellent case in point of the orienting power of expressed traditional goals. Over 200 constitutions have been adopted in the more or less 150 years during which the Latins have been at work on organic law. Most of the changes have been in the hortatory and the distributing clauses as one or another philosophy or this or that administrative gimmick has been experimented with. But the aspirations outlined in these documents have often served to condition the actions of future governments. As a Latin American jurist has said in commenting on the advanced theories contained in constitutional law, "After all, before you embrace a woman,

[1] Russell H. Fitzgibbon in "Pathology of Democracy in Latin America," *The American Political Science Review*, March, 1950.

you tell her you love her." Through the schools, law, the writings of impassioned leaders, Latin Americans have been told for almost two centuries that democracy is desirable. The writings of Locke, Bentham, and the two Mills, *The Federalist Papers*, the Constitution of the United States, and the Declaration of the Rights of Man, among many other such expressions of man's dignity, have all been imported to help in solidifying this predisposition. While the economic and social conditions in most of Latin America have not been of a type to support full-blown democracies, these political values have constantly served as a prod for the changing of the opposed root conditions. Small wonder, then, that the twentieth century is so often called the Age of Politics in Latin America.

It is thus no accident that included in the list of those countries which are most nearly nation-states are also to be found those usually considered most democratic. A noted American historian, Arthur P. Whitaker, suggests that "the countries which have approximated most closely to the democratic ideal have been—Argentina, Brazil, Chile, Colombia, Costa Rica, and Uruguay." A typology developed by a political sociologist (Seymour Martin Lipset, published in *The American Political Science Review* and subsequently in his book, *Political Man*) posits only two categories, "Democracies and Unstable Dictatorships" and "Stable Dictatorships." He puts in the former Argentina, Brazil, Chile, Colombia, Costa Rica, Mexico, and Uruguay, and in the latter all the rest of Latin America. While two categories are insufficient to explain all of Latin America, the reappearance of the first seven in high position on all three listings, "The National," "The Democratic," and "Democracies and Unstable Dictatorships," clearly indicates certain factors common to all. Nationalism plus the long belief in the value of democracy may well be in combination as the common denominator.

It should not be expected that such a fundamental change as the transformation of traditional societies into national democracies can occur without great disturbance.

THE USES OF FORCE

A Chilean political figure has written that some Latin Americans want "order even if in despotism" and that others want "liberty even if in anarchy." Before an ordering of liberty is attained, there will probably be much more trouble in Latin America. But the real amount of violence as such should not be overestimated. The number of revolutions in Latin America is accentuated by the North American, who tends to forget that there are twenty different republics all having their own troubles, and who does not understand the patterning of Latin violence, the often reduced number of persons involved, and the built-in limitations of the impact of civil disorder on daily life.

"Unpredictable" and "unstable" are the two adjectives most often applied to Latin American politics. The implications of both pejoratives are partially erroneous. First, to be "unstable" is not necessarily to be "unpredictable." As a matter of fact, one of the easiest things to predict is instability itself. And second, some types of revolutionary disturbance do not indicate instability. If the normal way of rotating the executive in a given country is by revolution, and if there have been a hundred such changes in a century, then it is not being facetious to remark that revolutions are a sign of stability—that events are marching along as they always have. A country can afford such adventures only if they are contained and if there are built-in safeguards against excessive violence. The right of asylum, recognized legally by all Latin American governments, is one of the insurance policies provided to cut down deaths by revolution. Top-level corruption—a kind of saving against a rainy day—is another of these insurance devices. In addition, very strong kinship ties, a sense of class identification, and colleague-ship all offer protection against the vicissitudes of politics. Many revolts, then, cost few lives, immediately affect persons only in the élite groups, and do not perturb the normal functioning of society.

In addition we should not forget that some countries have enjoyed very long periods without violence. Mexico has experienced peaceful political transitions for the last thirty years. Of the 105 years between 1839 and 1944, only three presidents in Guatemala occupied sixty-one years of the time. And yet, not to be too sanguine about the matter, some revolutions have been extraordinarily bloody and deeply disturbing, and there is little doubt that Latin American revolutionary activity is becoming more and more costly. Let us see whether some order can be breathed into this matter.

TYPES OF REVOLUTIONS AND THEIR INCIDENCE

There are many different families of violence, and their incidence depends absolutely on the type of society concerned. Here are the more common varieties, past and present:

The Simple Barracks Revolt. More outbreaks have been of this kind than of any other. Highly characteristic of the rudimentary bi-class societies, the army plays out the disposition of force, sometimes in its own name, or in that of a given leader, sometimes with ideological justification, and yet again in various combinations of these three rationalizations. The barracks revolt rarely causes much public commotion, even though at times substantive shifts in policy may emerge from one.

The Peasant Revolt.   Only in bi-ethnic countries, or where the rural group is maintained in deep subservience, do peasant revolts occur. They are rarely reported internationally, since by definition they take place in a restricted area and are not of direct significance at the national level. Very few are now seen, although they were quite common in the colonial and early independence periods.

The Regional Revolt.   Another type which now almost never occurs, regional uprisings were characteristic of the conflict period attending the rise of the centralizing *caudillos* and the liquidation of their provincial rivals. The history of Argentina, for example, is often written in terms of the "port," Buenos Aires, as opposed to the "interior," or the provinces. Brazil offers many examples, as does Colombia. Regional rivalries are now often played out in party politics through the activities of local bosses, who in many places have inherited the name *"cacique."*

The Complicated Barracks Revolt.   The commonest of all at present, this kind of insurrection involves civilian as well as military groups. The immediate events are largely in terms of military action, but the issues are clearly ideological and involve political parties and interest groups. The fall of Perón is a case in point, as well as the defeats of Pérez Jiménez in Venezuela in 1958, Rojas Pinilla in Colombia in 1957, of Argentina's Frondizi and Peru's Prado in 1962. This type can be somewhat costly in lives, although there are many examples (such as Guatemala in 1944) in which almost no one is killed. The issues may be entirely political, or the civilian participation may be so heated and widespread as to involve the attitudes and aspirations of social revolution, as was the case in Cuba with the overthrow of Batista in 1959. The Cuban example is on the border line, for although Havana fell and Batista fled as the direct result of an army defection, civilian opposition had previously so eroded the Batista govenment's power as to leave the military with little or no choice.

The Civilian Political Revolt.   Because of the active role of the military in politics, there is no abundance of this type of action. Chile, in its 1932 year of revolutions, saw the military discredited and many examples of entirely civilian action in forcing governmental changes. But this kind of undertaking becomes more difficult when the military are equipped with jet planes and tanks. The establishment of irregular armies and the practice of civilian terrorism were easier in the days when the rifle was the common arbiter. The general strike is the contemporary civilian phenomenon most closely allied to this category of revolt.

The Social Revolution.   The Mexican Revolution, at its most heated between 1910 and 1917, was the only relatively complete example of social revolution in Latin America before the installation of Cuba's revolutionary socialist Marxist regime. The Mexican experience combined all the other types, involving as it did simple and complex barracks revolts, a large measure of peasant protest and action, civilian participation at all levels, and regional disturbances. The result was to change the nature of the social hierarchy and partially to reorder it, thus, during its frankly violent phase, fitting the classical definition of social revolution. The Cuban Revolution, ostensibly fought in the name of the politics of Social Democracy, involved much less immediate violence than the Mexican case. But because of the more complex technology available to the Cubans, their extended communications network and relatively high degree of general economic development, and their susceptibility to Communist ideology, the social consequences promise to be much more immediately widespread and less evolutionary than in Mexico, and the tension of even longer duration.

Because of their failure to resolve many of the basic problems of even growth, all the intermediately developed countries of Latin America to one or another degree harbor the possibilities of social revolution, the most sanguinary and least predictable and thus potentially most dangerous of all forms of civil disorder.

Unstructured Violence. (1) The Street Riot: *Manifestaciones,* as they are often called in Spanish, usually take place to protest particular governmental actions, such as a rise in bus fares or the arrest of political or labor leaders. University students are very prone to this kind of disturbance; for example, the student riots in Mexico in 1958 and those in Chile in 1957 were both sparked by an increase in bus fares. Deaths are not uncommon in these incidents. (2) The *bogotazo:* This phenomenon takes its name from the mob violence in Bogotá in 1948, when the assassination of the leader of the Liberal Party touched off mass rioting resulting in wholesale looting, burning, and killing. These occurrences are undirected, a kind of explosive social vomiting. They indicate that the normal channels of access to the decision-making areas have been closed off for too long to bleed off protest pressures. The *bogotazo* is rare, but there are sufficient cases in history—and, dangerously, enough street riots which have had all the preliminary elements of the *bogotazo*—to make this category worth including.

Complicated barracks revolts, civilian political revolts, social revolutions and unstructured violence are all characteristic of periods in which the middle class is growing and seeking an adjustment. Those countries denominated as quite national (Chile, Uruguay, Argentina, Cuba, and Costa Rica) as well as those on the verge (Mexico, Colombia, Brazil, Venezuela, and the Dominican Republic) are susceptible to these types of disturbance, or already have partially outgrown them.

Since these nations have either large, complicated industrial cities or the self-conscious and cohesive landed peasantry of Costa Rica, civil strife is inevitably vastly punishing to major parts of the population, or at best a very grave threat. Bloodless strife is impossible to these countries; the best they can hope for, should they have recourse to revolution, is the stylized combination street fighting and barracks revolts of Argentina, an arrangement which may not hold even for that country should their troubles become more galling.

The more underdeveloped republics will tend to stick to the spread ranging from simple barracks revolts to complicated ones, probably with some peasant and regional difficulties thrown in, particularly in the cases of Peru and Bolivia. But no guarantees against a build-up to social revolution can be given even for the least developed countries, although the probabilities are against it. The uncontrollable factor here is the nature of international ideological and economic stimuli and the intensity of local reactions to them.

The prognosis must be for continued revolutionary activity in many of the countries as they shake their way further into this century. If Europe drew itself from mercantilism to capitalism by way of the French Revolution, Latin America is doing it by way of all those revolutionary conflicts in which so much valor, idealism, and youth are spent.

THE ROLE OF THE MILITARY

The military overthrows of the constitutional regimes of Argentina and Peru in the first seven months of 1962, as well as very public military pressure on the governments of Ecuador, El Salvador, and Venezuela in the same period, the role of the military in the resignation of Brazilian President Jânio Quadros and the subsequent change of the governmental structure in mid-1961, and hints of similar incidents in other lands—all have once again raised major international policy problems in the attempt to adjust defense requirements to the internal aspects of military organization.

The continuing intervention of the military in the politics of certain Latin American countries is a normal concomitant of oligarchical regimes, or of what may be called political underdevelopment. When government is the creature of only a part of the body social, the employment of overt force cannot be contained by a responsibly acting citizenry operating through the many institutions open to a participant and plural society. Even so, it would be erroneous to presume that politicized military groups in Latin America move in an entirely simplistic and uninhibited fashion. In carrying out their internal political policing functions, the military interact with their peer groups or with those to which they aspire. There is no divorce, then, between the armed forces and the social elements comprising the most effective civilian political groups; on the contrary, often the identification is all too close.

The patterns of military-civilian interaction change with the nature of the society and the development of the political value system. The historically first and simplest relationship is that described by the traditional caudillistic form, as in contemporary Paraguay, in which the leader is almost always an officer in the armed forces and uses this power position to cement himself into political office. Second, the modern variant of this practice appears when the military pretend to rule in trustee fashion but yet seek to sustain institutional forms and maintain a degree of impersonalism and aloofness from party politics, so that a *caudillo* does not emerge. This more complicated form of interventionism is what has recently become so popular, as the military assume the role of alleged defenders of constitutionalism and democracy. The governments which succeeded Perón in Argentina and Pérez Jiménez in Venezuela were of this type, and both prided themselves on their mission of preparing the country for the return to constitutional and civilian government which actually occurred. But Argentina has already witnessed another military coup against the person allowed to become president, and Venezuela is still perturbed by military elements from both the right and left.

A third variant is the military acting as the general orienters of policy. The Mexican situation is thus viewed by some specialists; that is, that the military defines the outside limits within which the constituted authorities may work, thus taking into its own hands only the ultimate tutelary role in partial control of the civil functionaries. The Argentine armed forces played this role in limiting the actions of President Arturo Frondizi from 1958 to 1962 with respect to the unions, communism, *peronismo*, and the Church. Closely allied to this category is the fourth variant, the situation in which no government can exist without at least the tacit consent of the military. Brazil and Guatemala are examples, at least for the moment. Any one of these first four situations is unstable, for slipping from one to another relationship is always a possibility unless social inhibitions against military interventionism have grown strong, as in Mexico.

Fifth, we find the military acting as a veto group only in so far as their own interests are concerned, but otherwise quite powerless politically. It may be that Chile fits this classification, or it may even fall into the sixth, in which the armed forces are professional and apolitical. Uruguay is in this last fortunate position. The ultimate possibility is that the military should be nonexistent. Costa Rica is the lone example, the only country in Latin America which has simply abolished its armed services on the dual grounds that the good citizen himself is enough to defend the country against any neighboring enemies, and that no one is able to defend it against the mighty nuclear weapons of the world powers.

Military intervention in political affairs is a long-standing impediment to the development of responsible government, a constant invitation to the dissatisfied to seek adjudication by bullet. Even though the military, armed with their World War II weapons, have not always been on the side of the devil, by and large they are a hindrance to the development of experience in the peaceful transfer of power. They can be hemmed in effectively only by the development of a complex of parties and pressure groups to orient the collective power of the citizenry. Certainly the growing complication of Latin American governments makes it ever riskier to entrust public administration to untrained and *ad hoc* military governors.

PARTIES AND PRESSURE GROUPS

PARTY SYSTEMS

The double class system already discussed also describes the dimensions of a profound clash between traditionalists and modernists that determines the basic nature of party ideologies in Latin America. In traditional societies individual behavior is prescribed for every situation, change is discouraged, and rigid hierarchy is adhered to in the stamping of all action with a moral as well as a secular sanction. Modern persons, on the contrary, encourage the making of deliberate decisions based in good measure on pragmatic considerations; they also seek to order and control change by institutionalizing it, and they strive for a pluralism and an eclecticism in social organization which tend to open society in answer to the demands for specialization and interdependence imposed by industrialization. The traditional-modern schism in Latin America is no less than the chasm between feudal and modern values, two dramatically opposed sets of world views.

The most important reflection of this strife in party politics is that consequently there are two different scales of Left, Right, and Center to match the two different class and value systems. The Right wing of the traditionalists is found in the classical Conservative parties; but there is also a little recognized traditional Left, composed of syndicalist and falangist elements who seek to contain the social and political effects of economic development by a corporativist ordering of man, imprisoning him within rigidly hierarchical institutions and denying him the kind of pragmatic individualism associated with liberal capitalistic societies. Thus traditionalists both of the Left and Right denounce liberalism as well as Marxism, and capitalism as well as communism, holding both the United States and Soviet Russia to be anti-religious and materialistic societies. On the other hand, the *modern* Right is normally composed of persons in the Liberal parties and in the Right wings of the Radical parties and other similar groups. And then the spread through Center to Left flows along the usual distribution of Radicals to Christian Democrats Socialists and Communists. This distinction between the traditional and modern concepts of Right and Left is of great importance in understanding the politics of such countries as Mexico, Argentina, and Colombia, which in certain characteristics of administrative organization as well as in the ideological constellation of important élite groups demonstrate the continuing appeal of corporativist solutions for the entire Latin world. Mexico's official party, for example, is a case in point of neo-syndicalist organization, as are parts of the Colombian labor movement.

What the parties espouse in terms of specific programs is also considerably varied. There are the well known "somebodyisms," the personalistic parties which identify with a charismatic individual. Thus arise such labels as *peronismo, batllismo, porfirismo,* and so on, referring to the conglomeration of attitudes, ideas, and loyalties surrounding Perón in Argentina, Batlle in Uruguay, and Profirio Díaz in Mexico, to take only three of numerous examples. An ideational tone accompanies these personalistic designations: a kind of Black Populism in the case of Perón; secularist, middle-class reform politics identified with Batlle; and the classical marriage of Liberal Positivism and *caudillismo* associated with Díaz.

Aside from propounding ideology and urging programs, political parties have many other functions, of course. They organize the electorate for their periodic interventions in decision making, if they operate within a democratic context. They serve to carry ideas back and forth between the government and the populace when campaigns and elections are not in process. That they also act as employment agencies is well known.

Not every Latin American group bearing the title *"partido"* is really a political party by these criteria. When what is called a party merely performs policing functions for a dictatorial government and serves as a housekeeping agency for the imposition of views from the top, then we are not dealing with a functional party. Of this one-way control type are the single party "systems" of such a country as was the Dominican Republic under Trujillo, or as Paraguay is today. The party is so closely identified with the administration that to be of an opposition group is to be subversive or even treasonous. Venezuela has also operated so in the recent past, as have other Latin countries in their periods of harsher caudillistic authoritarianism.

Mexico, however, offers the case of a single dominant party playing out its role without crudely repressive practices. There are opposition parties, the most important of which are the clerical PAN (National Action Party) on the right and the Popular Party on the left. Membership in these opposition groups is no crime, and they legitimately serve to organize dissident opinions. But they have no ability to win an election, even though they may campaign, publish, meet, and speak without interference. The PRI (Institutional Revolutionary Party), the official entity, embraces everyone from the industrialist to the government employee to the trade unionist. Sometimes it is argued that the PRI is analogous to the Democratic Party of the American South, in truth representative of many factions, with the real decisions among opposing views made in the primary elections. In Mexico, the arguments take place among the leaders representing their rank-and-file supporters, and then the party makes known its official position. PRI is not monolithic; it is part of the trust arrangement in which Mexico's development is held by the military, the intellectuals, the new economic élites, the trade unions, and the middle-class groups. Labor difficulties offer some hint that the PRI may eventually break into its component interest parts, but it would be a rash man indeed who would presume to predict when this split will occur.

Aside from the false and the real one-party systems named above, there are also a few two-party structures to be counted. Traditionally political development, as has been said, revolved about Conservatives and Liberals. In Colombia, where this division still exists, we have the most consistent case of bi-party politics. Uruguay, with its *Colorados* and *Blancos* ("Reds" and "Whites"), has been considered by many political scientists as not a true example of a two-party structure for the *Colorados* had won office uninterruptedly for almost a century. But in 1958 the Whites finally won a national election, and so we may presume Uruguay to be in the two-party class.

There are also mixed cases, in which two major parties contend at the national level, but a multiplicity argue over the municipal and provincial posts. Argentina is the most complicated case of this kind, for since 1945 only two major parties have presented themselves for the presidential elections. Unhappily for simplicity, they have not always been the same two parties. In 1945 there was the Peronista Party, with virtually all the opposition in a single coalition. The traditional Radical Party led the opposition in the hopeless elections of 1951, but later, in 1958, the Radicals split into their two historic blocs, the Intransigent Radicals and the Radicals of the People, they being the only two serious contenders. The Conservatives, Socialists, Christian Democrats, Peronists, and Communists continue to be forces of some consequence, however, so that Argentina is on the border line between a two-party and a multi-party system.

The electoral laws of Argentina, modeled as they are after those of the United States, including an electoral college, favor a two-party system even though social practice and the diversity of new interest groups favor a multi-party structure. Chile's laws, however, provide for proportional representation within the neo-parliamentary governmental organization established in the Constitution of 1925. The result has been one of the most stable multi-party systems in Latin America, running from Right to Left, from Conservatives through Liberals to Radicals in the center, and on left to Christian Democrats, various branches of the Socialists, and the Communists. The close similarity both in Chile and Argentina to the political spread of France and Italy is clear and is no accident, for both countries are deeply influenced by those two European idea sources.

The multi-party system of Brazil, however, is more indigenous in origin and orientation and also includes phenomena peculiar to the size and population of that huge country. The ideological distribution is strongly influenced by entirely internal considerations and is only peripherally liable to influence from abroad, while the extent and diversity of the country has been propitious for the development of sectional parties. Although these regional groups, or what are sometimes called "particularistic" parties, have died out almost everywhere in Latin America, including Brazil, the regional origins of a political party have much to do with setting present-day attitudes. The State of São Paulo has been particularly noteworthy in its influence on national politics through party mechanisms.

There is little meaningful relationship between formal party system and the social order, except in the most backward authoritarianisms. In those cases it is only by classificatory generosity that one can speak of parties at all. A better clue to political development is derived from party programs and approaches, rather than from counting the number of parties and relating them systematically. A reasonable hypothesis is that the more national a country, the less personalistic will be the parties, the more they will adjust conflicting interests within their own mechanisms, the greater will be their concern with institutional self-preservation and the winning of elections as a good in itself. As is to be expected, then, Argentina, Chile, Uruguay, and Costa Rica all have long histories of impersonal party politics, even though complicated by the traditional-modern value split. Castro Cuba rapidly succeeded in building a highly professional single party of authoritarian stamp, manipu-

lating the charisma of Fidel as a symbol, but otherwise quite impersonal for the Latin American ambience.

Professional parties coexist with single-interest and personalistic parties in Brazil and Venezuela; these nations are among those in the second level of adjustment to nation-state status. Mexico and Colombia,
heading the list of countries in the second level of adjustment, have
unique structures for Latin America, but their parties may with confidence be called impersonal, and broadly based in the interests they
represent, regardless of their ideologies. In Peru, Guatemala, Ecuador,
El Salvador, and Panama, the parties tend to be narrowly based, many
are short-lived, and in numerous cases little difference can be observed
between a party and the single interest it represents.

A preliminary non-public mediation of interest disputes is necessary
so that the electorate may choose among alternatives not at the level of
detail but of policy. Without an impersonal political party structure
aiding in the day-to-day mediation of disagreement, substantively good
voting is difficult if not impossible in anything more than a town situation. The weeding out of issues to simplify national politics is a major
party function which also has international effects. The introduction of
debate at the party level may slow down the process of diplomatic
negotiation but is necessary when a national consensus, rather than a
mere executive opinion, is required for lasting agreement on substantive issues. In brief, it is intrinsically more difficult to negotiate truly
important matters with democratic nation-states than with dictatorships. It is only good sense to make the effort, however, especially
when we recognize that the age of *caudillismo* is drawing to a troubled
close, as surely it is in Latin America.

MARXISM AND COMMUNISM AS SPECIAL CASES

Marxist thought and Communist ideology, as products of Western
philosophy attractive to the partially developed, have no market in pre-
industrial and non-national cultures. Naturally, then, the general social
and economic development of Latin America opens up possibilities for
the growth of communism as for the evolution of middle classes. Communists notoriously gain advantage in periods of turmoil, but only
sigificantly so in those upheavals connected with rapidly developing nationalism, or in cases in which social balance is denied by fanatical opposition to the full implications of the changes of development. Robert
Alexander, in his *Communism in Latin America*, for example, argues
that wherever a democratic trade union movement is allowed to flourish, the Communists lose their major source of mass support and are
driven back in upon their own professional core. He cites Mexico as the
most pertinent example, adding that in a period of national construc-

tion Communists may play a very important role, but thereafter they can be "withered away," to turn their phrase against them, by the open play of normal democratic politics. In formally organizational terms at least, the Mexican case seems most appropriate, for the Communist Party, although legal, has lately been unable to muster enough votes to get itself on the ballot.

But the play of Marxist politics in Latin America can no longer be effectively analyzed by an almost exclusive attention to persons formally members of the Communist parties and their fellow-travelers. The emergence of the "Marxist-Leninist" school of revolutionary socialism in Cuba has enlarged the scope of the revolutionary left by providing a living Latin example of a Marxist government, a training ground, and a factory of ideology. The effect has been to frighten less extremist individuals away from the revolutionary Socialist and Communist parties, but also to force a sometimes uneasy alliance between Socialists and Communists who previously had followed distinct policies and practices. The example of Cuba has also sharpened an awareness and recognition of the immediate necessity for a viable opposition to Marxist solutions, especially in the ranks of the democratic Left and Center. While the polarization has undoubtedly increased absolute Marxist strength in Latin America, the greater awareness of danger among opposition groups may have decreased their relative strength. The measure of the success of the Latin American role in the Alliance for Progress will be their ability to translate a recognition of danger into effectively affirmative policies of democratic development.

Statistically, the Communist role outside of Cuba seems small at first glance. Active membership in Communist parties is estimated at about a quarter of a million throughout Latin America; the U.S.S.R. maintains diplomatic relations with only five countries (Argentina, Cuba, Brazil, Mexico, and Uruguay), and Communist bloc countries account for only about 2 per cent of the combined imports and exports of Latin America. But figures of this type are increasingly misleading in assessing possible Marxist strength in Latin America. The fact that Communists *acting by themselves* have not the widespread popular support necessary to seize full political power anywhere in Latin America does not mean that rather more broadly defined Marxist revolutionary socialist regimes are not a possibility, as the case of Cuba has so clearly demonstrated. To quote from a prescient report released by a Senate investigating committee in 1959, and even more valid now than then:

> From the evidence at hand, the Latin American Communist parties are not, under normal circumstances, in any position to assume political power in any Latin American country. The exception to this general conclusion arises whenever there is a situation of political economic

confusion following the collapse of a dictatorial regime, with the new government in the hands of inexperienced and politically unsophisticated people. In such a situation, the Communists came close to seizing power in Guatemala in 1954. At present, Cuba may be following a similar pattern. . . . This situation holds danger—it can become a touch-and-go matter. Dictators may, and usually do, suppress the Communists—and the democratic political forces, too, as a rule. But dictators are no long run solution to the Communist threat. When the regime changes, and if democratic forces and traditions are weakened meanwhile, then the underground Communist group emerges as a potentially powerful force.

The Cuban example is all the more dangerous because it is not identified only with Communist parties; the Marxism-Leninism ideological tag was adopted by the present Cuban regime to indicate something native, something special to the Latin American experience and somewhat independent of the slavish devotion to Moscow which so long has characterized the policies of the Communist parties themselves. The Cuban line adjusts itself to the political configuration that often develops in times of nationalist revolution, when there is a tendency for all political groups of a nationalistic stripe to join for the attainment of their common national ends. This kind of alliance almost invariably takes place in times of acute political crisis involving all-embracing issues when polarization is the natural response to the utter massiveness of the issues involved. A similar coalition occurred in Mexico during the decade of the thirties, but the period of subsequent consolidation drastically reduced the advantages of alliance with the far left, with the results we have already noted. To broaden the base of the Marxist left inside the nationalist movements obviously increases their chances for consolidating the post-revolutionary regimes themselves as we are witnessing in Cuba. A distinction must then be drawn between Russian-oriented Communists and Cuban-type Marxist-Leninists to appreciate fully the new strength of this part of the Left in Latin America and thus the new task of the anti-Marxist opposition.

A third Marxist influence must also be noted—the vulgar Marxism, so-called, of that widespread and unsophisticated brand of economic determinism so common among educated Latin Americans. In areas where economic necessities loom large, where the example of the external world continuously pushes toward expanded consumption, to put primary attention on economic factors as the key to social change is only natural. The United States has also contributed to this kind of easy analysis by its past accent on only economic development and its ingenuous insistence that people with full bellies don't become Communists. It is not only Communists, Trotskyists, and left Socialists who have narrowly materialistic ideas; in an amorphous way, anyone who subscribes to the absolute premise that "Money Talks" contributes to a dime-store variety of economic determinism.

PRESSURE GROUPS

Interest or pressure groups are few in Latin America. Where caudillistic one-party rule holds sway, there is insufficient complication to give much room to variegated pressure groups. And where multi-party systems operate, except in the most developed countries, the parties represent small middle and upper groups and speak in the name of the economic interests themselves.

But still there remain some extremely important associations which can be called pressure groups. Foremost in rank is the Church, although some analysts go so far as to presume the religious institution almost an integral part of government. The intellectual ground here is very treacherous. Probably nowhere is the Church less than a veto group; i.e., it may not be able to innovate policy, but it can make action against it very costly if not impossible. In Ecuador, where the Church is at its strongest, it probably transcends veto status and can institute action, as it probably also can in Colombia. In other lands where the Church has great strength, such as El Salvador and Peru, it cannot act somewhat in the nature of a party as it does in Ecuador and Colombia.

Legal separation of Church and State exists in Brazil, Chile, Cuba, Ecuador, El Salvador, Guatemala, Honduras, Mexico, Nicaragua, Panama, and Uruguay. The Church is established in Argentina, Bolivia, Colombia, Costa Rica, the Dominican Republic, Haiti, Paraguay, Peru, and Venezuela. But this legal categorization tells us little, for while almost all the established churches have this legal status as a holdover from the rights of the Spanish monarchy and while the purpose of establishment is to make the religious institution subservient to the state, the degree of control varies widely. There has, for instance, been active persecution of the Church in Venezuela, in contrast to the impressively strong Church of Colombia. And where legal separation exists, the same range of attitude is also to be found, from the past bitter attacks on the Church in Mexico, to the comfortable adjustment in Chile, to Church ascendancy in Ecuador.

Another variable is the Church itself, which is by no means the same in its politics everywhere. The Gallican-influenced Churches of Brazil and Chile have very different political traits from the Spanish and Italian Church of Argentina. Most of the Chilean clergy now favor Christian Democracy; in the main, the Argentine clergy backed Perón for all but the last years of his regime and still support many of the ideas of *justicialismo*. The long-range trend everywhere is for the Church to throw in with the rising middle groups, to oppose *caudillismo,* gently to support labor, and to drift slowly toward the official support of Christian Democratic parties. There is much opposition within the Church itself to certain of these temporal decisions, of course, and it would be highly incorrect to indicate that there is a general Latin political consensus in the Church.

The students, notorious political actors that they are, also constitute a pressure group. Latin American universities, organized on the European system, introduce their students immediately to subprofessional life; the social class gulf between student and professor is also minimal, for almost all students in Latin American universities are of middle and upper occupational group parents; their chances to participate at reasonably high levels in the national life after graduation are thus high to begin with. University elections are often good indicators of public elections, a kind of academic Maine and Vermont. Political division among the students parallels that of the major political parties, and student political activities train youngsters for active life outside. There are few Church universities of high prestige in those Latin American countries where they are allowed to exist. Although students in religious universities are also political activists, the incidents about which one reads in the newspapers almost invariably are initiated in the state universities, citadels of the new, rising, nationalistic middle youth.

Other pressure groups are what one might expect: associations of landowners, mine operators, industrialists, chambers of commerce, and prestige social clubs edging into the political sphere. Then there are union groups, invariably politically militant if they are not subservient arms of the state. At times they are both. Where labor is fairly free of governmental supervision, it tends to group in Socialist, Communist, and Radical camps; and in three countries—Argentina, Chile, and Uruguay—unionism also has had its Anarchist contingents. The union movement of Mexico has been closely allied to the growth of the single party, whatever its name may have been at any particular period. In the most retarded countries, unions are *de facto* or even sometimes *de jure* illegal. Honduras, for example, legalized labor organization only as recently as 1954.

Another kind of occupational pressure group is the professional association, often intimately tied in with the universities from which they depend in many countries.

Groups-in-interest are another crucial index of impersonalism and maturity in the political process. To the extent to which they exist, a polity of countervailing powers becomes a possibility, assuring the operation of lateral controls in the political system and making possible government by decisions as the result of compromise through bargaining instead of by fiat through uncontrolled self-interest.

INTERNATIONAL ECHOES OF INTERNAL POLITICS

As we have seen, the wide variation in the political development of the Latin American republics precludes the application of overly narrow rules to the processes of interpretative analysis and policy making. But even this simple homily is difficult to apply in practice, for not only are Latin American countries broadly dispersed on almost any scale of social measurement, but also, in many short-run, operational respects, they are almost exactly what the United States is not, a fact which makes for difficulties in cross-cultural recommendations. The modernizing elements in Latin America in general want revolutionary changes, whether with violence or without; the United States is moderate in its views and skeptical of wrenching change. Latin American countries are in the early, romantic stages of nationalism; the United States is emerging into a cautious but firm commitment to internationalism. The Latin university student enjoys high social prestige and excellent chances for political power; his American counterpart is career-oriented and drawn from a very broad social spectrum. Latin American labor leaders are devoted to political unionism; American union officials are convinced of the advantages of economic unionism.

Most Latin Americans see the state as a legitimate agency for directing capital accumulation and investment; avowed American ideology is *laissez-faire*, despite the mixed economy of the United States. Latin Americans are more worried about their internal Communist parties than about the Soviet Union, and only as a result of Cuba have generated some relatively direct emotional involvement in the Cold War; the United States views the international clash with Soviet Russia as a struggle for survival in the deepest sense. Latin America wants steel mills and the other monuments of industrialization against a background of the technical full employment of underdevelopment; the United States is dealing with problems of automation and potential unemployment. Latin American governments are frankly tutelary; the American government is charged with the opposite task of reconciling numerous conflicting issues among laterally competing interests. The Latin American culture includes many Catholic as well as generically Mediterranean notions of collectivism and syndicalism; the United States is generally Protestant and individualistic in its approach to matters metaphysical. This list of divergences could be extended almost indefinitely. The major point is that North American groups cannot talk on the same attitudinal grounds as their Latin American peers, for the immediate aspirations and methods of each are not the same.

It is only in terms of broader and more long-range objectives that the community of interests may be made real. The ultimate dedication of the United States to democratic process is clearly reflected in Latin America. Unhappily, discord invariably appears over means to that common end, and the daily decisions of diplomacy suffer accordingly. The United States has often demonstrated itself insensitive to the currents of internal Latin American politics as well as to the variety of solutions possible to those countries. Too often have we defined private ownership as equal to capitalism without taking into account the importance to the maintenance of our system of competition and countervailing powers; we have viewed expropriation as equal to socialism, and nationalism as the same as supernationalism; the governmental authority of dictators has been treated as an honorable equivalent of legitimacy, and rote anti-communism as full partnership in the community of free nations.

Many Latin American countries, for their part, have dedicated themselves to a maintenance of the privileges of the old semi-feudalism at the same time as they seek the revolutionary advantages of modernism. Between the transcendental ideal and the grubbiness of daily administrative practice there is often a yawning gulf filled with ineptitude and corruption. Latin Americans have a long way to go to translate their notions of dignity and the good life into the reality after which they yearn. But, of course, that point is what this chapter concerns. The exciting variety of response being developed in Latin America is a most encouraging sign and at the same time a challenge to the scholar, the businessman, and the policy-maker. This variety cannot be understood by narrow ideologists thinking in bromides.

Many roads lead to democratic salvation.

3

THE NATION AND THE VILLAGE

Political scientists usually leave for anthropologists the study of the politics of pre-literate peoples. But as nationalistic groups in developing countries begin to pressure for the integration of total populations into a single social universe, the non-national persons find their traditional values and their way of life threatened with annihilation. Willy-nilly, under such pressure, they begin sometimes to respond to the same motivations as those who trespass against them; as so often happens, the victims adopt part of the same style as the victimizers. To the extent to which this process occurs and pre-national societies break down before the onslaught, they also fall prey to the techniques and theories of political science in its standard form. The tradition-bound village culture begins to be susceptible to questions concerning voting behavior, political participation, civil liberties, power groups, public administration, and so on.

Whether anthropologists or political scientists or anyone else does it, someone should be around academically to catch a village society when its inward-looking structure collapses, destroying traditional local government patterns and pushing aspiring youth to move away or to import revolutionary ideas from capital city or foreign land. It is precisely when a pre-national society begins to impel itself toward nationalism—or to be impelled thereto—that fundamental matters of social causation are laid bare for analysis, when the researcher can wrap his hands around the process of "history in the making," to use a hackneyed phrase.

In Guatemala some years ago I made an attempt to get at some knowledge of the range of diversity of nationalism from the village to the capital city.[1] Unfortunately it was impossible to complete the planned survey work in the capital, and what was left were two pilot studies of two Guatemalan towns, surveys initially designed as controls for the Guatemala City work. The purpose of presenting part of the data is to indicate the degree of political knowledge and participation which pertained in Guatemalan towns in the early part of the 1950's, after seven years of revolutionary government. Although political knowledge and degree of participation are not in themselves absolute measures of the existence of the value of nationalism as discussed in the previous chapter, when such knowledge and action circle around the conduct of national affairs and the affairs of nationalists, then it is safe to infer a relationship. Certainly to reverse the proposition and claim that ignorance of and apathy in national affairs indicate the absence of a nationalistic value structure would not be a daring theoretical statment. I take the results of these two surveys, then, to be indicative of degrees of the presence or absence of nationalistic feelings as those sentiments may be inferred from information known about national politics and the degree of participation therein.

Guatemala is a particularly apt theater for looking at the relationships between nationalistic and non-nationalistic groups living in the same country. Some 53 per cent of the population in 1950 was designated in the census as Indian; i.e., wearing Indian costume, speaking an Indian tongue, and characterized by themselves and others as being Indians. Except for a few Europeans and Negroes, the remainder are called *ladinos* or *mestizos*, mixed Europeans and Indians. There has been very little industrial urbanization, the capital having only 300,000 population, 10 per cent of the national total of 3,000,000. The second largest city, Quezaltenango, drops far down to 27,000 persons.[2] The economy is based on agriculture; corn, beans, and wheat are the three most important crops for internal consumption, coffee, bananas, and chicle for export. Of coffee and bananas, the former is overwhelmingly the more important, regularly providing approximately 80 per cent of the foreign exchange [3] and usually the same percentage of the national government's revenues.

[1] Parts of this chapter were initially presented in English as a paper read at the American Political Science Association convention in 1955. A Spanish version, including a theoretical statement concerning nationalism here omitted, was published under the title. "El Nacionalismo: Medida de su Crecimiento en Guatemala," in *Integración Social en Guatemala,* Seminario de Integración Social Guatemalteca, Guatemala, 1956, pp. 393–414. Commentary on the article by Drs. Frank Tannenbaum and Allan R. Holmberg appears in the same volume on pp. 415–34. A resumé of the article and the formal commentaries plus open debate appears in Vol. II of *Integración Social en Guatemala,* by the same publisher, 1960, pp. 279–326.

[2] Dirección General de Estadística, Oficina Permanente del Censo, *Sexto Censo de Población, 18 de Abril, 1950,* Guatemala: Imprenta Universitaria, 1953.

[3] *Boletín del Banco de Guatemala,* May, 1953, p. 32.

The ethnic situation is more complicated than a simple bi-polar split. Not only is there much linguistic and other cultural heterogeneity among Indians, but they are also found on different parts of the scale toward becoming ladinoized. There are thus Indians of the various village cultures, modified Indians, and ladinoized Indians all on the scale toward "Guatemalans." Although city people very often refer to the rural population as in its totality Indian,[4] urbanites sharply distinguish between Indians and ladinos on all matters of prestige and dignity, even though their physical conditions of life may be strikingly similar.[5] Indians are culturally and not racially distinguished; should they discard traditional costume, speak Spanish, and move from their village of birth, the transition to ladino status can often be accomplished in one generation. Since ethnic and cultural divisions are fundamental to attitude-behavior studies in the derivation of independent variables, it is obvious that the Guatemalan situation, complicated as it is not only by a class-caste system but also by differing urban-rural value systems, demands careful preliminary research design. In a voting study of Guatemala, for instance, we must start with two ethnic universes; these must be doubled for the sharp urban-rural difference; the addition of the sex variable provides eight categories before such other matters as occupation, income, or mobility factors can be considered.

With these ethnic complexities in mind, San Antonio Sacatepéquez and Cobán were chosen as the test towns for the questionnaire. The former has a population of some 800 in the county seat itself, of whom approximately 20 per cent are ladino, the remainder Indian. San Antonio is in a densely settled and highly Indian portion of Guatemala, and the town itself is composed of persons almost exclusively dedicated to agricultural pursuits. About 4,000 persons live in the entire *municipio*, or township, of which San Antonio is the seat. Cobán, lying in the coffee country north of the capital, is a municipio of almost 30,000 persons, of whom 86 per cent are Indian, but in the county seat itself, only 56 per cent of the population is given in the 1950 census as In-

---

[4] K. H. Silvert, *A Study in Government: Guatemala*, Part I, New Orleans: Middle American Research Institute, Pub. No. 21, 1954, pp. 61–63.

[5] See such anthropological studies as John Gillin, *The Culture of Security in San Carlos*, New Orleans: Middle American Research Institute Pub. No. 16, 1951; or Arden King, "Changing Cultural Goals and Patterns in Guatemala," *American Anthropologist*, Vol. 54, No. 1, 1952, pp. 139–43; or Melvin Tumin, *Caste and Class in a Peasant Society*, Princeton, N.J.: Princeton University Press, 1952, and many others. For an excellent description of village political practice among Indians in the Maya area, see Fernando Cámara, "Religious and Political Organizations," in Sol Tax and others, *Heritage of Conquest*, Glencoe, Ill.: The Free Press, 1952. Particularly appropriate is Richard N. Adams (compiler), *Political Changes in Guatemalan Indian Communities, A Symposium*, New Orleans: Middle American Research Institute, Pub. No. 24, 1957.

dian.[6] San Antonio is clearly a rural town; the large size of Cobán and its function as the seat of both the municipio and the departmental governments make it urban-rural in nature, especially since many who live in the town itself leave daily to work lands in the surrounding countryside. It should be emphasized that the questionnaire was not constructed for these towns but rather for Guatemala City, on the premise that the emergent social structure in the capital would bear resemblances to the "Western world," allowing then for the application of the techniques of that world. So one of the major reasons for the testing of the schedule in these towns was to see how badly it would work. Had it been a completely viable tool in an affirmative sense, then we should have to conclude either that rural Guatemala is Westernized or that the criteria of Westernization used in constructing the schedule were incorrect.

What was projected for the complete work was a horizontal comparison between Guatemala City and comparable nation-state situations, and a vertical comparison between Guatemala City and subordinate rural political units, in part to see in what degree they vary, in part to learn something of the background from which new arrivals to the city may come, and again in part to give a kind of quantitative historicism to the study, on the speculative presumption that certain urban-rural communities may give a clue to the Guatemala City of some years ago. All these ends, of course, were added to the use of the two areas for their primary technical purpose as pilot studies.

Two different types of samples were taken; in neither case, unfortunately, were the 1950 census materials available. In San Antonio an anthropologist in the midst of a community survey kindly administered the questionnaire. Every fifth house was used, the first chosen arbitrarily, leading to the completion of eighteen schedules including fifteen Indians and three ladinos. For Cobán an occupational count of only the nuclear urban area was made by two technicians on loan from the National Indian Institute, and on this basis and a decision to complete approximately sixty schedules, a list was worked out proportional to Indians and ladinos by occupation. The houses to be visited in each category were then chosen at random. Only heads of families, whether male or female or single persons living at the address, were interviewed. Sixty-two questionnaires were administered in Cobán.

[6] An excellent description of San Antonio may be found in Robert Ewald's doctoral dissertation, a community study of the town, University of Michigan, Ann Arbor, 1954. Other descriptions of San Antonio and Cobán may be found in K. H. Silvert, *op. cit.*, pp. 70–77 and 86–89. See also Arden King, *op. cit.*, for further Cobán material. Also, Robert Ewald, "San Antonio Sacatepéquez: 1932–53," and K. H. Silvert and Arden R. King, "Cobán: 1944–53" in Richard N. Adams, *op. cit.*

The political questions *per se* were divided into the following categories:

Formal participation. Covered topics: political party affiliation, voting record; if not a political party member, what party would be joined if individual so inclined; whether voted alone, in company with others, or taken by professional party worker to the polls.

Informal participation. Covered topics: whether individual has ever participated in a political demonstration, and how September 15 (Independence Day), October 20 (anniversary of 1944 revolution), and May 1 (which the government made a national holiday) are celebrated.

Informational knowledge. Covered topics: whether individual knows names of his deputies, has ever seen a President or attended a session of congress, has knowledge of national heroes and holidays.

Attitudes toward foreign countries. Covered topics: attitudes toward the Central American Union and where its capital should be; the Belice or British Honduras controversy with Great Britain, nationality of employer preference scale, and imperialism preference scale.

Political mobility. Covered topics: whether any Guatemalan has a chance to become president, whether respondent thought he or she could become a city councilman, syndic, mayor, deputy, or president, with reasons.

Special attitudes toward government. Covered topics: whether army should participate or not, whether respondent approves of a military man as president, whether church should participate in politics, etc.

General attitudes. Covered topics: attitudes toward unions, the Church, and open-ended wish fulfillment question at the end of the questionnaire.

Space precludes the inclusion of the correlations, in any event unnecessary, given the special purpose of this discussion and the homogeneity of the samples.

The San Antonio income data indicate Indians earning from $26.00 to $200.00 per year; the three ladinos fell in three separate categories, one between $251 and $275 annually, another between $401 and $450, and the third in the $901–$1,000 category. In Cobán, on the other hand, incomes ranged between $101 and $10,000. In San Antonio there were no employers in the sample; in Cobán seventeen of the sixty-two questioned were employers. The converse is, of course, that in San Antonio there were no *mozos,* or hired hands, to be found. Only seven occupations were represented in San Antonio, nineteen in Cobán. In the small town the highest reported income was earned by a carpenter, in Cobán by a merchant-large farmer. The results do not appear to be inconsistent with other studies.

The answers to the political information questions are fascinatingly spotty. At least one question failed almost entirely and thus fits our search for negative findings. It asked for a ranking of six Latin American political figures by fame; Simón Bolívar was included, as was Francisco Morazán, the hero of Central American Union, Justo Rufino Barrios, a great Guatemalan Liberal president, and three more Guatemalan presidents of this century, Estrada Cabrera, Ubico, and Arévalo. In Cobán 33 persons failed to answer the question at all. Of those answering, the number sequences chosen were too regular to be credible; e.g., 3-2-1-6-5-4, or 6-5-4-2-3-1. If it means anything, however, among those few who did respond, Barrios was far ahead, trailed by Arévalo and Ubico, the two most recent presidents listed. Poor Bolívar and Morazán vied for last place as the least distinguished.

Although not all the information questions failed so abruptly, the answers are all somewhat questionable. On the other hand, when specific behavior is concerned, the replies become predictable and internal checks in the questionnaire work. In response to a query concerning party membership, for example, we see only four persons affiliated in San Antonio, thirteen unaffiliated but willing to express a preference, and one unaffiliated and unwilling to express a preference. In Cobán a sharp and predictable distinction is seen, where thirty persons—almost half the sample—belonged to parties, seventeen did not but expressed a preference, and a suspicious fifteen gave no response at all. Of the thirty affiliated, twenty-one belonged to the major government party, eight to one minor government party, and one to the opposition; but of those seventeen expressing a preference, twelve voted for various minor government parties, two for the opposition, and only three for the major party.

The high percentage of Guatemalans who vote was also accurately represented by the responses, with very little difference showing up between Indians and ladinos in Cobán. But the ethnic difference revealed itself again in the following easily administered informational question:

Question: Do you know the names of your departmental deputies?

	San Antonio		Cobán	
	Yes	No	Yes	No
Ladino	3	0	33	5
Indian	8	7	7	16

There is no valid reason for continuing to divide out the three San Antonio ladinos, for the number is too small to be useful. But some further Indian-ladino differences for Cobán may be of interest.

Question: Do you think that the present government represents the majority of public opinion?

	Ladinos	Indians
Yes	24	6
No	3	2
No opinion or no response	12	15

In more compliant San Antonio, 15 said "Yes," none said "No," and 3 did not know.

There are some strong indications that avowed norms, what "ought" to be, come into clash with a recognition of what is.

Note:
Question: Do you think that the army should participate in politics?

	Cobán		San Antonio
	Indians	Ladinos	
Yes	1	10	2
No	17	29	14
No response or no opinion	5	0	1

Question: Do you prefer that the president of the republic be a military man or a civilian?

	Cobán		San Antonio
	Indians	Ladinos	
Military Man	10	20	13
Civilian	4	14	3
No response or no opinion	9	5	2

Again, an ethnic difference appears in the question concerning political mobility. Not one person queried in San Antonio thought every Guatemalan had a chance to be president, but twenty-seven out of sixty-two thought so in more ladinoized Cobán. But in matters of participation, as has been noted in connection with the physical act of voting, the responses are remarkably similar. In answer to the question, "Have you ever participated in a political demonstration, whether in favor of or against the government?" we find:

	Cobán		San Antonio
	Ladinos	Indians	
Yes	1	0	3
No	37	23	13
No response	1	0	2

Concerning the significance of September 15 and October 20, all queried in San Antonio were aware. In Cobán, in both cases, thirty-seven ladinos knew the national meanings of the dates and two did not; of the Indians, sixteen knew of September 15, five did not, and two did not respond, but eighteen knew of October 20 and the same five did not. But the manner of celebrating differed somewhat between Indians and ladinos. For those evincing knowledge, the manner of celebrating September 15 was as follows:

	Cobán		San Antonio
	Indians	Ladinos	
Dance or party	5	1	6
Does not celebrate	4	7	0
Gets drunk	5	0	1
Promenade	9	2	8
Parade	8	0	3*
Rest	6	13	0

* All three Ladinos answered this way.

In Cobán it is plain that the twenty out of twenty-three Indians who knew the significance of September 15 kept to themselves, either "not celebrating" or "resting."

The responses to the question, "List in order of importance those three countries which you believe are the most imperialistic," were interesting for their cognitive as well as attitudinal content. Given were Mexico, Great Britain, Japan, France, the United States, Soviet Russia, and Germany, with a space for others. In Cobán fourteen ladinos did not answer at all, leaving the ranking to be done on a basis of twenty-five; sixteen Indians did not respond, leaving six. In San Antonio eleven responded, electing the United States as the most imperialistic by a wide margin. Mexico and Great Britain tied for second place, but France was also surprisingly high, leading to the speculation that some, at least, ticked off the nations in order of familiarity, perhaps on the assumption that if a nation is much in the public eye, it must be imperialistic. In Cobán, where there is no word for imperialism in Kekchí, the language in which the questionnaire was administered to the Indians, the results were as follows:

| | Cobán | | | |
| | Ladinos | | Indians | |
	Mean Score	Rank	Mean Score	Rank
Mexico	—	0	—	0
Great Britain	5.7	1	5.5	1
Japan	2.1	5	3.5	1
France	—	0	—	0
United States	4.3	2	5.0	2
Soviet Russia	3.8	3	2.2	4
Germany	2.5	4	1.8	5
Others	—	0	—	0

The responses to this question merit some discussion. The high percentage of ladinos as well as Indians not answering underlines the common lack of information, introducing some likenesses into the ladino-Indian split usually not discussed by observers anxious to point out the differences. Further, although the manner of response indicates that some did not understand the question, it is just as obvious that some did. The high score of both the United States and Great Britain in both places, for example, probably indicates some absorption of government propaganda concerning the British Honduras issue in the first case and alleged Yankee imperialism in the second. Note, too, that Mexico is second choice in San Antonio and does not appear at all in Cobán. San Antonio is on the road to Mexico, there is much smuggling across the nearby border, and a long past history of frontier troubles. Although Cobán is physically close to Mexico, there is no overland communication and no history of traffic or bellicosity. But Cobán is close to British Honduras and ships out its coffee through Livingston, immediately south of Belice.

And again with this question there appears a discrepancy between avowed values and, in this case, desired practice. When respondents were asked by whom they would prefer to be employed, given equal pay and equal work conditions, only one ladino and one Indian in Cobán failed to respond, and the answer "North American" ranked first for both groups, "Guatemalan" second for both. In San Antonio only four persons ranked their answers at all, and sixteen put Guatemalans as their first or only choice. As further demonstration of some understanding and thought, in Cobán the Indians ranked the Germans, who own many coffee farms and stores in the region, as a good third, but among the ladinos the position of the Germans as a choice was insignificant. Both answers, as incomplete as the first one is, are partially consistent with historical reality.

For the curiosity value alone a few words may be said about the last question, concerning wish fulfillment. "If you had time and money enough to do anything you wished, what would you do?" Modest San Antonio chose as follows:

Go into business and buy a farm	11
Travel and live better	2
Buy own house and farm	2
Go into industry or be large farmer	1
Celebrate Saint's day and buy new clothes	1
Too old to wish	1

Every Indian talked in terms of owning land or a small business or both. Two of the three ladinos wanted to travel, and one elected to be an industrialist or large farmer. Recasting the answers in terms of more general concepts, we have:

	Cobán		San Antonio
	Ladino	Indian	
Better what one already has			
Change type of work	3	6	6
Go to Guatemala City	5	6	0
Ambition for children	2	2	0
Philanthropy	7	0	0
Stay but get conveniences			
Travel	10	4	2
Stop work, live like rich	4	1	1
Do religious work	1	0	1
Others	1	0	1

In the Cobán figures, if "Travel" is added to "Go to Guatemala City" and to give up work "and live like rich," then thirty-one persons, exactly half the sample, appear to have the desire to get out of Cobán in a literal sense.

This hasty and even skimpy look at some of the attitudes of pre-nationals in Guatemala should not be transposed without prior research into such other Indian countries as Ecuador, Peru, Bolivia, or Paraguay. But I suggest that this kind of work can be most fruitful, indicating as it does just what is the distance between those persons who work the machinery of the nation and those persons who fill the rural areas.

In areas of rapid social development the problem of easing the accommodation of new recruits to the integrated machine of the nation-state always presents itself. Unless one takes the comfortable *laissez-*

passer view that everything will work itself out, rational handling of the problem depends upon a knowledge of the origins of these migrants. This question is especially acute for *indigenistas*, the invariably nationalistic romanticizers of the Indian who dream of a nexus between Indian and European institutions, symbols, and artistic values. If individual integrity is to be respected, and cultural integrity preserved so far as compatible with national integration, then knowledge and its application are the only practical means of directing the tumbling rush of social change overwhelming contemporary Latin America. As to the possibilities of accumulating a sufficient store of data and of deriving suitable policies, I am pessimistic. Although I deplore the conclusion, I feel that *ad hoc* adjustments are the greater likelihood.

PART TWO

HISTORICAL INCIDENT AND
SOCIAL SYMBOLISM

In Part I the task was to define categorical boxes and indicate families of likenesses. In this section, on the other hand, the proposal is the complementary one of pointing out those differences in background which impart a unique flavor to each national entity. The historical sites are quite different: Argentina, an area of late settlement and extraordinarily heavy and influential migration from Europe, the most urbanized country of Latin America; Chile, a small, slowly populated, more *mestizo* country than Argentina, isolated from but intensely interested in Europe, with a *fin-de-siècle* atmosphere; and Guatemala, a Central American republic, backward but striving, supporting a heavy concentration of Indians, a "banana republic" in the eyes of the world. The social meaning of the unfolding of the histories of these countries is a function of the value significance with which the peoples concerned imbue those events. It is at this point that cultural differences work their effect on the train of human events.

4

REQUIEM FOR A NUMBER OF THINGS

Bitter riots in downtown Santiago in the first week of April, 1957, followed a classical pattern. An increase in bus fares was ordered by the government. University students, among others, objected. Sporadic violence broke out in Valparaíso, and finally on Friday, March 29, the Chilean Federation of Students began street demonstrations in the capital. Police (*carabinero*) contingents were reinforced and issued rifles and tear gas. On Monday night, April 1, the police fatally shot a twenty-three-year-old nursing student and wounded a fifteen-year-old secondary student demonstrator. Through Tuesday afternoon a mixed group of rioters—students and other elements—began stoning the police in earnest, breaking windows in buses, and committing other acts of violence. By late afternoon the situation had so deteriorated that the police, historical symbol of all evil to the students, were withdrawn. But it was not until several hours later that military units occupied the center of Santiago. At that late hour fringe elements in the city had already joined the festivities and looting and pillage became widespread. By Wednesday night the official figures indicated that almost a score were dead and hundreds hurt or wounded. Martial law was declared, a curfew imposed, the radio stations taken over by the government's information office, and newspapers were placed under censorship. Incidents virtually ceased by Thursday night. On Saturday the Senate voted special powers to the executive, and the fare increases were temporarily rescinded, pending study by a special commission. Public transportation resumed operation on Monday.

THE STUDENTS AND THEIR ROLE, HISTORICAL AND OTHERWISE

There are eight universities in Chile, counting the *Universidad Austral,* but it is the national University of Chile which remains the major center of higher education. When one says, "The students did so and so," the reference is invariably to the activities of the Chilean Federation of Students, or FECH, the student organization of the University of Chile.[1]

Although there is some argument about the exact date of its founding, the FECH probably came into existence in 1906, conceived, as one would expect, in a protest movement. An epidemic of smallpox in Valparaíso has been quelled with the aid of the volunteer services of the medical students of the University. On their return to the capital it was proposed that they be presented with medals in a ceremony to take place in the Municipal Theater. When the students arrived they found that the balconies had been reserved for their families but that the boxes had been set aside for the "best people." Enraged, the medical students walked out on the proceedings, and to make their objections felt they set about uniting the various *centros*, or student clubs, which already existed in various of the schools of the University. The result was the FECH.

The governing bodies of the organization are the Directorate, which discharges the legislative function, and the Executive Council, which administers the decisions of the former and acts during such times as the vacations when the Directorate does not sit. About 140 members compose the Directorate, made up of delegates from all University schools which maintain *centros*, and roughly in proportion to the size of the student bodies of each. The Schools of Law, Medicine, Architecture, Dentistry, Chemistry and Pharmacy, Engineering, and the Teachers' College are the the ones that are most active in the FECH. Also represented are Fine Arts, Nursing, Agronomy, and a few others not of university level but affiliated, such as the School of Male Nurses.

The Executive Council is composed of a president, vice-president, secretary, and four members, elected by popular vote from among the entire student body, all of whom automatically belong to FECH on matriculation. Since the University of Chile is state supported, tuition rates are very low (three to five or six dollars a year, depending on the school), but the economic factor is still strongly operative in the selection of students, because most Chileans must start to earn money as soon as possible. The FECH normally is supported with funds from the matriculation fees which usually provide it with a budget of approximately US$2,500. Sometimes the budget is increased by a special grant from the general funds of the University.

Obviously, some students are interested in politics and others are

[1] Mr. Frank Bonilla, a graduate of the Department of Sociology of Harvard, has prepared a doctoral dissertation on the FECH. I am indebted to him for aid in the preparation of this historical statement.

not. The FECH is not for the indifferent, for it is an eminently political body, closely tied into the national party structure and a training ground for future party leaders. This intimate identification with national politics has caused a chronic schism in the FECH. On the one hand are the "guildists" (*gremialistas*) and their plea that the FECH should concern itself with student problems alone and act as the conscience of the nation, above party; on the other are the politicalized ones, who are in favor of activist roles for the students as a preparation for later full citizenship and leadership. In the nature of things the latter must win, for it takes politicking to move to the forefront of the FECH in the first place.

The tradition of street demonstrations is an old one with the students. It is argued that they can get away with these activities because they are looked upon with fondness, their pranks being dismissed as in the United States we shrug our shoulders at panty raids. A more realistic way to look at it is that these young persons are, after all, the children of their parents. Their progenitors run the government, political parties, industry, commerce, the unions, and large-scale agriculture. The death of a student is shocking because the opinion formers can empathize with the student and with his family. Further, the students do historically express the liveliness which the older generation likes to feel nostalgic about, and so their "radicalness" is generally disregarded, if indeed they can be counted as any more radical than the country as a whole. As we shall see, these attitudes governed reactions to the fatalities which occurred in this bloody week.

The shooting of students anywhere in Latin America is usually judged a display of governmental weakness, indicating as it does a split between those responsible for the life of government itself, and elements of those very groups from which the governors tend to be drawn. The killing of the head of the student body in Havana in 1956 was widely interpreted as the beginning of the end for President Fulgencio Batista of Cuba. But the course of events obviously is not so automatic, and there are many cases of student deaths which have been quietly forgotten, at least for political purposes.

Chile has a long history of student street demonstrations and protests. Immediately before World War I the FECH distinguished itself by strenuous objections against a Papal nuncio who ostensibly had come to Chile to take Church property to Rome in the face of a rumored move to separate Church and State. In the course of the disturbances the nuncio's hat was stolen, and for a time the miniature representation of the headpiece was used as a lapel emblem to signify the victory of student fervor. In 1919 and 1920 there were many demonstrations (some in company with labor unions) to celebrate the end of the war and the new air of democracy then whistling through-out all of Latin America, and also to protest the economic difficulties of depression and inflation. In 1922 there was a strike in the medical school. In 1931 the students for a short time staged a sitdown strike in the University, demanding full restoration of civil liberties from President Carlos Ibáñez del Campo, then serving his first term. The student action may well have initiated the series of events which led to General Ibáñez' deposition in that year. In 1938 some sixty-three Nazi students were killed by *carabineros* as they tried to touch off another revolt. In 1944 the FECH ran a series of strikes designed to effect internal University reforms. In 1947, 1948, and 1949 students strongly protested against the government for its manner of dealing with strikes and for its passage of a law outlawing the Communist Party. Other demonstrations were against the rising cost of living and at least one, in 1949, against an increase in the bus fares. The year 1953 saw protests against a military pact between the United States and Chile and strong activity at the time of the Guatemala incident. In 1955 the students managed to get the government to give asylum to some political refugees from Peru. In 1956 they delicately played with the serious and threatening general strike of January, and in 1957 we have the case at hand. Since then the presidential elections of 1958 and 1964 were the cause of much street violence in which students acted directly as party partisans.

THE OVERT ISSUE

What touched off the incident under discussion was an increase in the bus fares from 10 pesos to 15 pesos in the capital, with some larger hikes in other places, such as Valparaíso. Ten pesos at the time were a little more than a penny and a half, and fifteen were about two and a half cents. An average minimum salary for an unskilled laborer in Santiago was then between Ch$12,000 and Ch$15,000 a month— US$20.00 to US$25.00. If we assume that such a person had to make twelve trips per week in getting to and from work, and further assume that any transfers were free, then he spent almost 4 per cent of his salary on transportation at the ten-peso fare. A New York commuter making the same number of trips at 15 cents each spends about the same percentage of a US$50.00 weekly salary. But since the Chilean worker lives so close to the margin, an increase in the amount he must spend on fare from 500 to 750 pesos a month, not including what his family spends on trips for the sake of diversion, obviously involves some hardship.

On the other hand, the buses could not be profitably operated on a ten-peso fare. All the equipment is imported, the gasoline costs the same as it does in the more expensive U.S. states, and the labor is less productive. True, salaries paid to transportation workers are much lower than those in the United States, but certainly not enough to account for the difference between a Santiago fare of one and one-half cents and even the uniquely low New Orleans fare of a dime. The matter would be simplified if the entire urban system were in the hands of the government or of one private company. The trolley-buses and the trolleys and the better buses all belong to a government system, the slack being taken up by a large number of private owners running different classes of buses.[2] If a singly managed network were involved, it could seriously be proposed that the system either be run as a commercial undertaking or frankly subsidized as a public service. New Yorkers will be familiar with the arguments on both sides, nostalgic as many are over the passing of the five-cent fare some years ago. But since the ownership and management situation is mixed and complex, and since the government had not the funds to buy out the private owners and subsidize the entire system even had it wanted to do so, there seemed to be no choice but to raise the rates.

As individuals, the students—whatever their grade—were unaffected by the rates, for by law they paid but one peso. There were many tales circulating that grammar school children actually were forced to pay five, ten, or even fifteen pesos by unscrupulous bus drivers. There is no reason to disbelieve the stories, but of course there is no way to know how widespread the practice was. As for the University students, they are big enough to take care of themselves and so paid the one-peso fare. Thus the FECH, in making its protest, was not concerned with an immediate student problem but rather with a matter affecting basic national economic policy. Since the Executive Council of the FECH is composed of representatives of political parties which range from being somewhat to being very anti-government, their attitude was never in doubt. Once their Valparaíso colleagues braved the weapons of the *carabineros* to go out on the street, the action in Santiago too was certain. The unknowns at the time concerned: (a) who else would get into the act; and (b) how strongly the government would react. Never was there any feeling that the move was revolutionary in motive. The students did not intend to attempt to overthrow the government, nor did other elements that might be expected to have had an interest in changing the government: the labor unions were without direction, having seen two levels of their leadership peeled off and exiled

[2] The state system alone has American, French, Japanese, and British equipment, raising monstrous maintenance and spare-part complexities.

to towns away from the capital; the political parties were thinking of campaigns and not *coups;* the military were content; and there were no loose leadership elements floating around in search of a public.

WHAT PEOPLE SAY HAPPENED

It is to be feared that the unknowns before the fact are still unknowns. There is wide debate as to just who did what to whom and why. The largest area of agreement is that by the end of Tuesday afternoon the students had in the main withdrawn as active participants and that thereafter the city was delivered up to vandals. Whether the latter are said to have been laborers on the loose, gangsters, drifters from the shanty towns, cleverly spotted Communist agitators, or even cleverly spotted government agitators depends on who makes the statement. The political right says the Communists organized the pillage and looting, once the students were out of the way. The left says the government purposely left the city wide open for two hours in order to encourage pillage and justify the shooting of gangster elements so that the populace would forget that a number of better-placed persons also had lost their lives.

I prefer the simple and matter-of-fact interpretations. In my opinion, nothing was plotted by anybody, but rather the incident grew spontaneously and grotesquely. The heel-dragging of the left in the FECH makes it probable that the Communists had not thought their way through to the point of attempting a concerted anti-government drive. They were willing enough to join the other students in the street demonstrations but were the recipients of bitter recriminations from some Radicals who berated them for not asking immediate reinforcements from Communist-led labor unions. Perhaps the Communists lagged because they were finding it harder and harder at that time to deliver unionists, given their then weak influence and the dispersion of their leaders. Or perhaps the extremely forceful measures President Ibáñez had taken in regard to illegal labor demonstrations and strikes persuaded them that martyrdom of the people they lead was not desirable at that particular moment.[3] In any event, this was one time when the FECH was led into the streets primarily by groups other than the Communists. Once the situation got out of hand, there is no reason to think that the Communists did not have something to do with keeping the ball rolling. There is no hard proof, but the conclusion would seem logical.

As for the government's setting up the whole incident in order to be able to get emergency powers, I discard that possibility. The gambit

[3] Pres. Carlos Ibáñez del Campo had been re-elected in 1952. His term expired in 1958.

was not worth it for the limited special powers the government actually got for a short time, and the play was much too risky. This incident was shocking and, the Chileans insist, unprecedented. That the government could have plotted it out and then have been able to control the confusing situation simply does not fit with what I know of Chilean procedures. It is easier to believe that the city was left open for the two fatal hours not in order to be able to kill more demonstrators but rather to be able to control them better by drawing out and bunching the rioting elements. The two-hour lag may even have been a simple military snafu, this being perhaps the easiest way to rationalize it. The *carabineros* are traditionally poison to the students,[4] and the police had been at it at the time of their withdrawal for almost five days. Their tempers were frayed, they were tired of dodging stones, and they had already tasted blood. When the military governor made the rounds in a jeep, proclaiming that the *carabineros* were to be withdrawn, he was greeted with cheers by the crowd. The withdrawal was probably a very justifiable move, but why it took the troops two hours to make their appearance is another question. The government insists that it took some time to bring the soldiers in, especially since they had little more than a *cadre* in Santiago itself. The opposition says it was planned, for the reasons given above. I suggest another possibility is that there was an ordinary Chilean version of a GI snarl.

There is the ring of truth in yet another version. The *carabineros* were in a huff because of the obvious hostility shown them. When they knew they were to be pulled off the job in favor of their military rivals, one story has it that they immediately left in a pet without waiting for their replacements to arrive. Their hurry was such that four policemen were left behind when the last truck departed from the central street (the *Alameda*) and had to shoot their way out of the mob.

Obliquely corroborative evidence of government indecision may be derived from accounts of a split which developed in the leadership of the Christian Democrats at the very time that the riots were moving into their ugliest phase. The story has it that the advisers of Eduardo Frei, this party's leader, were pleading with him to summon his followers to the street in order to halt the violence and then to regroup and march on the executive offices to demand repeal of the fare rise. Frei reportedly refused, an action that is said to have led to a temporary weakening of his party. Most significant, however, is the further report that such intervention from anywhere but the extreme left would have been very welcome at that particular time by the badgered gov-

[4] Another reason for regretting this incident is that the *carabineros* had notably improved in courtesy, efficiency, and *esprit de corps* during the years prior to the incident, and they since have somewhat reverted to earlier type.

ernment. But by Tuesday night it was too late for moderate means; the government had committed itself to shooting it out.

The stories of incidents were naturally legion. An Argentine checked into a downtown hotel, went out on the balcony to see what was happening, and fell dead of a rifle shot. A young housewife waiting to buy bread was killed by a wild shot aimed at a nearby group of demonstrators. Human interest was added when a nine-year-old child found wandering about in the midst of the *tiroteo* was solicitously returned home by the police. An Englishman shortly after the curfew struck was ordered by a patrolling squad of soldiers to stop his car, failed to do so, and died with a bullet through his heart. The proprietress of a well-known downtown eating establishment watching the events from her balcony was shot through the leg and suffered an amputation.

The atmosphere of the mobs on Tuesday afternoon, in the *mezzoforte* part of the proceedings, was one of mingled shame, relief at the outburst, and carnival. As the *fortissimo* was reached, ugliness invaded the crowd, and you have but to recall your favorite story of mob violence to be able to feel what happened. The police, too, met the affair in mixed fashion. Some were abashed, others workmanlike, others savage in their fright. The army units handled their chores reasonably well but seemed as though they were not quite certain that the situation in which they found themselves was real.

Make no mistake: the government's action was decisive, strenuous, and even harsh. The exact number of dead and wounded is not known, and probably never will be except to those on the inside. Official figures put the fatalities at about twenty, the seriously wounded at somewhat fewer than a hundred. Unofficial guesses run all the way to several thousand, a figure which certainly expresses sheer hysteria. To repeat, there is no way to be certain, but surely it would seem reasonable to guess that the deaths ranged between forty and sixty persons. Thousands of rounds were fired, and after Tuesday afternoon the orders to shoot into the air were rescinded. Although it is probable that at no time were there more than a thousand demonstrators or looters or pillagers in action, the events took three or four days to wind down, a period during which the military faithfully carried out their promise to repress the violence with gun, cannon, and tank, "no matter what the consequences."

The opposition complained that the government's measures resembled action taken against a foreign invader instead of against the very people of the country. Whether or not this accusation was just, certainly the charge that the forces of law and order did not act in a manner calculated to spare lives seems self-evidently true. The reason may well be that the police and the military did not know how to handle mobs. At least, those holding grimly to the myth of Chile's peacefulness interpret it so. Facilities to direct water under pressure were extremely limited. No mounted police were brought into action despite the known effectiveness of horsemen in quelling mobs, so long as the demonstrators refrain from throwing marbles under the horses' hoofs. Police threw tear gas but had no masks themselves, so the *carabineros* wept at least as much as the crowds and could accomplish no other mopping-up actions. After the mob phase ended and the cleaning up began, the roster of the dead and wounded continued to mount.

Nevertheless, there were no long lists of missing persons, nor did any party demand that the government produce any particular individuals. All but four dead students, too, were present and accounted for. There thus seems no reason to accept a mortality figure running into the hundreds.

Aside from comments on its amateurish toughness in handling the mobs, the government also incurred much criticism from all sides for its own flagrant abuse of civil liberties and property rights in what is universally thought to be its action in destroying the press which printed *El Siglo,* the Communist daily, as well as other non-Communist but opposition publications. Naturally the government denied that the wanton but expert destruction of linotype machines, a flatbed press, and even typewriters and furnishings could be laid at its door. But it showed no immediate inclination to find the culprits, and worse, some eighteen persons working on the destroyed premises were arrested—by the vandals themselves?—and several days later their names appeared on a list of persons exiled to the provinces. (They were subsequently allowed to return home.) There really was little doubt but that the action had to be laid to the government. Most disconcerting were the bland denials from responsible political personages which cast doubt on other official pronouncements, especially after the arrest of several detectives who had helped themselves to typewriters from *El Siglo's* office. A later investigation established officially the guilt of the police in this act of vandalism.

Aside from the damaged Communist press, what of all the normal businessmen whose property suffered extensive damage? A jewelry store was sacked, arms shops were broken into, windows were shattered wholesale. If the government left the two hours open as a tactical move, or if the *carabineros* withdrew early out of spite, does the government owe nothing to the individuals who indirectly paid as order was restored? In law, no, of course. Ethically the question is obviously debatable.

The looting caused a universal reaction among better-placed Chileans: rejection, disgust, and fright. In many of the outlying parts of the city there were alarms and talk of organizing civil militias to fight off rumored invasions from the shanty-towns. Children were often the carriers of the stories of the fear of the womenfolk, and men spoke of standing guard with a mixed air of fright, bravado, and vengefulness.

When it became evident that no Paris communes were to be established, sanity and its handmaiden, boredom, made their reappearance. Grumbling against the curfew began to be heard, and against the fact that all radio stations carried the same program, that of the national information service. It was a nuisance not to be able to drive to the center of town, go shopping, see a movie, or have parties unless accommodations could be supplied for guests until six o'clock in the morning.

Throughout it all there was little sympathy expressed for those who had been killed or wounded, unless they were from among the students or similar social groups. Time after time the sentiment was voiced that it was a shame that not more *rateros*—"lowlifes"—had been killed. "Chile has never seen such a thing. What can you do with such bums? *Pum-pum, no más.*" ("Bang-bang, that's all.") In a bi-ethnic country such as Bolivia or Peru, one commonly expects to hear such sentiments, where the members of the lower caste groups can be dismissed as not sharing the same human feelings as the more sensitive dominants. Similar opinions sound more shocking in a country like Chile where social division is not reinforced by racial difference. Such callousness and indifference certainly have their roots in the extremely sharp class divisions maintained there. All of my American friends in Chile commented upon this lack of human warmth, let alone indignation, in Chilean analyses of the occurrences.

The scabs of mythology immediately crusted themselves heavily upon the wounds. "This is the worst disturbance in Chile in this century." "I've never seen anything as bad in my fifty years here." "Vandals, low elements which exist in all countries are the responsible ones." "The police couldn't handle the matter better because we're not used to these things, like the other Latin American countries." "These people aren't real Chileans, they're just badly educated rabble." "It's a lack of 'culture' which leads to these incidents."

For international consumption, the inflation-social difficulties-subversion trilogy was trotted out. Chile had undergone an inflation of over 4,000 per cent in fifteen years. The obvious hardships induced by such economic disequilibrium can lead only to social distress, which in turn gives advantage to subversive groups. The implication, then, was that international intergovernmental credits had to be forthcoming to aid in the containment of subversion. Left unspoken in situations of this type is the question of how the use of loan funds will be organized for their social effects. Such moneys are almost invariably injected at the top to the accompaniment of pious hopes about the operation of an automatic trickle system which will slake the thirst of those on the bottom and presumably make them feel better about the social order. Certain it is, however, that the elements at various low economic levels who indulged their taste for violence in these happenings had little or nothing volitionally to do with the inflation. Banks, government, business, agricultural interests, international traders, and labor leaders all contributed.

To impede the continued price rise, it is plain that currency and credit restrictions and price and wage brakes had all to be employed insofar as possible. Since "insofar as possible" is the crucial phrase, it is again plain that the heaviest discomforts in halting the inflation have weighed on those least able to politick themselves out of governmental regulation. All of this may be regrettable, but it is also normal in almost any society that power will out. It can be argued that an inflation hurts the poor most because they are least able to defend themselves against it; and so, if the poor are asked to become poorer in halting the inflation (by fixing wages and not prices, which is what was done in Chile), it is all for their own eventual good, if they should manage to live so long.

The hitch arises when weaker sectors are denied more than they are willing to get along without. The breaking point of this willingness is not indicated by plain belly factors alone, as the oversimplified privation-subversion equation would seem to indicate. Since the Chilean wage earner is in a broad sense not a completely uneducated person, since he seems to have real aspirations to move upwards and onwards in the social scale, it is only with some difficulty that he can be pushed below what he defines as social subsistence. He is above strictly defined economic subsistence (that is, that situation in which the addition of one more mouth means the group can no longer reproduce itself) and not likely to fall below it. It may be conjectured that this social-subsistence maintenance is what is being threatened by fifteen years of inflation and a half a decade of depression. The obverse of this situation gives grounds for optimism. If this speculation is correct, then Chile has a population clamoring to share a wider economic base, to form the larger markets needed for more efficient production, to take the next step toward greater economic elaboration and more effective participation in a democratic political structure. The lower economic group thus is not inert, and this fact gives Chile a great advantage in flexibility over many other economically retarded areas.

Let us go further. The economically autonomous persons are those whose organization and values have expressed the power which made inflation at least tolerable for them, if not positively advantageous. Whether they have done their dark economic deeds out of conscious malice or ill will makes not the slightest difference. They have acted out of their pre- and misconceptions, out of their ways of thinking and doing business, out of their "natural" acquisitiveness as the modes thereof are established for them and as they themselves amend them. And once the process began, one had to adjust oneself, no?

The Chilean argument of, "We are poor, therefore we have discontent, therefore we have subversion, therefore lend us money," is a Woolworth version of economic determinism. The sugar coating is a little cloying, too, for ". . . therefore lend us money" is implicitly followed by ". . . for your own good, or the Communists will take us over, and you wouldn't like that a bit."

The problem for the United States should be a perplexing one, even if it is not viewed as one because of our wholesale subscription to the same kind of narrowly economically deterministic thinking. Assistance, as we all know by this time, is not just a question of money but also brings with it the problem of the administration of funds, the politics of money, which in turn is a matter touching at the very heart of sovereignty. Money badly used, moneys which increase social distance, can have an effect opposite to the political and military one planned. The administrative knot is a familiar one for anyone engaged in international aid programs. The ethical problem, too, is an old one for social scientists: self-conscious manipulation versus as independent as possible an interplay of the institutions of any cultural group.

Many Chileans threw themselves into the streets in April of 1957 because they could no longer stand what their own society was doing to them. Any American action which neglects this major premise will in the long haul be wrong.

5

GUATEMALA AFTER REVOLUTION

Guatemala is of special interest to the United States, if for no reason other than that it is of particular interest to other Latin American countries. The American government is commonly accused of having intervened in internal Guatemalan politics toward the end of eliminating the administration of Jacobo Arbenz Guzmán in 1954. Arbenz was widely viewed in the United States as either a Communist or a fellow-traveler. In Latin America he was usually regarded as a left-wing, nationalistic reformer. Certainly the United States participated in the overthrow of Arbenz in the sense that it openly frowned on his government and probably used its good offices in supporting the endeavors of rebel Castillo Armas in neighboring Central American states. Whatever the actual degree of American involvement, after the fall of Arbenz there seemed some reason for hoping that the worried little country would have its chance for social reform without the possibility of becoming deeply entangled in the Cold War or subjected to Marxist theory and practice.

Matters worked out otherwise. The United States did not choose to make of Guatemala a "showplace of democracy." Castillo Armas' administration turned out to be inefficacious and corrupt. Then Castillo Armas himself was mysteriously assassinated in 1957, and it was only after one fraudulent election and then another one to correct the defalcations that some stability returned to government with the election of conservative General Ydígoras Fuentes, who in his turn was deposed by military coup.

Some material on the immediate results of the revolution of 1954 is available in English.[1] But an objective and profound examination needs to be made of the entire course of events since 1954 with a view to revealing what happens when a reform government aborts, when exciting politics revert to boredom and lack of involvement. Studies of failure are all too rare.

I am not equipped to fill the lack just pointed out. What I can offer are observations on problems, persons, and events as they unfolded in 1955, a year after the assumption of power by Castillo Armas when it was still thought that Guatemala could be saved from its left and right extremists. My doubtful hopes for Castillo Armas at that time were snuffed out with his assassination; and my hopes for peaceful progress in Guatemala remain dim with what I know at second hand about the present regime. In any event, here are some observations which I have left as close to the original version as possible so that they will not lose their warmth and informality. My purpose is to transmit "feel," as I have already said, to unfold the little events of politics which make up a country's tone and which give the expert the background noise out of which he draws his stately themes and his pundit's declarations.

My first visit to Guatemala was during the summer of 1951. I returned to spend a year there between 1952 and 1953. After the fall of Arbenz I visited the country twice in 1955 and once in 1956, and since then have not returned—not out of pique, but simply because I became busied much farther to the south in Chile and Argentina. This chapter contains impressions of my 1955 visits, as well as some hindsight.

Between June 25 and July 4, 1955, everybody in Guatemala had something to celebrate. On the first date, law students opposing the government of Colonel Carlos Castillo Armas celebrated the death of a woman schoolteacher, martyr of the revolution that overthrew General Jorge Ubico in 1944 and led to the governments of Juan José Arévalo (1945–51) and of Jacobo Arbenz Guzmán (1951–54). June 27 was the first anniversary of the resignation of Arbenz, June 28 the eleventh anniversary of the overthrow of Ubico; July 3 ended the first year of the new Liberation Government of Castillo Armas. And the Fourth of July is a traditional national holiday in Guatemala, celebrated by *antiyanquis* in the name of Tom Paine and by pro-Americans in the name of either Franklin D. Roosevelt or Dwight D. Eisenhower, depending on how they feel about these things. In addition, the Fourth officially ushers in Guatemala's revolution month: not only are there Bastille Day to celebrate on the fourteenth and the anniversary of the

---

[1] See, for instance, Ronald M. Schneider, *Communism in Guatemala 1944–1954*, New York: Praeger 1958; or John Gillin and K. H. Silvert, "Ambiguities in Guatemala," *Foreign Affairs*, Vol. 34, No. 3, April, 1956, pp. 469–82.

assassination of Colonel Francisco Javier Arana, hero of the Castillo Armas government who was liquidated on July 18, 1949, but also respect must be paid to numerous plots, counterplots, revolutions, and counterrevolutions stemming all the way back to the victorious Liberal Revolution of 1871. Only proclericals celebrate the Conservative regime of 1839 to 1871, doing so without the benefit of national holidays.

The weather traditionally conspires to make July favorable for outdoor political activity. The rainy season, which starts in April, usually offers a partial respite during July—the *canícula*, a warm, dry, and beautiful *entr'acte*, is good campaigning weather, especially for a populace bored with inability to work outside during the preceding heavy rains and afflicted by an annual economic slump. In 1955, however, nature was uncooperative, holding back the rains until the last days of June, and then deluging most of the celebrations. The drought which was affecting almost all of Mexico and Central America had sharpened the pains of most of these governments. The corn and bean crops had been virtually ruined through the five Central American republics, with particularly disastrous consequences in El Salvador, Honduras, and Guatemala. In the last of these countries, corn sold on the open market was bringing as much as 15 cents a pound, as compared to a normal four cents, while the price of beans had risen almost as high. With El Salvador just entering a presidential campaign, Honduras laboring under a clumsily consummated executive exchange, and Guatemala not yet consolidated from one of a martial nature, the drought was potentially serious until shortages were relieved by imports from Mexico and the United States.

With revolutions come rumors of revolutions. In a small capital like Guatemala City, with a population of only 300,000, a normal electorate of at most 50,000, and a politically aware population of probably 20,000, the informal channels of communications are remarkably active and rapid but, regrettably, inaccurate. In the space of ten days rumor solved a murder for me, reported three separate political plots, explained the appointment of a new ambassador to El Salvador (he was unacceptable because he was being sued there), detailed how American corn shipped to relieve the shortage had allegedly been sold by government officials to El Salvador, dissected the love life of an allegedly hermaphroditic police official, and charged fraud in bidding between a German and a Swedish firm for a contract to expand the capital's telephone service (there were then only 5,000 lines in the entire city).

The following rumor, which came to me straight from a member of the government's inner circle and presumably fresh from discussion among the president's advisers, is a good example of the national hobby. It was said that a plot to invade Guatemala was brewing in Mexico, where there were many anti-government refugees. The Mexican government was reputedly cool to Castillo Armas. Both Guatemalan and United States intelligence sources, according to the report, were aware of the grouping of armed forces, but Castillo Armas wanted the invasion to take place so that he might destroy a center of infection and use the external pressure as an excuse to consolidate his domestic position. Guatemala, therefore, did not protest to the Mexican government. But the United States, anxious to keep Central America as quiet as possible after the turmoil of the previous year which seriously affected Guatemala, Honduras, Nicaragua, and Costa Rica, reportedly entered its protest to the Mexican government. The invasion was scheduled for July 3 and was planned to interrupt the victory celebration of the *castilloarmistas,* but the Mexicans reportedly apprehended thirty of the presumed invaders and handed them across the border to the Guatemalan officials at a town called Malacatán.

A neat legal question then is said to have arisen: what to do with these people? After all, they were guilty of no crime committed on Guatemalan soil. In addition, a public trial would be most embarrassing to the Mexican government, since Latin American states are not supposed to turn over political refugees to the prosecuting government, and there was a strong pro-Arbenz current in Mexico itself. The further reputed worry of the Castillo Armas government was the dispersal of a threatening nucleus which theretofore had been kept under observation. The government was seemingly particularly disturbed because the potential insurgents had eight planes which had disappeared. The report even detailed the planes, listing four Thunderbolts, two DC-3's, and two trainers.

Now, what is a neutral and objective observer to do with such a story? How is it to be verified? Were the source to be indicated, how would his future position be imperiled? Could he hope ever to get further information? An attempt to recheck the story three weeks later produced only blank stares. However, there was value in what must be classified as an unsubstantiated rumor.

First, it reveals some of Guatemala's mistrust of Mexico, whose embassy in Guatemala sheltered most of the important refugees of the former government, from Arbenz and his family down. *The Battle of Guatemala,* by Guillermo Toriello, last foreign minister of the late government, had already gone through six editions in Mexico since its first publication early in 1955. Refugees from the Arbenz government found it easy to obtain work permits in Mexico; and Lázaro Cárdenas, former Mexican president (from 1934 to 1940) and still a most eminent political leader, had publicly expressed his dissatisfaction with the course of events in Mexico's southern neighbor.

Second, there was and still is a great preoccupation with arms, and especially with airplanes, in all of Central America. The use of six Thunderbolt planes by Castillo Armas against the few trainers of the Arbenz government is often quoted as the decisive military fact of the revolution, whether it really was or not. The Guatemalan government was then displaying its few recently acquired P-51's as often as possible. The purchase of twenty-six Mustangs by the Nicaraguan government early in 1955, and its subsequent adventure against Costa Rica, resulted in general concern about comparative air forces. In Guatemala the P-51's were also used to symbolize the strength of the Castillo Armas government, its friendliness with the United States, and its sternly anti-Communist attitude. During the 1954 revolution the Liberation radio called the Castillo Armas fighter planes *sulfatos,* or laxatives, an amusing name which has stuck ever since. The public display of other arms was also encouraged. The police carried submachine guns when on regular duty; the clothes tree in the president's antechamber was decorated with four officers' caps and four tommy guns when I went to see him; the clothes closet of one of the secretaries of congress contained a number of suits, a military rifle, a submachine gun, two pistols, and a most tasteful record collection.

Lastly, the story demonstrates that there are few secrets in Guatemala, but also that there are times when it is virtually impossible to distinguish an open secret from a fantasy.

FREEDOM OF THE PRESS

There were, of course, other sources of information, but the general disturbance attending a change of administration had damaged many of the government's technical reporting services, such as the Office of Statistics, whose well-trained former head was then in Argentina. The exaggeratedly personalistic procedures of any new government were also strongly in evidence. In order to get a copy of the decrees issued during 1954, for example, it was necessary for me to see the Minister of Interior himself. After he heard my petition, and evinced disappointment when he learned I was not an expert in penal law, he extracted a key from his vest pocket, unlocked a closet, and presented me with two printed volumes of the decrees, taking them from huge stacks lining the closet walls. They were simply unavailable elsewhere.

The newspapers were rather useful in a limited sense for, despite the timorousness of the privately owned papers, a strong tradition of freedom of the press caused many outbursts and the expression of varying raw opinions and ideas. Guatemala's largest daily, *El Imparcial,* is notorious for its ability to live with any government, while the official newspaper, *El Diario de Centroamérica,* of course prints only approved governmental views. The numerous other smaller dailies and one weekly offer a reasonable spread of opinion. No single one of these papers has a great impact, however, since the largest, *El Imparcial,* has a circulation of only 21,000 to 23,000 daily, rising to 27,000 for the Saturday issue. But Guatemala's ten dailies (one an English-language advertising paper) and ten more or less regular weeklies were fruitful sources, given the fairly good measure of freedom of the press.

It is not the purpose of this report to show how difficult it was to get data about Guatemala but rather to say something of the informational limitations under which the Guatemalans themselves labored. The trouble is that many vital aspects of this country have never been studied. The problem is accentuated in the decision-making processes when changes in ruling personnel lose to the government the services of experienced and technically able persons.

In weighing Latin American revolutions, it is exceedingly important to find out how many persons were killed and how many exiled or otherwise dispossessed. No more than fifteen died when Ubico, the "Iron Dictator of the Caribbean," was overthrown in 1944. But, very conservatively, at least 300 were killed in nonmilitary action during the June 1954 revolt. At least another thousand fled. These figures must be taken very cautiously, for the claims are violently conflicting. In Toriello's book cited above (No. 39 in the famous Mexican *Cuadernos Americanos* series), 217 persons are listed as killed by the incoming Castillo Armas group (pp. 331–32). A few *arbenzistas* I spoke to in Guatemala claimed that the outgoing government killed some forty or fifty persons "in self-defense" and that the Toriello figure should be increased to at least 300. Although no official figures are available, the best guesses among informed government workers and foreign correspondents were remarkably similar: that the Arbenz government killed some 250 persons on the way out, the Castillo Armas group about fifty on the way in. Basing my conclusions on the veracity of the informants, I am inclined to accept the figure of 250 killed by the Arbenz regime, some of them first subjected to torture. But because most of the Castillo Armas killings occurred in the countryside, or at least out of the capital, my impulse is to raise the estimate of the number executed. John Gillin, then a University of North Carolina anthropologist, revisited the eastern Guatemala village of San Luis Jilotepeque [2] in late June of 1955 and reported that nine persons were removed by the invading Liberation Army and summarily executed. Eastern Guatemala, the Escuintla region between Guatemala City and the coastal port of

---

[2] See his *Culture of Security in San Carlos,* New Orleans: Middle American Research Institute, Pub. 16, 1951; and Melvin Tumin, *Caste and Class in a Peasant Society,* Princeton: Princeton University Press, 1952, for published studies on this town.

San José, and the banana area of Tiquisate probably felt the greatest brunt of this type of political cleansing, for these were areas of deepest Communist rural organization. It should also be noted that these are regions of heavy or exclusive *ladino* population.

The relatively large number of deaths is prima-facie evidence that we are not dealing with an ordinary *cuartelazo*, or barracks revolt, but with a phenomenon which shook more than political activists. A Chilean author, Edwards Vives, has spoken of the "aristocratic froth" to characterize the effective Latin American political actors; but in this case the froth took to embassies, to immediate flight, or to the protection of newly influential friends. For the first time since the religious upheavals of the last century, carpenters, bricklayers, and farmers were caught. On both sides these were the persons killed. Not one person of the policy level died on either side. Whereas the Arbenz-inspired killings included urban as well as rural persons, however, as has been said, the fewer Castillo Armas executions were outside the capital, but they effectively liquidated farm and labor union leaders. In Tiquisate alone, seventeen reputed union leaders were shot, according to private report as well as published information. To the credit of the Castillo Armas government, however, its period of reprisal was short, the worst being over in two weeks. An obvious result of this highly discriminatory action was that the government had grave difficulties in its attempt to reactivate the unions; there weren't enough labor leaders. Most unfortunately, many of the persons pulled into both rural and urban union activities were ambitious Indians and ladinos whose mobility urges were satisfied by these new avenues of self-expression which let them participate in activities of a national nature. Ideological factors above the level of strong feelings of nationalism may well have been erasable, however, saving lives and positively aiding the new government. Gillin told me of the case of the Peasants' Union leader of San Luis Jilotepeque, who had formerly been one of the few Indian lieutenants in Ubico's army and in charge of the famous Sunday drill designed to militarize the Indian population. He had been able to make the switch from *ubiquismo* to *arbenzismo*, but he did not survive the Castillo Armas revolution. Was he "really" a Communist, or could he have been educated to serve those nationalistic ends of the new government that coincided with those of its predecessor?

RELIGION AND POLITICS

A study of political prisoners brought from rural areas to the central penitentiary in Guatemala City, made by the pseudonymous Stokes Newbold, an American social scientist, indicates that the political outlook of the persons apprehended was very often naïve, but also was colored by a conscious self-interest. Convinced Communist leaders were, of course, in hiding or in embassies and thus unavailable; others, who may have been more dangerous or more disturbing than the people Newbold studied, were dead. The sample, thus, is biased, but the study is valuable, indicating why some persons on the social move can be influenced to accept the dominant ideological beliefs of the political elite. Some of Newbold's observations about mobility and political action are worth quoting:

> . . . among both labor union and agrarian committee members there was another significant trait (and one which was not characteristic of the membership in the political action groups); this was *mobility* or *low residential continuity* . . . The mere need for economic betterment . . . does not in itself make a group receptive to Communist propaganda and activity; there must also be some element in the population which has no traditional social relationship and no vested interest in the area . . . The whole picture of the Communist success in rural Guatemala must be measured . . . in terms of which groups became so interested in their activities that they became "self propelled," that is, continued without constant agitation by professionals . . . it is necessary to point out that it was specifically . . . [middle class] leadership . . . which provided the initial agitation and later the political guidance to groups of countrymen. Of equal importance, however, is that on the local level in the towns and countryside, local leaders developed to follow the lead of the ideologically more sophisticated agitators.[3]

Some of the other conclusions Newbold draws are that there ". . . is very little evidence that membership and activity in Catholic or Protestant churches was any serious deterrent to supporting Communist sponsored activities." My interpolation: Some superficial explanations may easily be found in the traditional anticlericalism of Guatemala, a country which successfully concluded its Liberal revolution eighty-four years ago and which even in 1955 had only 300 priests, or one for every 10,000 persons, the lowest percentage in any nominally Catholic country. Monastic orders, nunneries, and seminaries were forbidden from 1871 to 1954, as were religious educational institutions. The Protestants, in their turn, were drawn toward the Arbenz government because of its generosity in allowing missionaries to enter Guatemala. Protestantized Indians, themselves anti-Catholic, found here at least one area of agreement with the government. In addition such persons, forbidden to drink or otherwise take part in the activities of the traditional Indian religio-political community, began to partake of other

[3] Stokes Newbold, with the collaboration of June and Manning Nash, *A Study of Receptivity to Communism in Rural Guatemala.*

more generalized aspects of the Protestant ethic, such as attitudes toward work, and tended to move toward better economic positions. Their vested interests, therefore, became partially identified with the continued supremacy of the Arbenz government, at least in preference to a clerically oriented political structure.[4] The Castillo Armas government was also Liberal in orientation but in a precarious alliance with the Church because of a shared anti-Communism.

Another major Newbold conclusion is that:

> Poverty and landlessness were not characteristic of the sample population as a whole. Forty-three per cent were economically adequate and 36 per cent were land owners prior to the agrarian reform [in 1953] . . . While poverty doubtless plays an important role, it is neither the only factor nor necessarily the determining factor that may make a population susceptible to Communism.

My note: This comment should be juxtaposed with the previous one, emphasizing the role of the middle class in Guatemala as the supplier group for the previous government. Many men of means, such as the Toriello brothers, took an active part in the Arbenz administration, whose policy leaders were of predominantly European appearance. Castillo Armas, an obvious *mestizo,* was a shock to some groups in the capital after he arrived. Although the lines of social division in Guatemala are largely cultural and not racial, some snide comment arose about the "Indian" nature of many persons active in the present government. The shortage of cooks, for example, was sarcastically attributed to the fact that the new army officers were marrying them all. These criticisms cannot be taken too seriously, for they are part of an old and well-accepted pattern of political canards. In this connection, it is common in Guatemala and other Latin American countries to libel presidents as being narcotics addicts, as well as to question the legitimacy of many politicians. Since the rural illegitimacy rate in Guatemala is 60 per cent, the charges are sometimes correct.

It would be inaccurate to state that the Castillo Armas government was any more a product of the upper and middle classes than its predecessor. It is my opinion that many of the middle- and upper-middle-class persons so important to the Arévalo period (1945–1954) were not replaced by their social equivalents, and that the Castillo Armas government had a far greater proportion of lower-middle-class persons in its membership. This statement is not susceptible to proof, of course, and I repeat that it is a subjective determination.

[4] An attitude analysis of the population of Cobán, in the Department of the Alta Verapaz, by the author and his wife in 1953, clearly demonstrates the growing differences between Protestant and Catholic Indians even in such matters as the hours of sleeping and arising. Cf. Ch. 3.

Newbold's third principal conclusion is that the illiterates interviewed (66 per cent of the sample, as compared to a national average
of 72.2 per cent in 1950) showed "very little comprehension of Communist ideology or terminology. They were generally uninformed, but
where they did manifest knowledge, it concerned specifically Guatemalan and not foreign persons and events . . . In this particular population it seems that the ideological propaganda has not settled beyond
the local literate leader and, for the most part, people who were not
agriculturalists." His last point is closely related:

> It has been commented that "these people were being led like sheep";
> in the writer's opinion, this is not supported. It is clear that the popu-
> lation interviewed was in general interested in some phase of the past
> government's activities . . . It may be said that these people were
> being led like sheep in that they did what the Communists wanted; on
> the other hand, they were doing things which they too wished to do.
> The Communists were successful in identifying their goals with those
> of certain portions of the rural population; this can be laid to the clev-
> erness of the Communists, but not necessarily to the "sheep-like" qual-
> ities of the population.

A NEW CONSTITUTION

There is another possible interpretation of the evident willingness of
certain sectors of the society, both urban and rural, to cooperate with
the previous administrations. Some policies can be followed by governments of either the right or the left; such policies seem to be in the
nature of a given situation. Thus we do not find a legislative revolution
accompanying the political revolution of 1954. Although the Constitution of 1945 was dissolved, as well as the Agrarian Reform Law (Decree 900), almost every other social innovation of the past ten years
remained. The development corporation and the Guatemalan Social
Security Institute continued to operate, as did all the banks of a special
as well as general nature; the Labor Code (Decree 330) was still
largely in effect, although its administration tended toward much
greater favor for the employer than was the case before. The new constitution, still in effect, is in great measure merely an adaptation of the
old, with the addition of specific articles of a political nature custom-
built for the changed situation. The constitution, for example, continues to allow illiterates (commonly interpreted as Indians by the Deputies) to vote, although the Arbenz government had been criticized for
this practice. Essentially there was no legislative revolution because
those things accomplished by the previous government in line with the
normal development of modern nation-states also remained imperatives for the successor government. Many *castilloarmistas*, including

the president himself, came to prominence with the Revolution of 1944, and it was a major propaganda difficulty for them to decide whether to condemn "eleven years of Communism," as they officially said on more than one occasion, or whether to remain the true sons of the October revolution, which they also still celebrate as a national holiday. They were sure they were opposed to Ubico and to the Arévalo-Arbenz combine, but they still had not found a comfortable individual position.

Whether a Communist problem still existed was a matter of definition. That there were still some Communists and Communist sympathizers in Guatemala goes without saying; whether their numbers were large enough to matter was another question. A more subtle danger then lay in the meaning of the word "Communist" in Guatemala. Since it was used indiscriminately for almost five years to mean anyone connected with the former government or any of its policies, and formalized by naming the major opposition group the Party of Anti-Communist Unification (*Partido de Unificación Anticomunista*), the word was watered down and could be applied to many activities which were not peculiarly Communist, as the following story reveals. It seems that at Christmas, 1954, the first after Arbenz' overthrow, the newspaper *El Imparcial* failed to pay a bonus for the first time since 1944. A pressman is then reported to have told one of the reporters, "You see, when the Communists are not around to protect us, we lose our benefits."

Castillo Armas' avowed attitude was that the Communist problem was largely one for the police and not a political matter. During my interview with him on June 29 he made that statement and continued, "My government will smother them, not shoot them." Then he added hastily, "Of course, that does not include the torturers and the murderers whom we have in jail. They will be shot, but only after two or three years, and only after they have been tried in strict accordance with legal precepts, like the Rosenbergs in the United States." On August 5, two *arbenzistas* were shot for atrocities committed during the revolution. Castillo Armas admitted readily that many persons among his own supporters had complained that his government had not killed enough Communists or alleged Communists. Significantly he coupled this remark with the statement that Guatemala had received a bad press, especially in other Latin American countries, and that wholesale massacres were expected. Uruguay and Ecuador did not recognize the regime until almost a year after its taking office, and newspaper comment, especially in Mexico, was often most acrimonious.

On October 29, 1954, inaugurating the sessions of the new Constituent Assembly, the President stated his view on this matter:

> There has come to my attention the mistaken idea that the Government has not proceeded with the energy some may desire; our adversaries and even our supporters hoped that, after the unheard-of acts of terrorism and barbarity committed by the Government of Arbenz, incontrovertible proof of its weakness, an era of reprisals and vengeance would be initiated which would have been explained as a reaction against the crimes perpetrated by the Communist regime . . . Happily for everyone, my government has not fallen into that weakness . . . my policies, as a matter of conviction and of duty, will be developed equidistant from any extremist ideologies . . .

The opposition, however, still pointed to sporadic cases of violence. A former member of the Arbenz government, employed in the Indian Institute, gave as his sophisticated view that the government, which by its military and emergency nature should have been highly centralized, actually could not adequately control many country areas. For this reason, it was argued, many killings occurred in the provinces because the debility of the central government allowed revenge to be taken on a personal and *ad hoc* basis, with little regard for politics at the ideological level.

Political parties were still technically illegal during my 1955 visit, although nuclei of official and oppositionist parties existed and their attitudes were reflected in the newspapers. When asked how normal political processes could be restored and a loyal opposition created, the President, during our interview, said he favored a single official party, free organization of opposition groups, and the establishment of a civil service. Unfortunately, over a year had already passed, and the new constitution upon which a return to normal government depended was still at least three months away from completion and probably six months away from final promulgation. Further, the President had demonstrated a distrust of party politics, at least in the Guatemalan tradition. In the speech to the Constituent Assembly, cited above, he also made the following statement:

> I am of the opinion that it is of public utility and interest to limit in a rational manner—without violating the law—the constant political activities of the parties, and to abolish the unhealthy custom of subventing them with the funds of their contributors. I am also moved to eliminate those superfluous disbursements [from the treasury] which only make high public officials lazy and satisfy their personal vanity.

If past Guatemalan practice is any criterion, what the President meant is that the official party or parties would receive all their funds from the government and that the opposition groups would have to scrounge among their own members.

GUATEMALA'S ECONOMIC FUTURE

In answer to a question concerning diversification and improvement of Guatemala's economic structure, the President's answer could only be called disappointing. He put the hopes of his administration in three areas—oil, uranium, and roads, in that order. A new petroleum law was passed to encourage foreign investment, but since explorations had not been completed and not even a test well had as yet been sunk, Guatemala was many years away from enjoying the first royalty check. As for uranium, several areas are believed to have radioactive ores, but there are even now no formalized plans for extraction. The road-building program, emphasized and begun by the former regime, had been receiving the enthusiastic moral and financial support of the United States, so that work was already well under way. Initial appropriations to get the Pan-American highway under construction were reinforced by over $18 million from the International Bank at the end of July, 1955, and international bids had already been advertised for.

The road-building program was no longer a subject of great controversy. The previous Arbenz regime had not connected the Guatemalan roads with the existing paved Mexican highway to the border, presumably because of a desire to keep American tourists out and to prevent the use of the road as a military highway. Instead, they paved a road to the Pacific port of San José, asphalted the Pan-American highway for some seventy kilometers, as far west as a town called Patzicía, and then projected a new paved highway to the Atlantic, with its terminus in the recently constructed and nationally owned port of Santo Tomás. The purpose of the highway to the Atlantic was to compete with the International Railways of Central America, which the United Fruit Company controlled, since it then owned over a third of the line. It had been charged that the line imposed discriminatory freight rates and gave priority to bananas over all other kinds of freight. Further, the fact that the major Guatemalan Atlantic port, Puerto Barrios, is Fruit Company property was interpreted as giving that organization too much "threat" power in Guatemalan internal affairs.

The Castillo Armas government decided to go ahead with the entire Arbenz plan, adding to it the completion of the road to Mexico (now accomplished) and the paving of the whole strip from Mexico to Guatemala City through eastern Guatemala to El Salvador. It is now possible to travel on paved roads through Mexico and all the Central American republics to San José, the capital of Costa Rica.

Since some 80 per cent of the national budget rests on coffee export taxes and at least the same percentage describes the value of coffee annually in the total export picture, a drop in coffee prices in the

United States is a fundamental economic problem in Guatemala. Small wonder that a cold wave in Brazil leads to headlines in Guatemala. Although such an economy can survive depression without desperation in the predominantly rural population, the urban services depend upon foreign trade for gasoline, automobiles, breakfast cereals, and nylon stockings. The banana industry is not nearly so important to the nation as coffee, for the United Fruit Company employs only some ten to eleven thousand Guatemalans in its two plantations (Bananera on the Caribbean, and Tiquisate on the Pacific) and allied operations.

If Guatemala's economy has not produced a violent inflation, but has rather followed world trends, it also is obviously not of the type that can produce a surplus sufficient to afford the Guatemalan people a more interesting and varied existence. We may here be skirting close to the area of submerged value judgments. Let us say instead that this country's economic capabilities are limited; her broad areas of choice appear to be: (1) to stay more or less in *status quo,* riding out world storms as they may appear; (2) to depend upon extractive industries (all of which are away from the areas of high population density) to provide the foreign exchange with which to buy a wider array and greater quantity of industrial products than heretofore; or (3) to combine the second alternative with some attempt to establish small industries, such as furniture manufacture, the assembling of such articles as radios, badly needed cement manufacture to supplement the present supply, and the like. The decision of Castillo Armas was in favor of a combination of the first two possibilities, with yearnings for an impossible fourth—large industry. The country simply has no large supplies of raw materials with which to maintain a complex industrial setup; even if it had such resources, its labor supply would be inadequate in size and training to permit their exploitation.

PUBLIC HONESTY

Alleged corruption in Guatemala is as good a case as any to demonstrate the primary difficulty in getting facts mentioned above and even greater difficulty in analyzing them to show their relative significance or unimportance. Almost certainly the Castillo Armas government contained some very dishonest individuals. The corn scandals of June and July of 1955 were a case in point, as was a subsequent flour scandal, besides favoritism in letting bids for government contracts and the like. The corn problem was well reported to American readers. To recapitulate briefly, it was charged that a group of persons close to the President took advantage of the corn shortage resulting from the early-year drought to attempt to corner the market in this commodity. As the story went, the government's Development Institute attempted to buy corn from Mexico but was refused an export license by the Mexican government's price control agency. A hastily organized private concern, however, did get such a license from the Mexican entity (CEIMSA) and brought large shipments to Guatemala, the first of which was labeled unfit for human consumption by impartial technicians who tested samples. (Photostatic copies of these reports by a UN agency were published in the Guatemalan newspapers.) Castillo Armas himself was implicated when *El Estudiante,* a student weekly of the school of law, alleged that a check for $25,000 the president had received from the head of the corn importing company could have only one interpretation. The daily, *El Imparcial* ran the President's explanation that the check was merely in repayment of a personal loan under the very partial headline, "The Honor of the President is Resplendent," but many persons seemed to remain unconvinced, to judge by coffeehouse discussion.

Then there was the flour hassle. One of Guatemala's leading importers wrote his version of the story and gave me permission to use it. He is obviously an interested party, but his statement does not appear to be unduly inaccurate. Here is his account, just as he wrote it in English:

A year ago [late 1944] thru a defective decree a couple of "sharpies" booked (on paper only) the whole quota of imported flour destined for Guatemala under the International Wheat Agreement. Although anyone can usually buy Non-Quota flour, this decree specified that until the 25,000 tons of IWA flour had been imported, no other flour would be allowed into the country.

This gave these fellows automatically exclusive control of the flour imports. The then Minister of Economy . . . quickly issued a second decree calling this a "monopolistic scheme" and, to break it up, permitted anyone to bring in Non-Quota . . . flour—thus ending the monopoly completely.

A couple of months after this condition was normalized and all the trouble was eliminated, the new Minister of Economy . . . possibly thru the influence of law partner . . . (who by coincidence is also lawyer of the monopoly) issued a new decree reversing the law and abolishing the import of any flour except the IWA monopoly flour . . .

When the monopoly people realized they had won their battle, they decided to make all the money they could out of the chaos. Instead of bringing in the only flour allowed by Law—Patent Flours with not more than a .54% ash content—they began bringing in the poorest available grades of Clear Flour containing as high as .71% and more ash.

When samples from the local bakeries were privately tested and
proven bad the Health Department at the request of a small group of
importers acted to try and stop this flour from being released from the
Custom House. However, the Minister of Economy overruled the
Health Dept. Court and said that IF THE FLOURS HAD GOOD
CERTIFICATES OF ANALYSIS [his upper case] from the shippers,
they should come in, regardless of the Health Dept. Lab. report.

The newspapers have given no word of this scandal probably afraid of
possible political consequences or maybe because there are hundreds
of thousands of dollars profit involved that can work miracles anywhere . . .

Since this statement was written, however, the newspapers carried
the story; copying the above remarks is thus merely a recapitulation
of commonly available knowledge in Guatemala.

Businessmen in other branches of the economy also were affected.
During the summer bids were taken on an extension of Guatemala
City's telephone service. Rumors of bribes were everywhere. I played
bridge with one agent of a European telephone company who acted as
though he held the lead in a television spy drama and was quite free
with his charges that every company had passed bribes except, of
course, his own. An automobile dealer of my acquaintance was firm in
his determination that the government "had better be honest" in letting
its contracts for road-building equipment "this time." An importer of
machinery put bidding finagling as one of his major sources of discontent with the state of affairs.

It is easy enough to pass off this business by saying that the previous
governments of Arbenz and Arévalo were also corrupt, as they undoubtedly were. Our concern here is not to judge the morality of the
matter but rather to indicate why there was and is corruption and to
place the dishonesty within the culture concerned and to understand
its impact.

An excellent and amusing little book called *Precios, Salarios, y
Mordidas* (*Prices, Salaries, and Bribes*) is an attempt to discuss the influence of notorious and widespread graft on the economy of Mexico.
Does one include a bribe under "profits"? What type of business expense is it? Economic analysis under conditions of this kind can become understandably complicated. The author, Rodrigo García
Treviño, gives a short history of the Mexican bribe, called there the
mordida, or "bite."

If the post-revolutionary [after 1910, that is] understanding of the
verb "to bite" is new, the activity which originated it is ancient. If
"biting" was not practiced in ancient Anahuac [the Aztec empire],
there is no doubt that the conquistadors imported it and that it was

born together with the New Spain. Under Porfirismo [the long reign of Porfirio Díaz, lasting over three hundred years to 1910] it was a common practice . . . although an austere one. With the triumph of the revolution, the "bite" lost its austerity and . . . it was said, "to be able to have, one must have power." [This is an excellent Spanish pun, untranslatable: *Para poder tener hay que tener poder.*]

With that great boss of brilliant intelligence and festive spirit called Alvaro Obregón, they "bit" joyfully, not to accumulate, but rather to enjoy life, for otherwise, "Why did we fight?" . . .

Calles was the great statesman of the revolution . . . and therefore with his influence he stamped a new tone on everything. In his period, they "bit" perhaps less than under Obregón, but toward other ends. From among the politicians of that time and their friends and relatives began to be born the new bourgeoisie. Now they "bit" in order to accumulate. The progressive "bite" had been born! [5]

The author makes several very important points: The social character of the bribe or graft in general changes with the times; extraordinary rewards are a part of extraordinary sacrifices in gaining political power ("Why did we fight?"), and no matter what the ideology of government, at least in Mexico, imposing corruption has always been present. To a lesser degree than in Mexico, in all probability, the same things may be said of Guatemala. An American correspondent in that country told me, "This isn't Guatemala's worst government, but it is its most corrupt one." I should argue that it is the nature and type of these dark dealings that have given rise to so much publicity and discussion, rather than the number of incidents or even the amount of money concerned. To manipulate the prices of basic foodstuffs is to dabble in an area which immediately and totally affects the entire economy—a statement especially true of nonindustrialized societies. Corn is the basic item of the Guatemalan diet; the tortilla is both bread and utensil, both nourishing and satisfying. When corn prices rise, all the prices of those articles bought and sold by the numerous small farmers and tradespeople of Guatemala must likewise go up. Small wonder that a handful of string beans cost thirty-five American cents at the height of the corn inflation.

FOREIGN RELATIONS

The relationship of the Castillo Armas administration to the United States was also a matter of concern in Guatemala. That Guatemalan government was not popular with nationalists in other Latin countries, and it is accurate to state that it was abhorrent to the liberal national-

[5] Rodrigo García Treviño, *Precios, Salarios, y Mordidas,* Mexico: Editorial América, 1953, pp. 50–51.

ist. It is argued that Castillo Armas' government was the product of the United States—that without our moral and material support he would still be perspiring in Tegucigalpa. It matters little whether we did or did not really intervene directly, for practically nobody of any political color in Latin America—even fervent *castilloarmistas*—bothers to assume we did not.

Interventionism is an Old Latin American complaint against the United States. (It was only with the multilateralization of the Monroe Doctrine before World War II that the fears of the nationalists were stilled. We may have here the principal reason for the continued strong popularity of F. D. Roosevelt among Latin Americans.) In addition to this traditional plaint, however, there is another one against the revolutionary mode of Castillo Armas' accession to power. As stated in Chapter 2, now that the Latin American countries are becoming nations, barracks revolts cannot remain simple; more and more persons develop a stake in orderly process and in responsive government, restricting the ability of power monopolists to play without reference to immediate economic and social consequences.

. . . Twentieth-century technical development hit Latin America in 1946, as World War II closed, with hurricane force. Modern cities sprang up around the nuclei of the old, beautiful colonial capitals. The onrush of modern industry created large, sentient urban populations —sometimes too large—and brought with it complex industrial economics.

When varied industry enters, more than the personally directed force of powerful military generals or juntas is needed for permanent government, and capable South American statesmen know it. Economic distress means trouble; and you cannot compel economic prosperity with bayonets.[6]

The nationalistic Latin American has gone so far in his antipathy to the *cuartelazo* as the primary instrument of political change that he will sometimes be willing to accept a government hateful to him in preference to the overthrow of such a government by a device which is even more hateful. The Mexican imitation of *Time* magazine expressed this point of view most clearly with relationship to the Perón imbroglio:

Tiempo [that is, *Time*. The journal still uses its old title in the text, although now enjoined from using it on the cover.] never looked with favor on the political regime installed in Argentina by General Juan Domingo Perón, a matter which is easily understandable given on one

[6] Adolf A. Berle, Jr., "Latin America Moves Toward Stability," *The New York Times Sunday Magazine*, Oct. 16, 1955, p. 65.

hand the position of *Tiempo*, republican and liberal, and, on the other, the characteristics of that government . . .

. . . Whatever may have been the faults of the government of General Perón, there is not the slightest doubt about the constitutional origin of the regime he represented . . .

. . . in spite of his many errors, some grave by any lights, Mr. Perón carried out a transforming renovation in the Argentina nation, and if that wounded the secular interests of the cattle and landowning aristocracy, he tried at the same time to elevate the social condition of the economically weak classes.

. . . the Argentine armed forces . . . which . . . rose against the Peronist regime did not heed the most sacred of their duties when they overthrew the legitimate authority and the institutions whose protection was confided to them . . .

. . . few things can occur to a people so grave, in the political sphere, as the fact that the public force legally armed by it should break legal bounds, turning itself into the interpreter, arbiter, and executor of the national wishes and destiny, for what results from such a situation is always born with the stigma of being the spurious and violent fruit of arms which have been turned against the ends which justify them . . .

For all of which reasons, *Tiempo* concludes that, no matter the cloth one might wish to throw over the fact, General Perón's regime has succumbed to a military *pronunciamiento* . . . a lamentable happening in the opinion of those who follow the fate of the Argentine people with sympathy, even though at a distance.[7]

Guatemala's case is often viewed by persons of the above persuasion as parallel to that of Argentina, and perhaps as worse, because of the addition of foreign intervention. Arbenz in Guatemala was a legally elected president, although the first revolutionary chief before him, Arévalo, took office as the indirect result of a barracks revolt five months before. The point for the nationalist in Latin America is that at least constitutional processes seem to have started. There can be little doubt that the constitution itself was violated on many occasions by the Arévalo-Arbenz combine, nor can there be much doubt that Latins tend to confuse a constitutional regime with a democratic one. But even here the liberal Latin nationalist attempts to make a case for himself, arguing that the previous regime a year before its overthrow was more demonstrably democratic than the present one a year after its assumption of power.

Let me present this argument by paraphrasing a bitter former official

---

[7] Editorial, *Hispanoamericano*, Vol. XXVII, No. 699, Sept. 26, 1955, p. 3.

of the government who was once again on the national payroll in a lesser position in 1955. As he put it, under "democracy" (the quotation marks were in his intonation) there were no legally organized political parties and no organized opposition in congress. Under the "dictatorship" of Arbenz (again using his tone), rural elections had been rigged, but the cities returned from five to twelve opposition deputies, anti-government parties were relatively free, and for most of the 1945–54 period the municipal government of Guatemala City was run by the opposition, allowing for the training of the core of present governmental personnel. Under Castillo Armas the only frankly oppositionist paper was that little four-page student weekly mentioned above, *El Estudiante*. Under Arbenz every major private newspaper was anti-government to a degree, and some were bitterly so. Under Arbenz freedom of speech was virtually unlimited, as was freedom of assembly; drastic action was taken only in the event of actual participation in an uprising. Under Castillo Armas there existed a suprajudicial committee for the suppression of Communist activities—a violation of democratic tenets relating to the separation of powers and to civil liberties. Argenz governed under a constitution, however loosely; Castillo Armas still had not seen fit to bind himself, with no matter what reservations, to an organic law. And on and on in this vein.

To remonstrate about the final slaughter carried out by the Arbenz regime is to draw the statement from this sector of opinion that first, it's false, and, second, he should have killed more. If we limit ourselves to a discussion of the two regimes in what might be called "normalcy" —that year before loss and after assumption of power—then the above statement of conditions appears to me accurate. Again, interpretation is necessary. Was there relative democracy in the Arbenz period because the regime's goal was freedom *qua* freedom, or was democracy practiced for the purpose of developing a complicated middle-class society which then could be squeezed into a modern oppressive mold? Or would the development of civil liberties, by their nature, prevent the latter end? Were Castillo Armas and his government ideologically opposed to democratic solutions, or did they act as they did simply because they didn't know any better? Was it their lack of strength that caused the insecurities that prevented relaxation? Or was the task of weeding out extremist elements one which by its nature demanded oppressive techniques? These questions are factually unanswerable; the reader may exercise his taste.

I have thus far been referring to "nationalists" and "liberal nationalists" and have offered a few quotations to exemplify their attitudes. It is wise to be more specific. Probably few of us in this country realize the wave of resentment which swept these Latin American elements on the overthrow of Arbenz. The Mexican Congress passed a joint resolution censuring the action. Uruguayan schools closed down for a day of mourning and protest, and Americans stayed off the streets for a few nights (or so I was told). The Chilean Chamber of Deputies sent a protest to the United States House of Representatives. There is a long list of such incidents, and, unhappily for American prestige, happenings large and small indicate that the dissatisfaction continues.

Here are a few personal examples I ran into during that summer of 1955. At the lowest and most informal level, an incident at the Mexican Military Hospital may serve as an apt illustration. In one section of the hospital which I frequented on and off for four months, persons were initially interested when they found I knew something of Guatemala. As soon as they heard me attempt to explain Castillo Armas instead of condemn him, the interest evaporated. On the other hand, an intern spent two weeks in Guatemala visiting his father, a physician for an international agency, and on his return an informal forum was held in a corridor during which he raked the administration fore and aft. His opinion was automatically accepted as being "right."

I was told that during the summer signs appeared on the campus of the university at Guadalajara, "Yankee, Out of Guatemala!" In Costa Rica the conservative editor of one of San José's largest dailies told me, "I am glad the Communists are out of Guatemala, but Castillo Armas is, after all, a totally unprepared fellow and the present situation is probably making it easy for the Communists to return some day." Another extremely high-ranking official of the Costa Rican government summed it up for me dryly: "You people made an awful mistake." In the famous Mexican bookstore, Porrua, where I was browsing one day and buying books on Guatemala which were unavailable in that country, a salesman informed me that the store had, as of August, sold 1,500 copies of anti-Castillo Armas books since the revolution: 700 copies of ex-President Arévalo's work, 500 of ex-Foreign Minister Toriello's book, and 300 copies of ex-Foreign Minister Osegueda's book, which at that time had been out only a month. But Porrua had sold only five copies of *El Libro Negro del Comunismo en Guatemala* (*The Black Book of Communism in Guatemala*), the compendium defending the change.

CONCLUSIONS

The fact that certain elements of American foreign policy are not popular with some anti-Communists abroad is nothing new. I am not certain how to evaluate the adverse reaction to American relationship with the Guatemalan situation. On the one hand, it is plain that the United States has lost much sympathy among precisely those na-

tionalistic groups that either are in power in Latin America or are striving for it with excellent chances for success. On the other hand, a propaganda loss may make little difference when weighed against what
may be considered the other gain: that Latin America was warned that
its governments may not play with Communism, and that such toying
may incite the full range of unilateral United States action, as well as
whatever multilateral action the United States may be able to take in
concert with the Organization of American States. This corollary to the
Monroe Doctrine, which is what it amounts to, depends for its application and acceptability on definition. To win the propaganda victory
also, it is incumbent upon policy makers here to demonstrate that it is
really Communism to which we are opposed, and not liberal nationalistic development of what seems the inevitable and inexorable kind we
are witnessing in almost all underdeveloped areas. The Guatemala situation might well have lost some of its sting for us if Castillo Armas'
administration had demonstrated faithfulness to "legitimate national
aspirations," as the Latins always say.

In 1956 John Gillin and I concluded a short article on Guatemala
(already cited in the first note) with a paragraph which still seems to
me apt. It is as follows

> It is a considerably easier and shorter job to "liberate" Guatemala than
> to convert it to a fully democratic country of the modern world. The
> latter takes time, as well as enlightened leadership. The United States
> has much at stake and cannot afford to lose interest. Whatever the full
> truth may be, we are identified by much of the world as a conspirator
> in the Guatemalan Revolution of two years ago. If our first "Libera-
> tion" is to degenerate into a tawdry poorhouse of quarreling inmates,
> or another experiment in Communist infiltration, or a reversion to tra-
> ditional "banana republic" reactionism, many people are going to think
> that we would do better to remain out of the liberation business. Peo-
> ples of the underdeveloped areas outside the Iron Curtain, to say noth-
> ing of the satellites themselves, are going to judge the results of the
> Guatemala liberation in terms of their ideas of the better life, not by
> the immediate results of a few border skirmishes in June 1954.

6

POLITICAL LEADERSHIP
AND INSTITUTIONAL WEAKNESS
IN ARGENTINA

The oft-quoted testamentary remarks of Bolívar, his final despair, still afford us an excellent sentimental bench mark for a discussion of contemporary Argentina. "There is no good faith in America," said Bolívar, "either among men or among nations. Treaties are paper, constitutions books, elections battles, liberty anarchy, and life a torment." Bolívar went on to advise, "The only thing one can do in America is emigrate." These words and especially the sour parting admonition to move away are quite conventional in today's Argentina. Their academic reflection is found in a preoccupation with explaining why a country of such material promise, human richness, urban exaggeration, and past progress should now find itself stagnant, a prey to "tropical" politics in the upper reaches of society and to apathy and irresponsibility below.

The taxi-driver explanation is a condemnation of corrupt governments and more often than not a slurring of one or another of Argentina's numerous immigrant groups—Italians or Spanish Galicians or Jews or what not. Economists lament the fiscal illiteracy of the Perón regime, and most of them usually add complaints about Argentina's dependency on foreign markets, the mentality of landowners and industrialists, and the lack of productivity and morale of labor. Historians like to start with the 1930 intervention of the military in political affairs and then grimly trace the downward path of the juggernaut through intervening Conservative oligarchies, military dictatorships, the Perón adventure, and on to the present day via the interregnum of the Liberating Revolution of 1955 to 1958. Recently interpretations less concerned with symptomatology have begun to be heard, attempting to relate social disorganization to the more profound facts of national character, values, and social structure. The following quotation is typical of this new search: [1]

> Argentina today can be described as an economic enigma—a basically resourceful country that has undergone a period of economic stagnation during a decade of almost unprecedented economic expansion throughout most of the world, a country making a serious but largely unsuccessful attempt to take the road of steady economic growth . . .
>
> Of course, economic factors play an important role in determining whether or not economic development occurs . . . But Argentina's experience between 1945 and 1955 and its failure to recover, despite basically sound economic measures taken since then, suggest that something of more vital importance lies behind the troubles besetting the nation's economy . . .
>
> An analysis of the Argentine "national character," based on a study of the value orientation profile of the Argentine society, will demonstrate that some cultural traits of the bulk of the population are inimical to the emergence of social relationships which would enable individuals to act concertedly in the pursuit of common goals and interests. This feature, *i.e.*, the fact that Argentines are a "conglomeration" of people rather than an organic "community," together with the fact that those same cultural traits also constitute a powerful barrier to the appearance of "Western-capitalistic-like" economic initiative in the bulk of the society's members, is and has been in the past a fundamental impediment retarding the nation's economic growth. Of course, it would be unrealistic to assume that one element *alone* is the cause of Argentina's economic stagnation . . . [but] the basically passive, apathetic value-orientation profile of the Argentine society must be regarded as the *critical* factor limiting the possibilities of steady, long-run economic development.

Values and social structure underlie all social science disciplines. At this deepest level of generality, let us accept several still undemonstrated statements as working hypotheses descriptive of the Argentine way of looking at the world. We are concerned here with institutional and not value factors, but assumptions concerning the latter help us to define the limits of probable and perhaps even possible institutional

[1] Tomás Roberto Fillol, *Social Factors in Economic Development: The Argentine Case,* Cambridge: The M.I.T. Press, 1961, pp. 1–3 *passim.* For another recent publication underscoring the concept of "dilemma," see also Arthur P. Whitaker, "The Argentine Paradox," *The Annals of the American Academy of Political and Social Science,* Vol. 334, March, 1961, pp. 103–12.

change. These working premises are put in terms of those dilemmas, paradoxes, or contradictions with which so much of the recent literature on Argentina has been concerned.

1. A contradiction affecting the entire society is the clash between the leveling effects of mass communications and a very high degree of urban concentration and the opposing failure of the political mechanism to escape the corset of an extraordinarily narrow definition of interests. The almost universal view in Argentina is that no public measure can be good for almost everybody, that the benefit of one group is the automatic detriment of all others. Life is an inelastic pie, and a bigger piece for *fulano* means necessarily a smaller piece for *sutano*. Political discussion in Argentina, for example, takes it as axiomatic that increased freedom of action for lower economic groups in the *peronista* period implied a necessarily restricted freedom for others, and that with the fall of Perón nothing could have been more natural than a return to restriction of freedom for those below and a regrowth of freedom for those above. Such static views in the presence of the goads of radio, television, airplanes, and great cities must lead either to the purgatory of stultification or the hell of authoritarian direction.

2. Another inconsistency flows from the failure to adjust a fairly advanced degree of industrialization to responsible entrepreneurial attitudes and to an appreciation of the possibilities inherent in mass consumption. The impediment is once again the inability to see the society as in some respects total and interdependent. The power of industrialization, then, is employed to maintain a degree of social inequality preventing the growth of healthy markets and thus inhibiting the further economic development of the country. The results can again be measured against the poles of paralyzing frustration and rude force, rather than in terms of possible choice among positive policy alternatives.[2]

3. At the personal level the paradox describes the high degree of specialization, of functional articulation, demanded of the individual in Argentina's relatively developed economic situation and the opposing failure of the citizen to be guided by a system of impersonal loyalties toward all the others operating within the system of mutual dependency. The narrowness of the loyalty horizons weakens social institutions and invites autocratic personalism, whether for change or the mere continuance of the *status quo*.

[2] Easily available sources for a study of the Argentine economy are United Nations Economic Commission for Latin America, *El Desarrollo Económico de la Argentina*, 1957; the periodical statistical bulletins of the Argentine Central Bank; Ricardo M. Ortiz, *Historia Económica de la Argentina*, Buenos Aires: Raigal, 1955; and Leopoldo Portnoy, *La Realidad Argentina en el Siglo XX: II Análisis Crítico de la Economía*, Mexico: Fondo de Cultura Económica, 1961.

Why these localistic, sub-national views archetypical of the traditional society should manage to persist in a context of industrial urbanization must be the subject of speculation elsewhere. But their survival serves to afford a first explanation of the malfunction of social institutions, as measured by the criteria of the developed world. Because a working adjustment does exist, the Argentine situation does not fit neatly into the categories of social order as they have been derived from the major currents of European experience. The "paradoxes" of which we have been speaking are paradoxical only in terms of theoretical views of the elements necessary to social progress from folk to traditional to modern society; they are not paradoxical in the sense that they are incoherent or mutually incompatible in terms of the experiences of daily life. The resulting policy confusion, ultimate halt to economic growth, and resort to the politics of force is, of course, exactly fitting to the situation.

THE ARTICULATION OF THE POLITICAL MECHANISM

The most striking characteristic of Argentine politics is its simplicity. This lack of complication, this failure to achieve a high level of articulation of the functions of the state, is also in perfect consonance with the set of traditional values still pertaining. While the *structure* of the economic institution has managed a fairly high degree of modernization despite the continued rooting of certain *functions* in an older order, the political institution has remained much more intimately related to pre-national structures as well as to functions. Charisma, the charm factor of personalism, remains the only certain way of gaining mass support for political movements; if the manifest leaders do not possess charisma, then they must rely on the play of naked force to maintain authority. Recent history supports this statement unequivocally. The military dictatorship of 1930–31 of General José E. Uriburu, although based on a fair degree of popular support to begin with, ended as a mere military adventure. Succeeding Conservative governments depended on simple electoral fraud to give their governance a semblance of democratic legitimacy, but their authority stemmed from a combination of economic and military power.[3] The return of the military to direct government occurred in 1943, once again made possible and—to military eyes—seemingly "necessary" by the utter sim-

[3] It is not necessary to list the standard works on recent Argentine political developments. Specialists already know them, and any non-specialist can find them easily enough. I might mention only a recent work of merit, Alfredo Galletti, *La Realidad Argentina en el Siglo XX: I La Política y los Partidos*, Mexico: Fondo de Cultura Económica, 1961. Otherwise, see Fillol, *op. cit.*, and the appropriate works of A. P. Whitaker, G. I. Blanksten, J. J. Johnson, J. J. Kennedy, R. Alexander, *et al.*

plicity of the patterns of power distribution and the shrunken universe of political discourse recognized as pertinent. The emergence of Perón and his attractiveness to certain parts of the public—a political magnetism not seen in the country since the days of Radical Yrigoyen (1916–22 and 1927–30)—added other dimensions of power, but still the fall of Peronism was essentially a response to changes in the views of certain leaders and not to the complex, sweeping movements which one attributes to truly national politics. The succeeding Provisional Government of President Aramburu (1955–58) made no pretense of being other than a temporary military government, even though it earned widespread praise and support among middle- and upper-class groups. Succeeding administrations have also been unable to bank on the mechanisms of a plural society recognizing differing degrees and levels of approval and disapproval, instead being forced to play about among all too evident power centers to maintain an at times most precarious existence. For the past thirty-five years Argentine governments have shown either the hard surface of military rule or the mottled aspect of Machiavellian balancing, bargaining, and intriguing.

Perhaps nowhere is this disconcerting political absoluteness—another way of saying simplicity—made so evident as in the manner in which political parties see their own functions. Instead of viewing themselves as the guardians of a part of the truth and as holding a limited responsibility for the nation's destinies, parties are used either as the vessels of universal truth or as simple mechanisms with which to gain power. Even the quasi-official historian of the Radical Party, the most professional of all Argentine parties, permits himself these words:[4]

> . . . we are not just a political party . . . we are a force of national
> and continental history which consists in imparting constitutionality to
> Independence . . . in giving to the Nation through its people firm
> bases for its authentic development, which conceives of the Republic
> as a moral idea . . .

This messianic view of politics leaves no room for a legitimate opposition; the erection of an ideological structure on moral grounds viewed as universal condemns dissenting voices as heresy and not as mere human error. The dismaying inclusiveness of this view of radicalism is really no less than the bald statement made by General Rawson the day after he led the military to overt power in 1943: "Now there are no political parties, but only Argentines." In his turn Perón employed his newly erected party structure as a direct arm of government, as in

[4] From Gabriel del Mazo, *El Radicalismo: Ensayo sobre su historia y doctrina,* 2nd ed., Buenos Aires: Raigal, 1951, as quoted in Galletti, *op. cit.,* p. 40.

totalitarian situations. And even though the succeeding military interregnum actually encouraged a limited play of party politics, official proclamations deplored such activities, clearly implying a belief in the innately evil nature of parties.[5]

> . . . And finally, we appeal to all the inhabitants of the Republic to postpone all tendentious and partisan interest to the higher interests of the collectivity. Let republican austerity be the guide of our conduct and let solidarity in the common effort permit the prompt gaining of those ends for which our people long.

Even Arturo Frondizi (1958–62), the first civilian honestly elected to the presidency since 1927, demonstrated the same implied disdain for party politics by his constantly reiterated statement that he was the "President of twenty million Argentines," and not the exponent of a self-consistent and necessarily only partially valid set of views supported by a continuing, responsible, and extended party organization.

The directness of the manner in which political power is applied is also evident within the government itself. The strong executive pattern is a constant, the judiciary being relatively weak and without prestige, and the legislature never at any time having been able to exercise the deciding voice in the setting of public policy. Fundamental decisions are made within the executive establishment itself, where pressures continue to focus and where the true deliberative function occurs. Although there are rudimentary interest groups established outside the formal organization of government, pressure groups of importance extend their heads directly into the governmental structure itself. The military, the single most important source and avenue of pressure, of course represents other groups and ideologies as well as merely its own professional interests. As a consequence all aspiring interests attempt to exercise influence over the armed establishment; even far leftists sometimes wistfully speak of the possibility of talking some disgruntled level of the army over to their point of view. The Church, agrarian interests, industrial groups, and the labor unions all bring their plaints and their points of view to bear directly on the executive, at best using the legislature as a sounding board and the courts, when possible, as some kind of interim source of juridical legitimacy.

The workings of the mechanism are transparent, the channels of access clear, and the results plain to all through the activities of the media of mass communications and the pronouncements of the interested parties themselves. But this simplicity of articulation does not make the executive onmipotent. Executive decisions, however they may have been reached and with what concessions, may be in them-

---

[5] Message prepared by General Pedro Eugenio Aramburu on assuming the provisional presidency of the nation after the deposition of General Eduardo Lonardi in 1955, as quoted in Galletti, *op. cit.*, p. 209.

selves the decisive political acts of the state, but they are limited in their scope and effectiveness by the very simplicity of the structure. In short, the Argentine government is intrinsically weak,[6] a debility stemming from several fundamental causes:

First, the political institution is simplified, as we have been pointing out, so that not only are decisions a response to the crudest of pressures, but there can be no subtlety or refinement in the application of political measures throughout the society.

Second, the state is not established as the ultimate secular authority in Argentina. There are other competing institutions demanding men's loyalties which permit a high degree of protection from the dictates of the state. Although the Church immediately springs to mind, the matter is much more complicated. A failure to recognize the supremacy of the state in the mediation of secular dispute leaves many areas of life, such as the family, outside the reach of governmental determination. Class status also plays a fundamental part in the varying application of the law, as does simple economic position. The impunity enjoyed by the far-right scions of upper-class families for their racist demonstrations, shootings, bombings, and burnings are undeniable evidence of this statement.

And third, the combination of a simplified structure and a lack of acceptance of a broad social area as legitimate to political action reduces the amount of anticipated obedience any Argentine government can expect, increasing the need for direct police and military enforcement of the law, or else permitting a highly effective degree of *laissez-passer* in such daily events of life as parking a car or painting political slogans on walls. This executive dependency on the police and the weakness of the legislature were well exemplified in mid-1961 when the police peppered the Congress building with small-arms fire in a protest concerning equipment and pay, incidentally at the time Congress was considering charges of police torture. Their punishment was a salary increase.

Simplicity, party weakness, the immediacy of action of pressure groups, and an exaggerated dependence on direct sanction within a severely limited sphere all describe aspects of traditional Mediterranean political thought and practice, and especially of syndicalism. An innate distrust of the state coupled with the direct representation of economic and occupational interest in the government are destructive of party strength, erode pluralism, deny the sweeping grandeur possible to enlightened political action in its broadest senses, and lead easily to

[6] The fact that President Frondizi made an open and profound about-face in policy shortly after his election is rather a measure of weakness than strength, not only because the change was in partial response to alien pressures, but also because his own followers were powerless to stop him. If the Radical Intransigents had not the power to prevent the change, then it follows that they had not the strength to support their own president, duly overthrown in turn by the military.

such subsidiary ideologies as Fascism and Falangism, whose very symbols of course celebrate the tenuous tying together of vertical organizations. The denial of lateral identifications, the insistence on hierarchy, and a creole version of the *Führerprinzip* combine in Argentina to the detriment of decided and imaginative governmental action.

PERONISM AND LIMITATIONS ON THE LEADERSHIP ROLE

The Argentine leader cannot create a modern set of national values by signing a decree or speaking from a balcony. He can extend the effectiveness of his government by chipping at the power of rival institutions only through the exercise of great skill and effort. Unless he whips together a mass movement striving for frank and complete revolutionary change—an unlikely event at least for the immediate future—then he is restricted to the employment of two types of authority: he can derive his power from the existing play of intra- and inter-institutional forces, or else he can attempt to amend this situation by gaining external power through the mobilization of mass public opinion. In matters of program, as distinguished from the question of the configuration of his support, he is restricted to the path of administering the movement of the tides of the *status quo* or to a mild reformism. In explaining his actions to himself and others, however, he can indulge in the strongest of ideological statements from center-left to right in tone, or else be a simple eclectic. But no matter what his power basis, the profundity or the superficiality of his program, or the style of his explanations, the non-revolutionary leader cannot escape the limitation that he is leading a people of traditional values flexing the muscles of a substantially developed economy.[7]

These hindrances apply to Perón as well as to his successors. The

---

[7] Little attention is being paid in this analysis to the political left. The reason is that we are not considering the alternative of social revolution, rather limiting ourselves to the possibilities inherent to non-revolutionary governments. The Argentine left has but the scantest of chances to mount a full-blown revolution and has practically closed off for itself the possibility for sound parliamentary action. Leftist leaders are no less the captives of their culture than their political opponents. They have delivered themselves up to endless bickering, conspiratorial practices, unreal policies, and short-lived coalitions entered upon through wishful thinking instead of through a real concord of belief and interest. *Fidelismo* has also served to accentuate romantic dreams and to underscore the extra-national nature of the left in a country crying for healthy national integration. The dissolution of the left Socialists and Radicals, Communists, Trotskyists, and other left splinters was also hastened by the actions of President Frondizi, who succeeded in persuading many of them that he would be a left-leaning president, only to present them after his inauguration with much conservatism and a caricature of their own economic determinism. The left has little real hope of gaining the support of the former *peronistas* and their middle-class leadership by and large has made itself inefficacious in normal politics by a denial of elementary respect for the principles of Liberal political procedures, their only hope for a sound and productive political survival. And, of course, let us not forget the power and determination of their political opponents in their containment.

problem of categorization here becomes acute, for if the foregoing analysis is correct, then the Peronist government was not effectively totalitarian, whatever other unhappy things it may have been. A totalitarian state employs the political institution to work its will directly upon the citizen without the interference of intervening buffer institutions or of the restraints of a rule of law or a less than universal ideological justification. These institutional conditions simply did not prevail in Argentina between 1946 and 1955, although the lack of juridical and ideological constraint did exist and still does.

Even if we use secondary descriptive criteria of totalitarianism derived specifically from the European Fascist examples, the Argentine experience diverges in significant points. Specifically:

The middle-class base for German and Italian Fascism is contrasted in Argentina with the mass lower-class backing for Peronism, with significant middle-class groups also involved. As shall be seen later, even persons of upper-class extraction made themselves available for leadership positions

The relatively high degree of technology necessary for police-state control, eminently true of Nazi Germany, could not be said to describe Argentina; even Italian Fascism lost some of its effectiveness through an institutional "leakiness" caused by technological deficiencies.

Charisma was of great importance in the three systems, but in Argentina the full measure of organizational consequences did not flow therefrom, especially in the internal administrative operation of the government.

A mystical ideology of nationalism was also true of the three governments, but Argentine *justicialismo* was almost an afterthought, an intellectual appendage to justify the "leadership principle." Argentine nationalism was largely restricted to attacks on foreign countries in speech and press, and to mystical glorification of the nation, but devoted itself little to the task of assuring the relative position of the state as *the* supreme social institution.

Militarism was, of course, an important component of Peronism as of German and Italian Fascism, for Perón assumed power primarily as the result of his military position and previous actions of the armed forces. But both Hitler and Mussolini assumed power in some measure *despite* the military and employed their armed might for war, a purpose alien to the ideas of Perón despite brave words about Argentine hegemony in the southern part of the continent.

A controlled economy—the total identification between economic and political interests and the growing indistinguishability of controlling personnel in Italy and Germany—was not true of Argentina. Despite governmental interventionism at the highest level of Argentina's history, the Argentines did not succeed in surpassing the degree of control reached in Chile and Mexico, and perhaps even in Uruguay. Although Peronism did recruit some new millionaires from its own ranks, it is difficult to say whether the results were substantially different from this same kind of political corruption as practiced in other Latin American countries. In any event, Peronism contributed to building a new class of industrialists but stopped far short of dispossessing pre-existing wealthy groups or instituting total mobilization of the economy for national ends. The motivation for the economic measures of Peronism rested in nationalism as in the Mexican case, in statism as throughout Latin America, in anti-capitalism as an almost universal article of faith among both conservatives and leftists in Latin America, and probably only in a very minor degree on any self-conscious ideological principles concerning the economic role in a Fascist society.

Racism was entirely incidental to Peronism, even more marginal than it was to Italian Fascism.

Because Peronism went outside the pre-existing power structure to build popular support among lower-class groups herded into captive trade unions, some observers have attempted to save the totalitarian category by labeling the movement as "Fascism of the Left." S. M. Lipset, for example, writes: [8]

> [Another] . . . type of social movement which has often been described as fascist is Peronism . . . Unlike right-wing anti-democratic tendencies based on the more well-to-do and traditionalist strata and those tendencies I prefer to call "true" fascism—centrist authoritarianism, based on the liberal middle classes, primarily the self-employed—Peronism, much like Marxist parties, has been oriented toward the poorer classes, primarily urban workers but also the more impoverished rural population. . . .

> The phenomenon known as Peronism—anti-capitalist populist nationalism which appeals to the lower strata in alignment with the army—is, of course, not unique to the Argentine. In Brazil, Getulio Vargas developed the same theme a decade earlier, was also identified with fascism, and continued to retain the support of the workers after he left power . . . If Peronism is considered a variant of fascism, then it is a fascism of the left because it is based on the social strata who would otherwise turn to socialism or Communism as an outlet for their frustration

Several very serious quarrels can be picked with this statement, the most important being the loose and interchangeable use of "fascist," "authoritarian," and "totalitarian." All fascisms and totalitarianisms are of course authoritarian, but not all authoritarianisms are totalitari-

[8] *Political Man: The Social Bases of Politics*, New York: Doubleday, 1960, pp. 170–73 *passim*.

anisms and fascisms. Peronism employed the ideology and the public style of fascism but performed no revolutionary functions in a class or structural sense, governed internally by juggling already existing power centers in a fashion typical of states in immediately pre-national situations, and above all was unable to establish the unquestioned supremacy of the state. The regime even toppled in traditional semi-developed Latin American style, victim of a *coup d'état* led by a military vanguard and supported by an important and significant body of public sentiment.

Peronism did succeed in setting class against class more sharply than in any other period of Argentine history. It clearly counterposed liberty and authority and opted for the latter; it also in more hidden fashion opposed honesty to dishonesty, and also chose the latter in all senses. Reason, too, was made to cede to demagoguery. Peronism did not change the relative position of Argentina's social classes, although it did squeeze them together and temporarily reduce social distance in psychological as well as economic senses. The regime did not change the land-tenure system or the prevailing patterns of the distribution of great wealth. Although the style and ideology of leadership changed, the recruitment patterns changed only slightly, and the sources of succeeding opposition leaders were unaffected after all is said and done. Not even the prevailing distribution of opposition parties was effectively destroyed, for they all returned to their usual sickly bloom within a year after the fall of the dictator. These "accomplishments" of Peronism do not describe the workings of totalitarian fascism.

Peronism responded to several basic needs in Argentine political life and succeeded in betraying all of them. Any reasonably modern society must somehow recognize and make provision for the desire of large groups of citizens to participate in the civil experience; Argentina also urgently needs some kind of national, integrated identity and a means for the routine settlement of secular dispute. Perón gained outside support by promising to meet these desires and by devising a poor man's fascist ideology to explain his actions. But through inefficacy, a failure to understand why he really gained mass support, and his ultimate reliance on traditional sources of power, he perverted what might have been positive in his policies and left his country with the twisting legacy of a lower class infected with fascist political beliefs. And by denying even the traditionally thin Liberalism to which middle and upper groups had become accustomed, his kind of authoritarianism guaranteed the hatred even of wavering Argentine democrats.

The Argentine political tragedy resides in the fact that the political integration of the popular classes was initiated under the sign of totalitarianism which succeeded in providing, in its fashion, a certain experience of political and social participation in the immediate and personal aspects of the life of the worker, nullifying at the same time the political organization and the basic rights which constitute the irreplaceable pillars of any genuine democracy. The immense task to be carried out consists in gaining this same experience but relating it in an indissoluble manner to the theory and practice of democracy and freedom.[9]

Peronism, if this analysis is correct, boils itself down to an early and bumbling type of Nasserist authoritarianism, a self-conscious attempt by dissident members of the elite and near-elite to employ their power toward the end of creating politically nationalist, economically statist industrial societies, but in Argentina not really prepared to use their power to break traditional molds in favor of their ideological view of modernism, as appears to be the determination of the government of Nasser. Perón indubitably failed because his government did not understand the magnitude of its task, his ideological manipulation of the lower economic groups in the last analysis being no more than a cynical political ploy.

The importance of Peronism should not be underestimated, however. The effects were profound precisely in those two areas least strongly inhibited by institutionalized power—ideology and style. Unable as Perón was to change the basic contradictions in the structure of social values, economic practices, and mass versus traditional politics, his ideological prods and his simulacrum of populism have left these problems inflamed, a continuing source of infection and pain. Not only did the dispossessed become aware of their status and taste some of the fruits of a spurious participation, but now even the integrated middle and upper groups are willing to admit to the possible alienation of some of their fellow citizens.

Dismantling the work of the Perón administration in an organizational and immediate policy sense was not an inordinately difficult task and certainly nothing to compare with what would have been a transition from totalitarianism to limited democracy. Despite the damage he wreaked on the nation's economy, there is good reason to believe that many of the difficulties would have existed even without the maldirected interventionism of the Perón era.[10] The constitution of 1949 was calmly repealed, elections organized, and by early 1958 the government was legally reconstituted in regular fashion. Ideological confusion hinders leadership in gaining popular support, but since both policy horizons and public power remain limited, the play of politics

[9] Gino Germani, *Política e Massa*, Minas Gerais: Estudos Sociais e Políticas da Faculdade de Direito No. 13, 1960, p. 189.

[10] This view is common among many Argentine economists. See, for example, Leopoldo Portnoy, *op. cit.*, especially Chs. 2 and 3.

continues to deal with problems manipulatively and superficially. The great difference between the Perón and the post-Perón period lies in the present greater freedom of speculation, the enlarged area of liberties. Although large numbers of blue-collar workers continue to deny themselves the possibility of effective organization by clinging to their corporativism, and although anti-democratic forces continue to gain strength in many significant sectors of the society, the mere existence of even a little libertarian elbow room opens the range of political possibilities. Stable continued growth toward a more significant and truly institutionalized degree of mature democracy is still far from assured, however.

THE MANIFEST POLITICAL LEADERS: 1947, 1954, 1956, 1960

The preceding analysis of the area of action within which recent Argentine governments have acted cannot be validated only by an examination of the antecedents and occupational histories of political leaders. Even deep social psychological analysis would be inadequate, of course, for we should still be unable to relate personal intention to political product without prolonged research into many other aspects of political life. Sharp differences between Peronist and post-Peronist leaders, however, should lead us to suspect that perhaps the emphasis this paper is putting on ideological and stylistic differences and problem area and institutional likenesses is not well taken. Were Peronism the truly revolutionary government which a totalitarian fascism implies, we should expect young leaders, strong differences in educational background from their predecessors and successors, markedly dissimilar family antecedents, and extraordinary personal histories to support the hypothesis. In short, we should suspect that persons who reject an existing order strongly enough to attempt to change it by totalitarian means must demonstrate areas of great marginality; we should be able to infer resentments, unsatisfied desires, and great ambitions.

The task of determining who are the political leaders in Argentina is not a subtle process, even though the precautionary measure is being taken here of speaking only of *manifest* political leadership. Greater caution still might be exercised by drawing a theoretical distinction between leaders and the exercisers of power. But in Argentina manifest leadership is real leadership and also involves the power to make political decisions. Given the nature of the state and the strength of competing institutions, of course, many persons not formal members of the political institution obviously weigh heavily in the taking of such determinations as whether or not meat shall be marketed internationally through the agency of a governmental monopoly, or whether private universities should be allowed to grant degrees. This study does not concern itself with the "power elite" as a whole but only with that part of it which acts in formal governmental positions. As will be seen from an examination of some of the most obvious social characteristics of these persons, there is little reason to suppose that their extra-political colleagues are substantially dissimilar.

I have selected for examination persons occupying key governmental positions during four periods. The positions chosen were President and Vice-President of the Nation, Cabinet Ministers and Secretaries, Justices of the Supreme Court, members of the governing committees (*mesas directivas*) of the two houses of the legislature, governors (whether locally elected or appointed by the national executive) of the provinces of Buenos Aires, Mendoza, Córdoba, and Santa Fé, selected members of the board of the Central Bank, the Commander-in-Chief of the Army, and the federal Chief of Police. The periods selected were all for the month of July in the years 1947 (after the initial shaking down of the first Perón government, which took office in 1946), 1954 (one year before the fall of Perón to see the changes that may have occurred as his regime progressed), 1956 (in the midst of the rule of the Liberating Revolution), and 1960 (after twenty-five months of constitutional civil rule). There were 41 cases filled for 1947, 46 for 1954, 40 for 1956 when there was no Congress, and 41 for 1960; ten of the Peronist regime figures were the same in 1954 and 1947, although occupying different positions in all but two cases.[11]

Age distribution shows what is to be expected: the 1947 Peronist leaders were the youngest (median age 48 years and ten months), increasing to 50 years and nine months in 1954. The Provisional Government, tapping persons who in many cases had been prominent before the advent of Peronism, had leading members of a median age of 53 years and four months, while the administration in 1960 was still a little older, 54 years and three months.[12] These ages are relatively advanced for Latin America but of course to be expected in Argentina, where life expectancy among city dwellers is high and the tradition of maturity among political leaders of long establishment. We find essentially what we expect, of course, the Perón group being only a little younger and representing both in the military and civilian spheres persons who lacked the final step to cap their careers. Perón

[11] I owe thanks to the personnel of the morgues of the newspapers *La Nación* and *Clarín* for their assistance. Other sources of data were the Argentine *Who's Who* and *Blue Book*.

[12] The average ages, in contrast to the medians expressed above, are somewhat different because of the skewing effect caused by a few quite old leaders in their seventies, of course not counterbalanced by very young persons. The averages for the four periods respectively are 51 years three months, 49 years six months, 56 years one month, and 58 years one month. The median gives a more realistic impression in this case.

was a member of the so-called "Colonel's Clique," as will be remembered, a group which as its very name indicates was waiting to be invested with the insignia of general rank. But no true generational conflict reveals itself from these figures.

Birthplace holds only one surprise. In 1947 about two-thirds of the leading government personnel were born in the provinces, the remainder in Buenos Aires; in 1954 the division is about equal. The same more or less fifty-fifty split occurred in the Provisional Government, and in 1960 the government returned to a two-thirds preponderance in favor of the provinces. The 1960 increase in the number of persons born in the provinces appointed or elected to high position is a natural corollary of the return to civilian government and the ascendancy of a national political party owing favors to constituents throughout the land. The 1947 experience probably answers to the same considerations, for at that time Peronism was in the first blush of its pseudo-populism and appealing strongly for support to provincials. Probably the most significant aspect of these figures is that only two persons of the total of 168 were foreign-born, one in Italy (from whence about half of Argentina's recent migrants come), and one from Spain (providing about a third of the immigrants).

The relative similarity of ages and the astonishing failure of persons to emerge from the great numbers of the foreign-born to assume high political office are preliminary indicators of a similarity of style throughout the four periods suggesting the stubborn narrowness of the terms of political availability in Argentina. This striking likeness holds throughout the succeeding analysis. Unfortunately the data on social extraction of the leaders are insufficient to permit us to speak with surety about their mobility paths. This lack is lamentable, especially because of the possibility that many of the Peronists were sons of immigrants seeking the political or the politico-military path to assure a social status equal to the economic positions of their fathers. What information can be trusted on the social position of parents indicates that during the Perón period at least half the leaders were from middle-, upper-middle-, or upper-class parents. A very few were from modest surroundings. A reasonable guess would place those concerning whom we do not have full information also in the middle and upper groups, whether at the provincial or national levels, particularly because of their occupations and educational levels, as will be seen immediately below.

The 1956 group appears more heavily weighted in favor of persons of traditional upper- and upper-middle-class origins, with perhaps a slight tendency to spread downward once again in 1960. Certainly the thesis cannot be entertained that Peronist leadership was of humble origins; there can be no question but that the heavily preponderant source of Argentine leadership during the four periods was from among the children of middle- and upper-class parents, more or less evenly divided between provincial and Buenos Aires families.

This conclusion is strengthened by a glance at the occupational and educational histories of the leaders. In 1947 some 81 per cent had graduated either from a university or from one or another national military academy; in 1954 the figure was 83.5 per cent; the Liberating Revolutionary period saw 95 per cent in these categories, and in 1960 the figure went to a round 100 per cent.

EDUCATIONAL RECORDS OF ARGENTINE LEADERS IN SELECTED YEARS

	1947		1954		1956		1960	
Type of Training	%	No.	%	No.	%	No.	%	No.
University	59	24	70	32	60	24	83	34
Military/Naval/Air	22	9	13.5	6	35	14	17	7
Secondary	5	2	6.5	3	2.5	1	—	—
Primary	5	2	2.5	1	—	—	—	—
Not ascertained with surety	10	4	6.5	3	2.5	1	—	—

An examination of the principal occupations of the leaders naturally reveals conclusions parallel to those concerning education: the heavy preponderance of persons with higher education during Peronism climbing steadily to the absolute of 1960 accompanies a similarly growing number of professionals and career military officers. These two categories (professionals and military) accounted for 70.2 per cent of the leaders in 1947, 80.5 per cent in 1954, and 95 per cent both in 1956 and 1960. The objective breakdown is as in the following table:

PRINCIPAL OCCUPATIONS OF ARGENTINE LEADERS IN SELECTED YEARS

Occupation	1947	1954	1956	1960
Lawyer	15	12	12	21
Career Military Officer	9	7	14	5
Physician	4	8	4	2
Manufacturer	3	—	—	1
Dentist	1	1	—	—
Agronomist	1	—	—	—
Professor	1	2	3	3
Accountant; Economist	1	3	1	2
Rancher	1	—	—	—

Occupation	1947	1954	1956	1960
White-Collar Employee	1	3	—	—
Labor Organizer	1	1	—	—
Professional Politician	—	1	1	—
Journalist	—	—	—	1
Engineer	—	3	4	6
Diplomat	—	1	—	—
Secondary Teacher	—	1	—	—
Career Police Officer	—	1	—	—
Not ascertained with surety	3	2	1	—

The commanding position of lawyers is to be expected, as is the varying number of military men, naturally reaching its peak with the military government of President Aramburu. The greater occupational spread under Peronism is once again in response to his function as a partial innovator and the builder of a new political party, while the later shrinking to a more limited and standard occupational distribution reflects the return to normalcy and more complete traditionalism. Because the chart is restricted to principal occupations, those persons who may be physicians as well as large landowners, for example, or who denominate themselves as "lawyers, professors, and diplomats," are counted only once. Multiple occupations are much more important in the 1956 period than in any of the others, as is to be expected, and of course there are many more persons owning estates than appears. The criterion of "principal occupation" for non-professional politicians was essentially that from which the individual's primary prestige derived and to which he devoted most of his time; in the case of the professional politicans, their principal source of income during periods when they were out of office was allowed to govern. Only one person on the list earned his income directly from party sources. Thus President Frondizi, a professional politician, of course, was listed as a lawyer because it was through the exercise of this profession that he earned a living before taking office.

The career paths of the professionals and the military are almost exactly the same for the four periods, except for the accidents of history which caused some to interrupt their careers at one time, others at another. In almost every case professionals have dedicated themselves to teaching, some beginning at the secondary level, but most initiating their academic careers as assistants to distinguished professors. Some have worked in the provinces at the beginning of their careers, even some persons born in Buenos Aires, but virtually all have reached the pinnacle of their professional careers in some kind of intimate association with the capital. Extensive travel is common to almost all; few have studied formally abroad, but international conferences see these persons in steady attendance. Some have gained international repute in their professional fields, and at least half have authored books. Without exception the civilians who participated in the 1956 and 1960 governments had to suspend their public activities during Peronism; they withdrew or were discharged from their university and governmental positions and a few went into exile, although most of them continued to pursue their professional careers privately. Civilians who served in the Perón governments also found themselves cast out of formal political office, if not in worse condition, when the wheel turned.

The military line divides itself in two: those who pursued relatively normal careers throughout the Peronist period and thus were in a position to mobilize troops, airplanes, and ships when the moment for the overthrow came, and those who went into retirement, in almost every case immediately following or within a year of the ill-fated "Menéndez Revolt" of 1951. Once again we find great consistency: overseas missions and positions as military or naval attaché usually serve as the first really marked opening into high prestige status, with subsidiary careers developing as professors in the various training academies, troop or ship commands, and so forth into the ministerial level or the "interventorship" of a province. The major difference between Peronist and post-Peronist military officers is that most of the former took their last steps upward during the course of the Perón regime, while those of the latter who continued on active duty through the Perón period had their "careers made," as they also say in Spanish, by the time of the revolution. Those who retired in 1951 and 1952 and then returned to important positions enjoyed almost immediate promotion, of course, and many were granted reinstatement with seniority as of the date of their retirement.

The relatively small number of persons in the Peronist governments who did not follow these normal life paths sprang from many diverse origins, owing their ascent to their own ambitions and attitudes as well as to the need of the government to support its "black populism" with individuals to fit the style of the ideology and to serve as living demonstration of the identification of the lower groups with the exalted sphere of government. These persons define the very limited extent to which the Weberian definition of the charismatic corporate group implanted itself within the administrative machine itself.[13]

The corporate group which is subject to charismatic authority is based on an emotional form of communal relationship. The administrative staff of a charismatic leader does not consist of "officials"; at least its

[13] Max Weber, *The Theory of Social and Economic Organization*, tr. by A. M. Henderson and Talcott Parsons, Glencoe: The Free Press, p. 360.

members are not technically trained. It is not chosen on the basis of social privilege or from the point of view of domestic or personal dependency. It is rather chosen in terms of the charismatic qualities of its members. The prophet has his disciples; the war lord his selected henchmen; the leader, generally, his followers. There is no such thing as "appointment" or "dismissal," no career, no promotion. There is only a "call" at the instance of the leader . . . There is no hierarchy . . . There is no such thing as a definite sphere of authority and of competence, and no appropriation of official powers on the basis of social privileges

How little the Peronist leadership group really responds to this definition of the charismatic corporate type is evident, except for the reduced number of special cases. The growing normalization of the bureaucracy is apparent even in the course of the decline of Perón and of course comes to full bloom in 1960. The rules of the career game were preserved in their essence throughout the thirteen years of Argentine history we have been examining. The leaders continued to adjust themselves to the appreciation of the attributes of prestige common to Argentina; those who rose into the political hierarchy on the wings of the Peronist appeal used their positions to advance their careers as university professors, to travel, to complete the prestige image. The institutions conquered them, willing as they were; they themselves changed the institutions very little, and certainly not enough in the case of the Peronists to guarantee their own survival—obviously.

THE PRESIDENTS AND THEIR ALTER-EGOS

No word has yet been said about famed Eva Perón whose presence and ideology imparted so much of the tone to her husband's administration until her death in 1952. She does not enter into our statistics, for she held no formal position fitting our definition of "manifest" leadership. Her attempt to present herself as a vice-presidential candidate in 1951 failed before the pressure of many within the Perón camp as well as without, but plainly she was a person of power and a key figure in the leadership constellation of the regime. Had she appeared in the statistics, her presence would have changed the averages: she was young, dying at the age of 33; she had little formal education; her occupation was that of entertainer. Her personal history is in sharp contrast with that of her husband, whose military career followed quite normal Argentine lines. Perón was born in 1895 in a small town in the Province of Buenos Aires. Some doubt concerns his origins, but at least his father was well enough placed to see his son graduated from the National Military College in 1913. After the military coup of 1930 his star began to shine brightly. In that year he became the private secretary of the Minister of War, a post he held for five years, and also was

appointed professor of military history in the superior War College, a
chair he occupied until 1936. In that year he was appointed military
attaché in Chile. After a few intermediate incidents he was sent to
Italy from 1939 to 1941, where he bettered his professional knowledge
of mountain fighting and sought to learn some political lessons. Returned to Argentina, he was given troop commands in Mendoza,
nestled in the skirts of the Andes. With the military revolt of 1943 he
assumed important political posts and then, with imposing difficulties
here and there along the way, swept into the presidency in the elections of 1946, winner by a solid majority.

The partnership was plain: as his primary task the President kept the
institutional store, while his wife took a populist ideology to the lower
class and funneled power back to the government. Rarely indeed are
we privileged to watch a contradiction work itself out to the last resolv-
ing chord, as in the fall of Perón. With Church, military, landowners,
and large parts of the middle class ranked against him at the end, he
had clearly to choose between the ideology he had espoused and the
institutional loyalties to which he had remained tied. He could have attempted to distribute arms to the trade unions, a step which would
have unleashed the class war his ideology propelled and his measures
were too ill-designed to make unnecessary. Instead he chose to continue
juggling among the clusters of formal power and, of course, guaranteed his downfall.

In a strange fashion the two succeeding administrations we have
been examining also were headed by presidents who made use of extremely important leaders to round out what we may call the personalities of their governments. General Pedro Eugenio Aramburu, Provisional President from 1955 to 1958, was seconded by Admiral Isaac F.
Rojas as Vice-President, both differing in styles and certain political
policies. The two men had distinguished careers, acting as attachés
overseas and as professors and directors of academies, as well as having important commands entrusted to them. They both also remained
on active duty throughout the Perón period and thus took important
parts in the rebellion. President Aramburu dedicated himself to a re-
structuring of constitutional rule and insisted on holding two elections,
the second of which returned the presidential election to a person not
favored by the provisional rulers. Vice-President Rojas is what is
called in Argentina a "gorilla." Although the term is a relative
one, changing with the times, it refers primarily to a person who believes in the forcible institution of Liberalism, who is extremely anti-
Peronist, and is willing to see the military enforce political measures on
the nation if need be. Although Aramburu also qualifies as a "gorilla,"
of course, his position was much more moderate than that of Rojas. In

the interaction of the Provisional Government, Aramburu represented the center moderates and certain sectors of the democratic left, while Rojas appealed more to the traditionally Liberal right.

The same Janus-like appearance characterized the Frondizi administration in 1960, when the President was backstopped by a Minister of Economy (also called the Prime Minister in jest) who earlier had been a most severe critic of Mr. Frondizi. The President, born in Corrientes in 1908 of immigrant parents who had achieved a comfortable position in the provinces, was graduated from the School of Law of the University of Buenos Aires in 1929. He then embarked on an active life as lecturer, practicing attorney, editor and publisher, and politician. He was a national deputy for the capital from 1946 to 1952 and ran for the vice-presidency in 1951. He was elected President of the nation in 1958 against the desires of the Provisional Government with a reputation as something of a left-leaning intellectual, anticlerical, and so forth. For a series of reasons still mysterious to many, Frondizi soon after his inauguration adopted a series of conservative economic and social policies. To guarantee his integrity in this change, he had to appoint an electoral opponent, Alvaro C. Alsogaray, an outspoken and indubitably honest exponent of a purist's version of economic Liberalism. Mr. Alsogaray, born in 1913 in the province of Santa Fé, first went through military training and on completion studied engineering at the University of Córdoba. He taught in military schools, addressed himself to private undertakings, was President of the Argentine Merchant Air Fleet from 1949 to 1950, and then retired from public life until his reappearance as Subsecretary of the Ministry of Commerce in 1955; he was also Minister of Industries from 1955 to 1956. Appointed Minister of Economy by Frondizi and given a guaranteed free hand, his function was not only to redirect the economy along *laissez-faire* lines but also by his presence and his conviction and his known personality to inspire faith in the new political look.

In all three cases we find the same—the unsolved problems below, the immense weight of institutional continuity and essential governmental weakness pressing from above, and the necessity to explain actions of one kind with ideologies of another. These three immutable guides to Argentine political life help to explain the continuity of the three regimes and to condition our views of future possibilities.

To attempt to discriminate among several types of authoritarianism is no mere intellectual game. In both professional and lay spheres there has been too much lazy satisfaction with simply dividing the world into good democracies and bad dictatorships, with the added modern fillip of welcoming some dictatorships because we like them or because we say nothing else is possible to certain lands other than one kind of dictatorship or another. But of course there are few things so important to developing nations as the kind of authoritarianism they have, or to put it in perhaps less loaded words, the kind of a-democratic situation under which they must live. Certainly to confuse a fascist totalitarianism with a Nasserist or Peronist dictatorship has important consequences: it is a muddling of our thinking, to begin with; we make it difficult to judge events as they are occurring in Asia and Africa; and we confuse our ethical ability to judge good and bad, assuming we wish to permit ourselves a judgment. We also trammel our analyses of the leadership function, for what determines policy is not only the interplay of leaders and followers but also the power of the governmental institution being employed.

There are degrees and degrees of constraint. An authoritarian government which is the least authoritarian it can manage to be is what we should favor if we like democratic solutions. Peronism was by conviction totalitarian, by practice a kind of caudillistic police state, by social philosophy cheaply paternalistic, and by economic doctrine a kind of semi-state monopolistic pre-capitalism. The successor governments have been less authoritarian than they could have been and not so libertarian as they should have been.

PART THREE

INTELLECTUALS AND THEIR
INQUIETUDES

Karl Mannheim's concept of the function of the intellectual fits the Latin American case very closely. He wrote: *

> One of the most impressive facts about modern life is that in it, unlike preceding cultures, intellectual activity is not carried on exclusively by a socially rigidly defined class, such as a priesthood, but rather by a social stratum which is to a large degree unattached to any social class and which is recruited from an increasingly inclusive area of social life. This sociological fact determined essentially the uniqueness of the modern mind, which is characteristically not based upon the authority of a priesthood, which is not closed and finished, but which is rather dynamic, elastic, in a constant state of flux, and perpetually confronted by new problems . . .
>
> . . . The specific social position of this stratum can be quite adequately characterized. Although situated between classes it does not form a middle class. Not, of course, that it is suspended in a vacuum into which social interests do not penetrate; on the contrary, it subsumes in itself all those interests with which social life is permeated . . .

The nature of social change in Latin America depends in important measure on these formulators and definers of problems.

* *Ideology and Utopia*, New York: Harcourt, Brace and Co., 1946, pp. 139–40.

7

THE SOCIAL ORIGINS AND POLITICS

OF UNIVERSITY STUDENTS

The profundity of change and the immense difference among coexisting groups in Latin America, both inside and outside the university, are what make of most political disagreement there an intense and sometimes total clash. Rural Latin America is occupied by persons living in hunting and fishing cultures, in stable isolated agricultural towns, and in fiefs; there is also the small rural aristocracy professing the religious universalism of the medieval upper class. Urban Latin America, by and large, is inhabited both by traditionalists who respect hierarchy, oppose change, and judge all social action by religious precept, and by very different persons of modern temperament and relativistic ideas who are willing to accept some compromise of social issues and are ideologically committed to at least a limited secularism.[1]

University students represent many but not all of these social segments. They are recruited overwhelmingly from urban centers. They are not by definition a modernizing element; indeed, they may form part of broader social groups whose strength powerfully inhibits development. But whatever the students' basic value commitment, they are in a world where disagreement goes far deeper than any explicitly ideological division. Two ways of life, two ways of thought, oppose

[1] For a fuller statement of the traditional-modern dichotomy being used here with special reference to the Latin American city, see Gino Germani's construction in Philip M. Hauser, ed., *Urbanization in Latin America*, New York: International Documents Service, 1961, pp. 47–48. My amendments to these views appeared in UNESCO, *International Social Science Journal*, Vol. XV, No. 4, 1963, pp. 560–70, under the title, "National Values, Development, and Leaders and Followers."

each other in the Latin American city, and the accommodations tenuously lacing them can be only temporary, an adjustment forced by the need to maintain the mechanics of urban and quasi-national life. In the absence of a single national community to which all citizens unequivocally belong, Latin Americans are split into qualitatively different kinds of loyalty patterns. Villagers are concerned first with family and tribe, traditionalists with family and church and friendship commitments, and the modernizers with building the impersonal mechanisms of national, industrial society. Given this situation, no single set of criteria of legitimacy can provide the consensus from which flows the power necessary for stable public institutions. The Latin American university student must make a more or less conscious choice from among a set of worlds, for he cannot merely fit himself into an already established and coherent community embracing all his peers.

Mediterranean traditionalism can coexist for relatively long periods with some degree of modern social and economic organization. Indeed, all of Latin America's more economically developed states offer persistent demonstration that the required payment—giving up the privileges of the old order in return for the benefits of the new—can be deferred for quite a while. But the price of this indulgence is a weak institutional structure which is unable to guarantee either continuity or predictability and thus inhibits contained and ordered change. The power that Latin American student groups have demonstrated since the first decades of this century is then in inverse relation to the strength of governments and the efficacy of the university administrations themselves. The relative influence of organized student movements must be heightened by the essential fragility of societies in transition toward modern nationhood.

CLASS AND THE NATURE OF STUDENT POWER

Weak social institutions make more salient the power of any organized group, whether it is composed of students, military officers, or clergy. The sharp class distinctions of all Latin-America also serve to protect rebels against the established order if they enjoy the power of high social status. The Latin American university traditionally has served to certify the elite position of the sons of the upper class. Access to higher education is still so restricted for the general population that it is apparent the student-selection process in most Latin American countries still effectively excludes the economically underprivileged. The educational pyramid narrows so abruptly that such a conclusion is inescapable. As recently as 1950, for example, 49 per cent of the population over fifteen years of age in Latin America had no primary schooling at all or had failed to complete the first year; 44 per cent had more than a year of primary education, but only 8 per cent had completed it. Six per cent had some secondary school training, and 2 per cent had graduated; only 1 per cent of the population over fifteen had attended an institution of higher learning.[2] This steep decline in school attendance was expressed graphically in the Mexican ten-year educational plan submitted to President Adolfo López Mateos on October 27, 1959:

. . . According to recent information (1956), of every thousand children who manage to put their feet on the first rung of primary school [on the same base, 460 more never get even that far], only one reaches the last grade of the professional school . . . During the course of the first six grades . . . no fewer than 866 are left on the road. Only 59 get to the threshold of secondary education; but of these, 32 drop out during the three scholastic grades of secondary, prevocational, and special education, who, added to the previous ones, give us the figure of 973. Only nine arrive at the *bachillerato,* vocational education, and the professional cycle of primary normal instruction, of whom three drop out in the two or three grades involved . . . with whom the total of desertion rises to 994. And, finally, only six get to higher education, but of these five drop out. . . . In summary, through the course of the sixteen grades that comprise a complete educational scale, 999 abandon their studies and only one finishes. . . . [To this we must add] the alarming circumstance that 471 abandon school . . . in the first grade.[3]

The survey adduces reasons for non-attendance and abandonment that are a direct function of class position: it estimates that at the time the report was prepared, 600,000 children then of school age had never attended school and that an additional 366,000 had abandoned school for economic reasons, while 175,000 were out of school because of illness. Because the Mexican data are certainly not atypical,[4] we may reasonably conclude that despite important differences in primary and secondary school attendance between, for example, Haiti at one extreme and Argentina at the other, higher education as such remains the privilege of the few. The favored, moreover, come largely from families in the middle and upper-middle occupational categories in the national capitals; a somewhat smaller group comes from the same occupational levels in smaller cities; and a still smaller element is from the homes of higher level workers and artisans, almost invariably from the

[2] Oscar Vera, "La situación educativa en América Latina," paper read at a UNESCO meeting on the Social Aspects of Economic Development in Latin America, Mexico, December 1960, pp. 2–3.

[3] As quoted in Mexican news reports of October 28, 1959.

[4] See Eduardo Hamuy, *El problema educacional del pueblo de Chile,* Santiago, Ed. del Pacífico, 1961, esp. Ch. 5, for Chilean experiences analogous to the Mexican problem.

capital. Numerous studies confirm the generality of this pattern, despite a few variant situations, mostly in provincial areas. For example:

> The group which receives higher education is naturally very much smaller than the "middle sectors," but in all the Central American countries it is observed that the majority of university students—as well as secondary school students—come from those urban middle sectors comprised of professionals, businessmen, and white collar employees; and an important minority from artisan or worker groups.[5]

A 1961 survey of the law students in the University of Panama [6] showed that about a third of the sample had fathers in the ranks of skilled, semi-skilled, and unskilled labor. It is worth adding here that only in Argentina, Chile, Cuba, and Panama, of all the Latin American republics, is the modal point of the educated population among those who have completed from four to six years of primary education. To put it another way, it is only in these four countries that there is a sufficiently broad base of persons with primary education to provide some social heterogeneity to the student body passing through secondary education into the university—a fact which goes far toward explaining the relatively high percentage of persons of lower occupational origins in the Panamanian law school.

There should be no presumption, however, that the Latin American university in general serves as an important group mobility channel for lower-class persons. Students from working-class families rarely attend the most prestigious faculties or complete the full course of study. Further, it is probable that students with "worker" fathers have a life style move characteristic of the lower middle classes than of the working class. The situation at the University of Chile accurately reflects the general state of affairs:

> The University's 13,000 students constitute no more than 1.5 per cent of the young people between 17 and 25 years of age in Chile, and the sons of working class families have little hope of reaching any of the major professional schools. But this is not because of anything inherent in the University itself but rather is a reflection of general economic conditions and the desperate poverty of Chile's rural and urban

[5] Marshall Wolfe, "Las Clases Medias en Centroamérica; Características que Presentan en la Actualidad y Requisitos para su Desarrollo," CEPAL, Comité de Cooperación Económica del Istmo Centroamericano, October 18, 1960, p. 29, mimeo.

[6] Daniel Goldrich, *Radical Nationalism: The Political Orientations of Panamanian Law Students*, Bureau of Social and Political Research, Michigan State University, May, 1961, p. 30. Robert C. Williamson has also completed a study of students in the National University of Colombia which clearly supports these statements as well as many of those which follow. See his *El estudiante colombiano y sus actitudes*, Monografías Sociológicas of the Univ. Nac. de Colombia, Bogotá: 1962, esp. p. 16 and pp. 75–76.

masses . . . the University remains a stronghold of Chile's middle class, many of whom themselves are hard pressed by need and are able to stay in the University only with great sacrifice.[7]

Student leadership also reflects this class influence. The only large-scale empirical study of student leaders in Latin America, an inquiry into the Chilean Student Federation (FECH), unequivocally establishes the middle-level occupational origins of those student leaders since 1920.[8] The relatively large number of leaders coming to the capital from provincial cities, however, suggests that we should look to physical mobility as a probably significant element in the more general social picture.

The well-advertised interest of some Latin American university students in practical politics is a direct consequence of the introduction of new middle elements into full social participation in the more developed countries after the turn of the century. The symbol of their emergence is the Córdoba Reform of 1918, a declaration of academic independence and political intent. Wherever stimulated by the Argentine initiative, the Reformists adopted a populist tone reflecting the identification of newly integrating groups with all alienated elements, in a pattern not unlike the all-embracing national spirit of the French bourgeoisie in their own revolutionary day. The Reform created an elaborated body of doctrine that has been in constant use throughout Latin America ever since

The traditional élitist social function of the university was by no means in direct contradiction with the thoughts of the newly mobile who had assumed the responsibility of assisting their less fortunate fellows. The politics of the situation, however, were violently wrenched. Instead of producing only leaders of stasis, the university also began to create leaders of change. Within their academic environment the two elements mingled in fashions quite like the new strata developing in society as a whole. Rightists, forced into activism to maintain their positions, fomented the importation of new ideologies of conservatism from Europe, partially accounting for the Nazi and Falangist strains in the politics of Chile, Brazil, Argentina, and many other countries in the 1930's and 1940's, and still in full bloom in Argentina. Meanwhile, leftists seized on the traditions of élitism to justify a tutelary stance in anticipation of the reality of the victory of populist democracy.

Eduardo Frei, leader of the Christian Democrats in Chile and a leading exponent of "government by technician" in Latin America, provides

---

[7] Frank Bonilla, "The Student Federation of Chile: 50 Years of Political Action," *Journal of Inter-American Studies*, July, 1960, p. 313.

[8] Frank Bonilla, *Students in Politics: Three Generations of Political Action in a Latin-American University*, a doctoral dissertation for Harvard University, April, 1959, mimeo.

this contemporary expression of the university as an agency for training élites:

> The University cannot isolate itself from this historical process [of modernization]; and in its fashion it can be a decisive factor in its orientation. Is it prepared for it, or does youth follow one set of paths, the University others, without giving them any reply? Is it only a machine to produce professionals who on leaving the University feel themselves frustrated . . . ? . . . The University is a social force and a great moral reserve . . .
>
> It is now time for the University to provide ideas and cadres of responsible men capable of recognizing and stating the truth in an objective manner, and capable of elaborating and utilizing formulas that do not rest on intuition or on ambition disguised as "ability." . . . The University can provide the governing élites for this decisive historical crossroads, giving them a vision of the world and of our own America.[9]

The conscious acceptance of direct social responsibility by the new university students is an implicit identification of themselves as actual or aspirant members of an expanding élite. If there is some negative correlation between group size and élitist attitudes, then the exclusiveness of higher education in Latin America would seem to contribute importantly to the psychology of leadership. In the mid-1950's there were in all Latin America only about 350,000 registered students in institutions of higher learning, both state and private.[10] Of this number, 40 per cent were registered in Argentine institutions, and almost half of them matriculated in one university—the National University of Buenos Aires. And once again it should be recalled that the drop-out rate is extremely high, so that very few of even these small numbers will ever be graduated.[11]

There is some disagreement about these figures, for criteria concerning which institutions and which students should be considered of university level vary widely among countries and experts.[12] Some estimates, for example, exclude schools of fine arts, theology, and other

[9] Eduardo Frei Montalva, "La Universidad, conciencia social de la Nación," *Prólogo*, Oct.–Nov., 1962, pp. 8–11 and *passim*. *Prólogo* is a Christian Democratic review published in Buenos Aires.

[10] These figures are estimates based on the various charts in UNESCO, *La situación educativa en América Latina*, Paris, 1960, as well as Frank Bonilla, *op. cit.*, for the Chile data missing in the UNESCO survey. Comparable reliable data for Bolivia, also missing in the UNESCO monograph, were unobtainable.

[11] The drop-out rate is discussed on pp. 115–16.

[12] For example, Juan Mantovani, "Idea, forma y misión de las universidades en los países latinoamericanos," *Política* [Caracas], No. 21, (April–May, 1962), p. 39, estimates the number of institutions of higher learning as 88 universities, 31 technical schools, and "another 114 higher schools of university category, not counting those of theology, fine arts, music and physical culture."

institutions dedicated exclusively to the humanities. The student count is also a problem, for in many countries the central national university has some degree of administrative responsibility for the college preparatory work in the secondary school system, and sometimes the universities either run the entire system or maintain one or more prestigious secondary schools. In any event, the highest enrollment figures given do not exceed 550,000 for 1960,[13] still a very small figure when compared with the United States (four million students in higher education on approximately the same population base), and of course made even smaller by the high drop-out rate. On a percentage basis, the above figure is very small, especially when viewed against the large urban populations of many Latin American countries. Yet in absolute numbers it is large enough to cover a broad social spectrum including significant middle elements and some marginal upper-lower ones. Relative smallness and objective largeness justify ideologies of planned development, reinforcing the students' view of the university as a training center for the future holders of the power they expect at least partially to create for themselves.

THE STUDENT IN THE LARGE STATE UNIVERSITY

Available information is much too sparse to permit a detailed discussion of differences between students in private and religious institutions and those in the state-operated universities. With few exceptions the only student organizations that historically have had important roles in political life are those of the major national universities in the capital cities. However, where regional universities do experience student convulsion, they, too, are almost always within the state system. The State University of São Paulo, for example, has been consistently involved in national politics, and it contributed not a few martyrs to the anti-Vargas cause during the early days of his experiment in authoritarian populism. Other cases could be cited of significant student activities in the regional public universities of Argentina, Chile, Peru, and Mexico, but even so their effect on national life is usually indirect. This generalization holds true even though it was the regional university of Córdoba that played host to the delegates who promulgated the Reform of 1918. The ideal of the academic republic promulgated on that occasion had more profound ideological effect outside Argentina than within it. Nevertheless, even there the influences of the Reform were felt more strongly in other parts of the national university system than in Córdoba. As one Argentine authority summarized the results of the *Reforma* in his country:

[13] See, for example, the editorial in *Panorama*, OAS Task Force for Programming and Development of Education, Science and Culture in Latin America, Bulletin No. 9, Washington, D.C. (December, 1962).

In truth there was no such reform, for the structure of the university, substantively as well as legally, was maintained. There were, on the other hand, statutory reforms, all tending toward seeing that the universities acquire a more flexible and efficacious rhythm of life.[14]

The same author points out that within twenty years the national university system doubled in size, while administrative reform promoted a fresh academic spirit of freedom and innovation. The point here being made is that only the politics of national integration and development have stirred significant student action in this century. This ideological commitment behind student action explains why it is that institutions, whether secular or religious, are of little importance in general student movements, and why only major national issues have served to arouse students of the regional universities.

Of all Latin America's universities, the University of Buenos Aires is by far the largest, having something over 70,000 students. It had about one-fifth the total university enrollment in Latin America less than a decade ago, and it now has probably no less than 15 per cent of the total.[15] This institution merits detached discussion here not only because of its mammoth size but also because the Student Federation of the University of Buenos Aires (FUBA) has long been politically active as well as formally participant in the administration of the university. Many of the generalizations hurried travelers make about Latin American universities and students are in reality but extensions of impressions of the famous case of the University of Buenos Aires.

Exactly 58,684 students were tallied in the census of October 1958 count of the University of Buenos Aires from which the following statistical profile is derived. Seventy-five per cent of the students were males, although the ratio of sexes varied widely from school to school within the university. In Philosophy and Letters, which embraces the training of teachers, the sex ratio was reversed, while only 2 per cent of the Engineering students were female. Ninety per cent of the students were less than thirty years old, the modal age being twenty years for the university as a whole, twenty-one in Engineering, twenty-two in Medicine, and nineteen in Philosophy and Letters. These figures, being not significantly different from those for any large United States university, cast some doubt on a widely accepted stereotype. They make

[14] José Babini, *Historia de la ciencia argentina*, Mexico: Fondo de Cultura Económica, 1949, pp. 131–32. See also Arthur P. Whitaker, *The United States and Argentina*, Cambridge: Harvard University Press, 1954, p. 74, for an easily available summary statement in English of the echoes within the general Argentine university system of the Reform.

[15] All figures in this section are taken from University of Buenos Aires, *Censo Universitario*, Buenos Aires, 1959. The census was taken in 1958.

one wonder how many "professional students" there actually are in at least this Latin American university. Ninety-one per cent of the students held Argentine citizenship; 4 per cent were from other Latin American countries, and the rest were resident non-citizens. Seventy per cent of the students were born in Greater Buenos Aires and 13 per cent in the surrounding provinces. Only 2.2 per cent were born in towns of less than 2,000 population. The secondary school record of the students makes the urban nature of the student body even more apparent, for 80 per cent completed high school in Buenos Aires. Seventy-five per cent attended public secondary schools, while only 11 per cent were graduated from secondary parochial schools; the remainder were from secular private schools. As a group, then, the students were of normal university age, urban origin, and secular training.

Over 85 per cent of the students were single; 90 per cent had no children, and only 3 per cent had two or more children. Ninety per cent of them lived in a family situation, either with parents or a spouse. Thirty per cent were supported entirely by the family, a figure rising to 52 per cent in medicine and 58 per cent in Dentistry. There were also 514 members of the armed forces registered. Only .6 per cent of the students were employed in blue-collar occupations!

Twenty-seven per cent of the students' fathers and 33 per cent of their paternal grandfathers had been or were in employer positions; 10 per cent of the fathers and 5 per cent of the grandfathers had been or were professional. But only 5.4 per cent of the fathers and 8.3 per cent of the grandfathers had been or were of the laboring group.[16]

Few of these students will ever receive their degrees. Approximately 30 per cent were in the first year of study at the time of the census, though this figure varied considerably by faculty. In Law the freshmen were 49 per cent of the total. With 58,684 enrolled students, the university granted only 3,324 degrees in 1958.[17] Normally the proportion

[16] Later statistics indicate that now over 10 per cent of the students have blue-collar fathers. But again, over one-half of such students have one or more white-collar grandfathers.

[17] These figures are not unusual in Latin America. In Lucio Mendieto y Núñez and José Gómez Robleda, *Problemas de la Universidad*, Mexico: Biblioteca de Ensayos Sociológicos, 1948. Chs. 1 and 2, we find a desertion rate of 53 per cent for the University of Mexico. From 1931 to 1943 the University granted only 7,532 degrees. Total enrollment in 1931 was 9,722 and in 1943 was 22,230. As late as 1953 the *total* enrollment in all universities in Mexico was 27,200, and the University of Mexico continued to serve about 20,000 of these. The Asociación Nacional de Universidades e Institutos de Enseñanza Superior, in *The Teaching of Engineering in Mexico*, Mexico, 1962, pp. 21–23, now gives the total student population in higher education at 101,236 for 1961, of whom 44,319 were in the National University of Mexico. This figure does not include 23,561 students in the preparatory levels controlled by the University of Mexico.

of degrees awarded to freshmen registered is about 15 per cent. Dropout rates for recent years vary from as much as 80 per cent in Architecture to 64 per cent in Law and 44 per cent in Medicine.

In terms of party affiliation and attitudes toward the university, the students seem close to the Argentine national norm. A poll taken in 1957 in the Faculty of Letters (often considered quite leftist) indicated that over 50 per cent of the students clustered about the center; 7 per cent said they were Communists, 8 per cent chose one or another of the conservative parties, and 22 per cent did not reply. Only 1 per cent avowed themselves Peronists. This student body has consistently returned Reformist (center and left) student delegates to office, but only Exact Sciences has in recent years elected frankly Marxist student officers. Indeed, in the last two student elections the choice in the majority of faculties has fallen to the center and the right, and the Reformist left and center-left have been forced to support moderate candidates in order to retain some power in the university administration. In short, the University of Buenos Aires reflects all the political schisms of the upper and middle groups in Argentina. It is hardly surprising that Peronism, a lower-class political movement, finds few supporters in this haven of the middle- and upper-class Argentine.

Although the usual majority grouping of students calls itself *reformista*, in deference to the Córdoba Reform, splits for electoral purposes are common, and there is even striking evidence that some of the basic academic tenets of the Reform are now being rejected by the Buenos Aires students. Democratization of the university and its establishment as a kind of autonomous academic republic governed by students as well as faculty remains the goal of most students and professors. But apparently there is much backsliding from some of the pedagogical precepts implicit in these ideals.[18] Only 1 per cent of the students receive scholarship assistance, for example, and certainly the scramble for grades and academic advantage in Buenos Aires is as heated as in many United States universities. On the crucial question of whether the university should have entrance examinations (strongly opposed by orthodox Reformists), fully 70 per cent of the students supported some kind of entrance examination or qualifying year of studies. Significantly, in the most "popular" or socially least prestigious school, Economic Sciences, 47 per cent opposed any entrance requirement beyond the requisite secondary schooling.

[18] See John P. Harrison, "The Confrontation with the Political University," in Robert N. Burr, ed., *Latin America's Nationalistic Revolutions, The Annals of the American Academy of Political and Social Science*, March, 1961, pp. 74–83, for a concise and easily available digest of current understandings of the Reform. The writings of Gabriel del Mazo are usually considered the most definitive Spanish sources on the Reform.

FUBA has been politically restrained for the past several years, because of the general political instability of the country and the consequent threat of military intervention to force the government to oust the elected university administration and appoint a new rector and deans. The last major political student action of a public nature was a massive demonstration in 1958 against permitting Catholic universities to confer legally valid degrees. FUBA lost, and Argentina now has three more or less regularly functioning clerical universities, two in Buenos Aires and one in Córdoba. Otherwise the fairly close collaboration between majority faculty and student groups has thus far prevented major incidents and saved the university from intervention.

There is logic and relevance to the drift by Reformists into a more professional attitude toward the university and into a politics of coalition and limited compromise, activist but not narrowly fanatical. A recent survey [19] conducted among freshmen, seniors, and graduates of the Faculties of Economic Sciences, Medicine, and Exact Sciences show unmistakably that there is a strong correlation between those taking a modern view of society (and who also are likely to be Reformists) and those students accenting the vocational and technical aspects of learning.

> Taken as a whole, about a third of each sample [from Medicine] favored education for good citizenship and the building of a national spirit [the view of the old aristocracy as well as of the *reformistas* of 1918, although with a changed ideological substance], while the remainder favored a more vocational and generally cultural orientation. The figures as taken by mobility . . . indicate that with fair consistency the upwardly mobile tend to respect more highly the practical and vocational functions of education, as do those who rank highly on the national identification scale [the measure of modernism]. Low scorers on the national identification scale are consistently above average in their desire for the formation of good citizens and the national spirit . . .[20]

These correlations held constant through the Faculties of Economics and Exact Sciences as well. It is only reasonable that technological change, the necessity for a high degree of specialization, and emphasis on economic development should lead modernizing Argentines to insist upon improvement of vocational training at the university level, even if at the apparent expense of some cherished notions of the "popular university." This attitude explains a seeming contradiction in the literature concerning Latin American student movements. John P. Harrison, for

[19] Tentative findings are reported in K. H. Silvert and Frank Bonilla, *Education and the Social Meaning of Development: A Preliminary Statement*, New York: American Universities Field Staff, 1961, Part II.

[20] *Ibid.*, p. 100.

example, states, in an article on the "political university," that "while all of the aims of the reform movement mentioned above touch directly upon the university as an institution, it is readily apparent that none of them is concerned with curriculum revision or in improving the professional training of the student." Several pages later the author points out, however, that reformism and curricular improvements are not necessarily mutually exclusive. "There has been, if anything, even less interest in reforming university curricula and professional training to meet mid-twentieth century needs in those universities that closed their doors to the reform movement than in those where it found fertile ground."[21]

Several interim conclusions would seem justified at this point: first, that the Reformists of 1918 inherited the elitist notion of the university from their predecessors; second, that because of their class origins and general changes in the political environment they imbued their assumption of an élite role with a populist and nationalist ideology vastly different from the ideals of their traditionalist predecessors; and third, that with the passage of time the traditionalists have continued to conceive the university's role as that of forming citizens in the Greek sense, while the Reformists have begun to value the quality of education as indirectly contributory, through broader social processes, to nation-building. In an important sense, then, the innovating student is approaching the prevailing view of academicians in developed lands, while still continuing to place a greater weight on the immediate applicability of learning. This view was given strong expression by Risieri Frondizi, brother of ex-President Arturo Frondizi and rector of the University of Buenos Aires from 1957 to 1962:

> The Argentine university has wasted much of its energies in the search for ingenious solutions to administrative questions, without becoming aware that the problems of the university are of a pedagogical nature. . . . [It seems not to] matter that the university does no research, that one turns one's back on the needs of the country, that there are no professors fit to teach many courses, that the students still keep on repeating by rote the worn-out notes of past years . . . that there is no university life . . . the university . . . should not be at the orders of a governor—or of a political party or an ideology—but rather ready to serve society, the people, who maintain it. Not to give it what this or that person demands through his political spokesman, but what it [the society] needs for its progress, enrichment, and material and spiritual elevation.[22]

[21] John P. Harrison, *op. cit.*, pp. 77, 80.
[22] Risieri Frondizi, "La Universidad y sus misiones," *Comentario*, Oct.–Nov.–Dec., 1956, p. 309, *passim*.

STUDENT POWER AND POLITICAL ACTIVISM

The ascription of great political influence to student organizations implies that these organizations are surrogates for other interested social groups. It also suggests that if young persons can gain sufficient influence to change, on occasion, the course of national political life, then, as already noted, other power centers must be in such disarray as to elevate the relative power of any organized group. This argument has often been advanced to explain the prominence of the military's role in Latin American politics; it holds as well for student groups.

The following propositions may serve to explain relative student political strength in a more specific and functional sense:

1. All Latin American countries, with the possible exception of Cuba, are still in a pre-national phase. Government is thus by definition weak; it can count on little anticipatory adjustment to law and thus, by the same token, has few means for the unequivocal imposition of regulation and sanction.

2. Instability and disorganization are characteristic not only of governments but also of all interest and occupational associations. But because not all fall into disarray—or the same degree thereof—at the same time, the significance of and the relative power generated by the very fact of group organization vary from time to time and place to place.

3. The very explicitly defined class divisions, reinforced by tradition and custom, promise the university student an elevated chance of success in life. He comes from a middle- or upper-class family; he is acquiring the social certification of achievement and status. Even though he may be disappointed and fall into the "intellectual proletariat," his life chances are still very high, and he is realistic so to recognize them. The following views expressed in the previously cited study of Panamanian law students imply that at least some students use politics to bolster their already high chances for attainment:

> Their [the Nationalists'] expectation of success is high, and they seem to have a stronger motivation toward achievement than do the Moderates—radical nationalism may thus have been embraced because the success of the movement would mean the expansion of socio-economic opportunities and because the Nationalists have projected their drive for achievement onto the nation as a whole.[23]

4. Traditional as well as modern persons place great stress upon the need for adequate leadership in Latin America; the university is viewed as a necessary element in the training of leaders, and within

[23] Daniel Goldrich, *op. cit.*, p. 19.

the university the faculty of law continues to produce the greatest number of political figures. As we might expect, during the Aramburu government in Argentina (1955–58) 95 per cent of all high policy-making government officials were graduates either of a university or of a military academy, and this figure rose to 100 per cent in 1960. Even during the quasi-populist Perón regime (1945–55), about 85 per cent of the policy-makers had higher degrees. Over half the persons at this level in 1960 were lawyers, and even during the Aramburu military interregnum the career officers outnumbered the lawyers only by fourteen to twelve in the top positions.[24]

5. Youth is a relative concept to a certain extent. The exclusiveness of the university, coupled with strong family and class identifications, makes of students apprentice professionals from the moment they matriculate. Thus the word *universitario* denotes anyone connected with the university, whether student, teaching assistant, professor, or graduate. The Latin American student is, then, not considered so callow as his North American counterpart and may be trusted with public power at an early age. For example, eight years after a revolution in which law students had played an important role, half of the deputies in the Congress of Guatemala were thirty-five years old or younger. Only six of fifty-four deputies were over fifty years of age.

6. The strong desires for development on the part of major urban groups in Latin America create a demand for a new socio-economic ideology. The university is the natural site for the *pensador* and for the diffusion of his ideas.

7. The needs of Latin America's new industries have already impelled curricular revision and expansion in many Latin American universities in such fields as business administration and the sciences. But at least as important have been the effects of governmental commitments to partially planned procedures of economic growth, now given formal approval as an announced requirement of the Alliance for Progress, but a long-standing administrative practice in such countries as Uruguay, Costa Rica, Mexico, and Chile. Economic planning has naturally force-fed the growth of faculties and departments of economics, but its effect has also been felt in engineering, sociology, and public administration. Increased demand for technicians has fortified the power of the universities in these areas and has at the same time increased the certainty of success which imbues the student. The invitation to early manipulation of public power is quite explicit.

8. These circumstances, taken in sum and added to the social propinquity of the university situation, provide the conditions for the creation of student organizations that parallel the national parties.

[24] See Chap. VI.

Wherever studies have been made of the politics of students, it has been found that only a minority (albeit usually a large one) "belong" to national parties in any positive sense. Student leaders, however, usually have some party coloration, if not a firm identification, and factions within universities have at least a tenuous identification with national parties.

> To say that the student organization is "captive" or riddled with political factions is not to say that it is a passive instrument of more powerful and experienced politicians. The Fech [the Student Federation of the University of Chile] is really in the hands of students with strong political convictions, who have a firm sense of dedication and allegiance to their parties. The University political groups enjoy considerable independence within the broad framework of basic party policy and organization. They are able to influence party decisions through their dominance of youth sections and by allying themselves with sympathetic elements in the party hierarchy. They ordinarily experience no conflict between their loyalty to party and their responsibilities to fellow students because they believe their parties offer the only acceptable solutions to the problems of youth and the nation.[25]

9. Latin America has always been a hearty consumer of European ideas and practices, and the university has long played a vital part in the process of importation, adaptation, and propagation. The present search for ideology, technique, and science has broadened the university's role in the mimetic process. Even though this imitation means that "much research is accomplished by waiting for the mail," as several Latin American university administrators have sarcastically put it, the postman brings ideas that increase the power of the university establishment.

The nine foregoing propositions suggest the basic reasons for the inherent institutional strength of Latin America's universities in relation to other social groupings. Not all students, however, attempt to use institutional power for public ends, nor is the manner of employment the same among activist students. Attitudes toward the proper use of power vary widely.

In the study of Argentine students already cited we find, for example, that medical students engage in little overt political activity. Well over half of them report that they argue politics with friends and acquaintances, but only 6 per cent of the freshmen and 8 per cent of the seniors attest to any party activity, and only 20 per cent of the former and 15 per cent of the latter attended a student association meeting during the six months preceding the interview.[26] Only 17 per cent of the practic-

---

[25] Frank Bonilla, "The Student Federation of Chile," *op. cit.*, p. 330.
[26] For all the material in this paragraph, see Silvert and Bonilla, *op. cit.*, pp. 104, 114–15, 127–28, and 237, 256, 276.

ing physicians reported they had attended professional association meet-
ings during the same period. Students in the Faculty of Exact Sciences
take a much more active part in student organizations than those in
Medicine, but their level of participation and involvement in politics is
not much higher. A strong sense of school identification and the famili-
arities fostered by small enrollments help to explain this higher level of
student-oriented political activity.

The most surprising findings of all relating to political activity are
those that reveal the numbers of students who participated in some
sort of street rally or demonstration during the six months prior to the
interview. For the three groups in Sciences (freshmen, seniors, and
graduates), the percentages were 39, 11, and 12 respectively; for Medicine, 16, 15, and 10, and for Economics, 14 per cent among freshmen
and 18 per cent among graduates. The time period covered was one of
quite intensive national political activity, and an affirmative answer
may have meant only that the respondent listened to political speeches
in a public plaza.

The study appears to show that few students participate extensively
in either university or public political activities; that normally at least
half of the students in all the groups studied were passive, and that between one-quarter and one-third of the students constitute an "immediately available public," ready to be tapped for special occasions. This
potential for action is paralleled in the community at large. It is estimated, for example, that at least 250,000 persons in Buenos Aires demonstrated in favor of religious higher education in 1958, with another
300,000 appearing later to oppose it. That half a million persons in a
city of approximately seven million demonstrated on the Church-state
issue in a period of only normal political tension indicates the large
reservoirs of readiness to respond to the leadership of university students and professors of Catholic as well as secularist persuasion.

THE EFFECTIVENESS OF STUDENT POLITICAL ACTION

To this point we have sought to describe the nature of student political activity and to link student power with social organization and the
institutional nature of the university.

Unless the unique historical development of each country is taken
into account, however, attempts to categorize the range and effectiveness of student participation in politics may appear simplistic. For example, the location of the national university in Nicaragua outside
Managua, the capital city, certainly has something to do with the relatively little one hears of Nicaraguan students. The much more important case of Brazil is strongly conditioned by the very late start that
country had in higher education, which only came with the inauguration

of several professional schools in the nineteenth century.[27] The Reform was already two years old when the Brazilian government decided to merge existing schools of medicine, engineering, and law to form the nucleus of the University of Rio de Janeiro. In 1937 the University of Brazil finally emerged, a combination of the University of Rio de Janeiro and an embryonic Federal Technical University, and by 1959 Brazil had twenty universities plus some private institutes. This delayed development clearly affected the growth of a student political tradition.

Still, it should be possible to derive a set of categories sufficiently flexible to give realistic play to each unique case, yet precise enough to be meaningful. We know that students have been important in political events in Cuba, Colombia, Venezuela, and Guatemala—in each of which they have participated in the overthrow of a dictatorial regime. In the same countries the students subsequently lost whatever decisive power they may have had. Probably the most realistic appraisal is that in no case were the students the decisive element in the overthrow, but rather participants in a broad national movement involving the military, the clergy, businessmen, industrialists, and labor groups, as in the ouster of Perón. The intellectual community, including the students, provided the rationale for action, but the physical power to overthrow constituted authorities lay elsewhere. The effectiveness and the potential results of student action may be judged broadly according to the following scheme:

Situations of Stable Traditional Societies. In very rudimentary, almost bi-class social structures, necessarily governed under crude dictatorial forms, students normally play a very limited role in innovation and political activity. This was the situation in the colonial era, and present-day Nicaragua, Haiti, and Paraguay fall into this category.

Situations of Beginning Modernization and Disarray. As the city begins to grow, as an industrially oriented middle class emerges, and as the politics of change begin to operate, students assume a most important role in the importation and adaptation of ideology, in the organization of power as well as of ideas, and in government itself. Factionalism is one of the earliest signs of modern pluralism. El Salvador, Guatemala, Ecuador, Peru, the Dominican Republic, and Panama are currently in this stage. In a world of political factionalism, more than in any other social milieu, the student, as one of the aspirant elites, finds a situation sufficiently simple so that he can exercise relatively great power over political events.

More Mature Situations of Temporary Resolution. When the social

[27] Robert Moreira, *Educação e desenvolvimento no Brasil,* Rio de Janeiro: Centro Latinoamericano de Pesquisas em Ciencias Sociais, 1960, pp. 192–93.

structure is relatively complex, politics turbulent, and at least interim political decisions are made with the immediate future in mind, student groups are usually very active but limited in their role by other established interests. In such situations student activity can still be of great importance in defining issues and precipitating incidents or even full-scale revolts. But usually the university as an institution begins to turn inward, preparing to meet the demand for professionalism that always arises in times of rapid economic and political development. Colombia, Venezuela, and Bolivia, for varying historical reasons, all fall into this category

Situations of Institutional Complexity and Relative Strength. Where the student finds himself in a plural-interest structure and complex class system, his relative power becomes even more limited. The Mexican experience is a useful case in point. For some time the Mexican student has had little organized voice in national affairs. The bus strikes of 1958, which broke a peace that had lasted almost a generation, had little significance. Only the Technical University—the "poor man's University of Mexico"—has given the authorities much difficulty, and then only on matters having principally to do with the school's internal administration. The strength of the Mexican government, the ideological weight of the Revolution and the institutional expression of this ideology by the state, the single governing party, and the intellectual community all combine to strip from the students much of their political reason for being. To take another example, active as the Cuban students were against the Batista regime, they are now contained by the ideological as well as military strength of Castro's modern dictatorship. In Argentina, even though the country exhibits institutional disarray, effective student action in public affairs is impeded by the massiveness of Buenos Aires, the strength of the competing interest structure, and the complication of motivations and values. In these situations the students may and usually do have much influence over university policy and affairs, but in national politics their role must of necessity depend on other, more primary definitions of interest. Brazil, Mexico, Argentina, Uruguay, Costa Rica, Chile, and Cuba are all within this category.

Ideological orientation, too, will vary with the kind of developmental problem the country faces and with the particular student body involved. Ideologies of nationalism are felt but weakly, if at all, by the public at large in the least developed countries of Latin America. But the intellectual and modernizing student caught in the midst of the disorder of rapid change may indeed become impregnated with nationalistic views. Only certain students and student groups, however, will embrace exclusivism, impersonalism, anti-imperialism, and other of the more extremist views implied by nationalist ideologies. Students in Catholic and other private universities tend toward conservatism; *i.e.,* they are opposed to nationalism, secularism, and the impersonalism of modern society. They may be anti-American as well, hostile to both capitalism and Protestantism as Latin conservatism traditionally has been. The state universities, ahead in the modernization of the traditional academic disciplines as well as in their growing dedication to the physical sciences and empiricism, attract the innovators—and thus the nationalists—in much greater measure than such schools as the Catholic University of Chile or the Javeriana (Jesuit University) in Colombia. This political array is common to some degree throughout Latin America, describing students as much as other politicized groups. The nationalistic student of the state university draws more attention to himself than any other non-party group of ideologists, since he is also the innovator, the modernizer, the politically concerned, and likely to be pursuing studies closely involved with the developmental process. This constellation of attitudes and practices accompanies modernization everywhere, for wherever economic and social development has occurred, the nation-state has been its political vehicle.

SOCIAL CHANGE AND THE STUDENT

A complex mythology of the Latin American student has grown up in the United States, in large measure fomented by the excited findings of observers scurrying to make up for irrevocably lost time. We hear that the Latin American student is a radical, uninterested in study, the pawn of professional agitators, the persecutor of his professors, and the bane of responsible university administrators. Some students are all these things. Others are serious and questioning young people working well and serenely in rapidly improving faculties and departments. Still others are apathetic playboys, or yearners after the glories of National Socialism, or social climbers thirsting to become oligarchs, or desiccated youths who aspire to no more than the routine life of the bookkeeper. Probably the majority of students in the state universities are more secularist than not, more nationalist than not, more middle-class than not, more center and left-of-center than not, and more worried about their individual fortunes than the fate of the state. They are the reservoir of modern men and women upon whom the nation can draw for its development, susceptible to national leadership and willing to take the risks demanded when societies break from one world of thought and action into another.

The Latin American university student is the child of his parents. To assume the student is but a hot-eyed revolutionary is to presume that somehow registering in a university is sufficient to cut family ties, break class and other group identifications, and produce a special kind of creature divorced from his society. The intellectual community can be "ahead" of society as a whole, but it must have identifications with some sectors of the community and can pull along only those people susceptible to its particular suggestions or prodding. To single out the Latin American student for special disdain is to forget that it is truly debatable whether he is more irresponsible, rapacious, corrupt, and foolish than his elders on the farm, in government, the bank, or the trade union. Indeed, there is some reason for advancing the thesis that the student is at least temporarily a better citizen than his elders.

The simple fact of youth also crucially distinguishes the Latin American student from his parents. He still remains free to believe in and to attempt to apply the long-held ideals of the old Liberal aristocracy, those desires for freedom, dignity, growth, and progress so often honored in the breach since Independence. With whatever ideological superficiality, misplaced enthusiasm, and youthful conviction of ultimate right, the Reformists have preserved and modernized these ideals and often have displayed a courage and selflessness in their defense that merit admiration rather than contempt or condescension.

> Over and above nationalistic feeling and the commitments to party, there exists a set of canons governing and inspiring student action. In Chile these are not often articulated but they are recognized as going back to the very beginnings of the student federation. . . . They include the courage to hold and defend a point of view on fundamental issues, a readiness for self-sacrifice, loyalty in friendship, love of country, hatred of dictators and distrust of the military, a sentimental identification with the working classes, and solidarity with the youth of other Latin American countries. Students have been a force of progress within the university; their dedication to democratic ideals, their readiness to protest injustice, and their resistance to political repression have helped keep Chile politically moderate.[28]

The university is a propitious place for demonstrating the relationship between freedom and development. For long the *reformista* and neo-*reformista* students have instinctively linked the two in their hatred for authoritarianism on the one hand and their search for modernization on the other. If they have been tempted to adopt ideologies that the Western World rejects as totalitarian, it may well be that they have been offered no other seemingly viable alternative, have heard no objective and authoritative voices reaffirm the convictions of 1918, and have seen corruption and dictatorship blessed with international respectability. To leave the university and to "grow up" means to accept measures of conduct in contradiction to those avowed social ideals the

[28] Frank Bonilla, "The Student Federation of Chile," *op. cit.*, p. 315.

student has been taught in civics texts, the speeches of his leaders, and the writing of the *próceres* (Founding Fathers). Rarely indeed is the gulf between ideal and real behavior so broad as it is in Latin America. But a major reason for hope lies precisely in the insistent presence of those concepts of free inquiry whose routine application must be a part of the modern university if it is to accomplish its pedagogical and research functions. There will always be tension between academia and the public so long as the bold pursuit of ideas is hampered by cultures that fetter minds with archaic measures of hierarchy and demand ultimate commitment to unchanging standards of the good.

8

ARIEL AND THE DILEMMA OF THE
INTELLECTUALS

"Uruguay is the Switzerland of America." Sometimes it is made the
Denmark, or the Belgium, or even the New Zealand of the New World.
But those who are intent on comparisons all fall short of the mark
. . . Uruguay is Uruguay. Most people probably mean it as a compli-
ment to the South American country to call it the Switzerland—or the
Denmark or Belgium or New Zealand—of the Western Hemisphere,
but those European and Pacific countries could consider themselves
complimented by the comparison. Let us not forget that . . .

Spend a little time in Uruguay—it need not be a long while—and you
gradually get an impression of national well-being, a sense of maturity,
a feeling of adjustment. It is fluid, invisible, and highly subtle. It is not
something you can put your finger on; it is simply there in the air you
breathe, in the social radiations and emanations from city and countryside. Spend a little time in thinking about the matter, after it gradually obtrudes itself from the subconscious into the conscious, and you
almost inevitably come to the conclusion that it is to be explained on
the ground that *Uruguay is an integrated country*.[1] [The emphasis is
not mine.]

British and American attitudes toward Uruguay are very generally this
kind of panegyric. And indeed, Uruguay is very refreshing in its free
press, in its abundant civil liberties in general, in its political militancy
when it comes to dictatorships at home and in the Western Hemisphere. Latin American attitudes, however, are not so glowing toward
Uruguay as Anglo-Saxon ones, even though the same justified belief in

[1] Russell H. Fitzgibbon, *Uruguay: Portrait of a Democracy*, London: George
Allen and Unwin, 1956, pp. 264–65.

the abundant freedom of the country is not lacking. Argentines like to think of Uruguay, the "eastern coast" of the Plata, as a wayward province, rather economically retarded and localistic in sentiment. They are grateful for the aid extended to the democratic movement in Argentina if they happen to be anti-Peronists, but think that Uruguayans tend to be rather simplistic in their politics, inclined to glossy generalizations and a lack of realism. Argentines enjoy referring to Uruguayan democracy as an arranged affair, an elaborate game of make-believe in which the entire nation conspires. This judgment to my mind is unfair, even though the formal play of Uruguay's democracy can be so explained, for it neglects the real amount of daily freedom which Uruguayans have and fully exercise, even if the result is sometimes rudeness to guests of the nation or the university.

Every Latin American country is in greater or lesser degree different from every other one, and despite the fact that Montevideo is across the river from Buenos Aires, there are notable characterological variations between the two cities. Uruguayans are famed for talking right up in direct and unmistakable fashion, and indeed pride themselves on doing so. Their respect must be earned by hard work; the accused is considered despicable unless proved worthy of dignity. I should like to spin a dubious hypothesis to explain this phenomenon. Uruguay is a small country, and one with a large middle group. According to recent estimates, there are only 2,500,000 Uruguayans, and to boot about 40 per cent of them live in the capital city. Uruguay is more a city-state than a nation-state.

The rector of the University of Montevideo tells a most revealing story about Uruguayan political stubbornness. He was born in a small town in the hinterland into a family of White political persuasion. (There are also Reds, the major opposition to the Whites, and reds who are Communists, and Socialists, or Trotskyists, and several major splits in the Reds and Whites themselves.) When the rector as a young man went to Montevideo to attend medical school, he suffered a political transformation and became a Socialist. Now it seems that in Uruguay one simply does not change his party but accepts his politics as a birthright. So, on a visit home, the rector was pointedly spurned by one of his favorite aunts, who said to him when she learned of his new Socialist affiliation, "Aha! So you sold out!" (This kind of thing is unnerving to a Chilean, who spends his political life sampling the wares of one party after another.)

ANTI-IMPERIALISM AND ANTI-AMERICANISM

Opinions conflict as to whether Uruguay is generally for or against the United States. Because Uruguay early and decisively aided the

Allied cause in World War II while Chile and Argentina dragged their heels until the closing days of the conflict, and even then entered grudgingly, Uruguay is thought to be the most pro-U.S. of the three. But it can also be held that the country has one of Latin America's richest anti-American literatures and a long history of practical and polemical anti-imperialism, both based on the early emergence of nationalist and separatist attitudes. Uruguay's participation in the war is solid evidence for that time at least that she was much more strongly pro-democratic than anti-U.S.

The years 1957 and 1958 were especially bad ones for Americans in Uruguay because of an acrimonious debate over the closing down of the Swift and Armour packing plants in December 1957. I have no intention of going into the unpleasant and long history of the controversy, but the conflict has been extremely intense, involving as it does basic clashes of interest and system. The crystallized truth of the matter from the viewpoint of the companies is that they had to close down because they could no longer make as much money in Uruguay as in other meat-exporting countries. The land has about the same number of head of cattle now as fifty years ago, while the population has more than doubled.[2] Worse, the Uruguayans have a great and seemingly increasing appetite for meat and lead the world in consumption per capita according to available figures, such as they are.

The shortage of cattle restricted the companies' operations, and so in their last years in Uruguay they squeezed as much work into two or three months as they could, allowing the plants to lie idle during the remainder of the year. The Uruguayan side of the argument is that the past profitable operations of the companies produced a national vested interest in their continued existence, for not only were foreign exchange needs satisfied by the meat exports, but in addition thirty thousand persons lived directly off the plants' operations. This figure is derived by taking the five thousand workers of the packing plants and adding in their families, plus the tradesmen (and their dependents) who dealt directly with the meat packers. The government argues that just because things were bad at the moment was no excuse not to hold out and help the country to recover. Simple expropriation of the pri-

[2] According to Guillermo Bernhard, *Comercio de Carnes en el Uruguay*, Montevideo: Aguilar e Irazábel, 1958, p. 14, the number of head of livestock is as follows:

Year	Cattle	Sheep	Pigs
1860	3,630,000	1,990,000	5,851
1900	6,820,000	18,600,000	23,900
1908	8,190,000	26,280,000	180,100
1924	8,430,000	14,440,000	251,200
1946	6,820,000	19,560,000	274,400
1956	7,305,462	22,954,230	

vate holdings is not an easy solution, not only because of a lack of money and expertise, but also because the withdrawal of the companies implies a related lack of the necessary refrigerator ships to transport to overseas markets whatever meat may be produced by a nationalized company or a co-operative.

Aside from this disagreement, at the very heart of matters commercially ideological, there was a constellation of second-level irritations. The companies and the union had been at loggerheads for years. Armour and Swift accused the Uruguayan government of partiality, and the government charged the company officials with cunning, deceit, and worse. When the companies finally abandoned Uruguay, anti-Americanism boiled over into anti-Nixon and Eisenhower demonstrations, protests against the Chessman execution, and so forth.

But anti-imperialism has long been an imperative in daily Uruguayan political expression, a symbolic necessity with the weight of history and the influence of powerfully prestigious hero figures behind it. Although the United States is the long-standing and favored object of Uruguayan nationalists, England too comes in for its share of opprobrium, for the British have been involved in the Plata region for much longer than the Americans and even made two forceful attempts to colonize at the beginning of the nineteenth century. The United Kingdom is still the largest buyer from Argentina and Uruguay, although the United States has moved into the favored-supplier position. Railroads, banks, commercial houses, generating plants, and packing houses have all demonstrated the long and vital British interest in the area, so extended as to give rise to the popular saying about Argentina that it is "a British colony in which a lot of Italians talk bad Spanish." And yet the British are not nearly so harshly attacked as the Americans. In a long citation quoted below from a famous Uruguayan tract, a cultural rationalization is advanced for this phenomenon. In truth, the matter is not so easily explained and would be an excellent subject for a doctoral dissertation on "Objects of Anti-Imperialist Hatred Compared."

For all practical contemporary purposes, anti-imperialism in Uruguay is largely the generalization derived from anti-Americanism. Eudocio Ravines, author of the well-known *The Yenan Way*, in another work says the following on the subject:

> Notwithstanding the profound change which has been bettering the relations between the two Americas, it is a massive and tangible fact that Latin American political and social life as it develops is being shot through with an attitude which goes from resistance to non-collaboration and from antipathy to hostility with respect to the United States. The rich diversity of feelings derived from this sentiment goes under

the general name of anti-imperialism. A Latin American anti-imperialist will always be *antiyanqui,* actively or potentially, and to distinguish one from the other would be to embark on a sea of subtleties
through which it would be easy to anchor on all possible sophisms.

One could argue a great deal about the existence, the non-existence, or
the survivals of imperialism, but what does not allow for discussion is
the operative and militant existence of Yankee anti-imperialism as a
real sociological category, as a political current, with incessant and
multiple activities in all the countries without exception.[3]

ANTI-IMPERIALISM AS DOCTRINE

Latin America's most famous literary and quasi-philosophical attack
against American utilitarianism was written by a Uruguayan, José
Enrique Rodó, in 1900.[4] *Ariel,* as this short book is called, takes the
form of an address by Prospero to his students after the conclusion of
the year's studies. In elevated language and sophisticated thought,
Rodó urges his readers to the life of reason and spirit, the rejection of
irrationality and materialism. He exhorts youth to develop the integrity
of the being, to be "unmutilated examples of humanity, in which no
noble faculty of the spirit is obliterated and no higher interest . . .
should lose its . . . virtue." Rejecting an egalitarian notion of democracy, he argues that the truly democratic state must grant equality of
opportunity in order to make possible the unequal development of
each individual according to his capacity and will. The end of such selection must be a higher capacity for love.

Fortunately, so long as there exists in the world the possibility of ar-
ranging two pieces of wood in the form of a cross—that is to say, always—humanity will go on believing that love is the foundation of
any stable order and that hierarchical superiority in such an order cannot be other than a higher capacity for loving.

To the spirit of *Ariel* which he sees as compatible with the Latin appreciation of life's values, he opposes the Caliban of the utilitarian
United States. With great acuity and much insight he launches into a
devastating attack on "The American Way of Life." The conclusion is
an impassioned plea to Latin youth to reject facile imitation of North

[3] *América Latina: Un continente en erupción,* Buenos Aires: Editorial Claridad,
1956, p. 15
[4] Rodó was born in Montevideo on July 15, 1872. He became a professor of
literature in the University of Montevideo and also a member of Congress, although
a political career held little attraction for him. A very popular lecturer, he was
the object of an impressive public demonstration of affection when he left Montevideo in 1916 for Europe as a foreign correspondent for a local review. The
following year he died in Palermo, Italy. *Ariel* and his *Motivos de Proteo* (1909)
are considered his most important literary works.

American manners and standards, to remain faithful to humanistic traditions, disinterested love for the things of the spirit, art, science, religious sincerity, and idealistic politics.

Fresh editions of *Ariel* appear regularly. The book, still widely viewed in Latin America as an accurate portrayal of American democracy, is also a required part of any discussion of Latin American political thought.[5] I am going to quote extensively from the last third of *Ariel,* so that the reader may see some of Rodó's thinking in depth and taste of his style.[6]

Their [American] culture, which is far from being refined or spiritual, has an admirable efficiency so long as it directs itself practically toward realizing an immediate end. They have not incorporated within the acquisitions of science a single general law, a single principle; but they have made science a wizard through the marvels of their applications, they have made it a giant in the realms of utility, and they have given to the world in the steam boiler and the electric generator billions of invisible slaves who multiply by hundreds the power of the magic lantern to serve the human Aladdin . . . Puritan liberty, which sent them its light from the past, joined to that light the heat of a piety which still lasts. Hard by the factory and the school their strong hands have also raised the temples from which spread the public prayers of many millions of free consciences. They have known how to preserve, amidst the shipwreck of all ideals, the highest ideal, keeping alive the tradition of a religious sentiment which, if it does not fly on the wings of a delicate and profound spiritualism, still partly holds to the firm kingdom of moral sense amidst the rough and tumble of utilitarian tumult.—In the midst of the refinements of civilized life, they have also known how to maintain the mark of a certain primitive robustness. They have the pagan cult of health, of skill, of strength; in their muscles they temper and sharpen the precious instrument of the will; and obliged by their insatiable urge for domination to cultivate the strength of all human activities, they model the torso of the athlete for the heart of the free man. And from the concert of their civilization, from the coordinated movement of their culture surges a dominant note of optimism, of confidence, of faith, which fills their hearts, pushing them into the future under the suggestion of a hard and arrogant promise . . .

. . . You see that although I do not love them, I admire them. I admire them, first of all, for their formidable capacity *to want,* and I bow before the "school of will and work" which . . . they have instituted . . .

[5] See, for example, Rex Crawford, *A Century of Latin American Thought,* Cambridge, Massachusetts, 1944.

[6] The edition I have used here was published by Imprenta Balmes in Buenos Aires in 1947. This edition also includes other critical essays. The translation runs from p. 95 *passim* to the end on p. 124.

. . . If anything saves them collectively from vulgarity, it is that extraordinary show of energy they carry everywhere and with which they impress a certain character of epic grandeur even on struggles for material interest . . .

With the sincere recognition of how much is shining and grand in the spirit of that powerful nation, and so having earned the right to completing a just appreciation with respect to it, a question charged with interest asks to be put.—Is that society carrying out, or at least tending to carry out, the ideal of rational conduct which fulfills the legitimate demands of the spirit, of the intellectual and moral dignity of our civilization?—Is it there where we must go to point out the approach to our "perfect city"?—That feverish inquietude whose embrace seems to multiply the movement and the intensity of life, does it have an object which merits it and a stimulus sufficient to justify it?

Herbert Spencer, extending his salute to American democracy with noble sincerity in a banquet in New York, pointed out the fundamental trait of American life as that same uncontained inquietude which manifests itself in an infinite passion for work and relentless material expansion in all its forms. And he then observed that in such an exclusive rule of activity subordinated to the material ends of utility there was revealed a conception of life, tolerable, without doubt, as a provisional character for a civilization, but one which now demanded rectification, since it tended to convert utilitarian labor into the end and the supreme object of life, when in no case can it rationally signify anything other than the mere accumulation of elements serving to make possible the total and harmonious development of our being . . .

American life effectively describes that vicious circle pointed out by Pascal in the grasping pursuit of welfare when this pursuit does not have its end outside itself. Its prosperity is as great as its impossibility of satisfying a mediocre concept of human destiny. A titanic work because of the enormous demonstration of will it represents, and because of its unheard of triumphs in all spheres of material aggrandizement, it is undeniable that that civilization produces, in its totality, a singular impression of insufficiency and emptiness. And so it is that if, exercising the right conferred by thirty centuries of the history of evolution presided over by the dignity of the classical and the Christian spirits, one asks what is the guiding principle, what is the ideal substractum, what is the purpose behind the immediate preoccupation for positive interests which shapes that formidable mass, one finds only, as the formula for the definitive ideal, the same absolute preoccupation with material victory . . . that people has not known how to substitute idealism inspired by the past with a high and disinterested conception of the future. It lives for the immediate reality, the present, and for it subordinates all its activity to the egoism of personal and collective welfare.—Of the sum of the elements of its wealth and power, it may be said . . . that it is a pile of timber to which no one has found a way of setting fire. What is missing is the effective spark to make the flame of a vivifying and restless ideal arise from the abundant fuel. Not even national pride, failing higher impulses, not even exclusivism and pride in race, which are those which in antiquity transfigured and glorified the prosaic hardness of Roman life, can have glimmerings of idealism and beauty in a people where cosmopolitan confusion and the *atomism* of a badly understood democracy impede the formation of a true national consciousness.

It might be said that the productive positivism of the Metropolis has suffered, on being transmitted to its emancipated sons in America, a distillation depriving it of all those elements of idealism which tempered it, reducing it in truth to the crudeness which in the exaggerations of passion or satire has been attributed to the positivism of England.—The English spirit, under the harsh coat of utilitarianism, under mercantile indifference, under Puritan severity hides—it cannot be doubted—a select poetic awareness, and a profound veneration for sensitivity which reveal . . . that the original basis, the Germanic basis of that race, later modified by the passion for conquest and the habit of commercial activity, was an extraordinary exaltation of the senses. The American spirit has not received in inheritance that ancestral poetic instinct . . . The English people have in the institution of their aristocracy—no matter how anachronistic and unjust it may be from the point of view of political rights—a high and impregnable bulwark to oppose to the mercantilism 'round about and to the invading dullness . . . In the situation of American democracy, the spirit of vulgarity does not find before itself heights inaccessible to its power to rise, and it extends and propagates itself as though over the flats of an infinite plain.

Sensitivity, intelligence, customs—all are characterized in that enormous people by a radical ineptitude for selection which, alongside the mechanical order of their material activity and of their political life makes for a profound disorder in everything pertaining to the world of idealistic arts.—It is easy to follow the manifestations of that ineptitude, starting with the most superficial and apparent, then going on to others more essential and intimate.—Prodigal with his riches . . . the American has succeeded in acquiring fully with them the satisfaction and the ostentation of sumptuary magnificence; but he has not succeeded in acquiring the select note of good taste. True art has been able to exist in such surroundings only as a result of individual rebellion. Emerson and Poe there are like examples of fauna expelled from their real medium by the force of a geologic catastrophe . . .

The ideal of beauty does not move the descendant of the austere Puritans. Nor is he moved by the ideal of truth. He deprecates all exercise of thought lacking an immediate finality as being vain and unfruitful. He does not bring to science a disinterested desire for truth, nor has he ever manifested himself in any case as loving it for itself. Research is for him only the preparation for utilitarian application.

—His glorious efforts to spread the benefits of public education are inspired in the noble purpose of communicating the fundamental elements of knowledge to the greatest number; but they do not reveal that . . . there is care taken to select and elevate such education to aid the effort of the superior ones who have the desire to rise above the general mediocrity. The result, thus, of their stubborn war on ignorance has been universal semiculture and a profound languishing of higher culture . . . Here is the reason for the history of their thinking activity being a decreasing progression of brilliance and originality. While in the period of the Revolution and their [national] organization there arose many illustrious names to represent the thinking as well as the will of that people, a half century later Tocqueville could observe . . . that *the gods are going*. When Tocqueville wrote his master work, there still irradiated, nevertheless, from Boston, the *Puritan citadel*, the city of the learned traditions, a glorious galaxy possessing . . . universality in the intellectual history of that century. —Who, later, has picked up the heritage of Channing, of Emerson, or Poe?—Mesocratic levelling, hurrying its desolating work, tends to dissipate the little character which still remained to that precarious intellectuality. It is a long time since their books have been borne to the heights where it would be universally possible to recognize them. And today, the most genuine representation of American taste, so far as letters go, is in the dirty linen of newspapering which does not remind us of what once *The Federalist Papers* gave us.

With respect to moral sentiments, the mechanical push of utilitarianism has come up against the moderating force of a strong religious tradition. But one should not therefore believe that the guidance of conduct has been subordinated to a real principle of disinterest.—The religiosity of the Americans . . . is nothing more than an auxiliary aid to criminal law . . . The highest point of their morals is that of Franklin: a philosophy of conduct which finds its end in what is mediocre about honesty, in the utility of prudence; from whose womb never will arise saintliness or heroism . . .

Public life is, of course, not exempt from the consequences of the growth of that germ of disorganization which that society carries in its entrails. Any ordinary observer of their political customs will tell you of how the obsession for utilitarian interest progressively tends to enervate and wither the sense of right in their hearts. Civic virtue, the old virtue of the Hamiltonians, is a steel sheet which is rusting, always more forgotten among the cobwebs of tradition. Venality, which begins with the public vote, is propagating itself to all institutional areas . . . Democracy . . . has always tended among them to the abominable brutality of numbers, minimizing the greatest moral benefits of liberty and annulling . . . respect for the dignity of others. Today, furthermore, a formidable force is raising itself to counteract the absolutism of numbers in the worst possible manner. The political influence of plutocracy represented by the all-powerful allies of the trusts, monopolizers of production and masters of economic life, is, without doubt, one of the traits most worthy of interest in the present configuration of that great people. The formation of this plutocracy has forced one to think, and probably very correctly, of the rise of that enriched and haughty class which, in the last era of the Roman Republic, was one of the visible antecedents of the ruination of liberty and of the tyranny of the Caesars.

. . . it is in that West, growing formidable before the old states of the Atlantic and demanding hegemony in the immediate future, where one finds the clearest representation of American life at the present moment of its evolution . . . Utilitarianism empty of any idealistic content, cosmopolitan vagueness, and the levelling of bastard democracy will there . . . arrive at their ultimate triumph.—Every noble element of that civilization, everything which links it with generous remembrances and buttresses its historic dignity—the legacy of the crewmen of the *Mayflower*, the memory of the Virginia patricians and the gentlemen of New England, the spirit of the citizenry and the legislators of emancipation—will stay within the old stages where Boston and Philadelphia still maintain, as has been expressively said, "the palladium of the Washingtonian tradition." Chicago is preparing itself to reign . . .

In the same measure as the utilitarian genius of that civilization thus is assuming more defined, franker, and narrower characteristics, there increases with the intoxication of material prosperity the impatience of its sons to propagate it and attribute to it the predestination of a Roman rule.—Today, they openly aspire to first rank in universal culture, to leadership in ideas, and they consider themselves the forgers of a type of civilization which will prevail . . . Underneath their declared spirit of rivalry with Europe is an ingenuous disdain and also the profound conviction that they are soon destined to overshadow Europe's spiritual superiority and its glory, thus complying once more, in the evolution of human civilization, with the iron law of the ancient mysteries in which the initiated killed the initiator . . . It would be useless to try to convince them that the works carried out by the persevering genius of the European Ariel for the last three thousand years . . . can not be equated with the formula *Washington plus Edison*. They aspire to revise Genesis so they can occupy the first page.—But in addition to the relative insufficiency of the part which has been given them to carry out in the education of humanity, their very character denies them the possibility of hegemony.—Nature has not conceded them a genius for propaganda nor an apostolic vocation. They lack that superior gift of *amiability*—in the highest sense—of that extraordinary power of sympathy with which the races blessed with a providential trust of education have been able to make of their culture something similar to the beauty of classic Hellene, in which everyone imagines he can recognize traces of his own.

And take note that when, in the name of the rights of the spirit, I deny to American utilitarianism that typical character with which it would like to impose itself on us as the sum and model of civilization, it is not my purpose to affirm that the work realized by it has been entirely lost with relation to what we might call *the interests of the soul* . . . The work of American positivism will serve the cause of Ariel, in the last analysis. What that people of cyclops have directly conquered for material well-being with their sense of the useful and their admirable aptitude for mechanical invention, other peoples will convert, or they themselves may do so in the future, into efficacious elements of selectivity . . .

. . . Let us hope that the spirit of that titanic social organism, which up to now has been *solely will and utility,* may also some day be intelligence, sentiment, idealism . . .

. . . A great civilization, a great people—in the meaning which has value for history—are those which, when they disappear materially in time, leave vibrant forever after the melancholy arising from their spirit and make persist into posterity their imperishable legacy—as Carlyle said of the souls of his "heroes"—*as a new and divine portion of the sum of things* . . .

A definitively organized society which limits its idea of civilization to accumulating abundant elements of prosperity, and its idea of justice to distributing them equitably among the partners, will not make of the cities it inhabits anything which can be distinguished, essentially, from the anthill or the beehive . . . thus the quantitative grandeur of the population as well as the material grandeur of its instruments, of its arms, of its houses are only *means* of the civilizing spirit, and in no case results with which one may content himself.—Of the stones which composed Carthage, not a particle remained transfigured into spirit and light . . .

Great . . . is the city when the suburbs of its spirit reach beyond the heights and the seas and when, its name evoked, there illuminates itself for posterity an entire period of human history, a whole horizon of time. The city is strong and beautiful when its days are something more than the invariable repetition of the same echo . . . when there is something in it which floats above the crowd; when among the lights which are lit during its nights is the lamp which accompanies the solitude of the vigil made restless by thought and in which is incubated the idea which is to bloom in the light of the next day converted into the cry which gathers the force to lead souls.

Only then can the material extension and grandeur of a city give the measure to calculate the intensity of its civilization . . .

In our Latin America there now exist cities whose material grandeur and whose sum of apparent civilization push them with accelerated pace to share in the first level of the world. It is necessary to fear that the serene thought which is about to break upon the fatuous externals, as on a sealed bronze vessel, will evoke the disheartening noise of emptiness. It is necessary to fear, for example, that the cities whose names were a glorious symbol in America, who had Moreno, Rivadavia, Sarmiento, who took the initiative in immortal Revolution; cities which made the glory of their heroes and the words of their tribunes lengthen throughout the extension of a continent, as in the harmonious unfolding of the concentric circles raised by the stroke of a stone on still water—can end in Sidon, in Tyre, in Carthage.

It falls to your generation to prevent it; to the youth which is coming, blood and muscle and nerve of the future . . .

. . . not like Hartmann, in the name of death, but rather in that of life and hope themselves, I ask you a part of your soul for the work of the future.—To ask it of you, I have wanted to take inspiration in the sweet and serene image of my Ariel . . . Ariel is reason and higher sentiment. Ariel is that sublime instinct for perfectibility, for whose virtue that human clay by the side of which his light lives, is magnified and converted into the center of things . . . Ariel triumphant signifies idealism and order in life, noble inspiration in thought, disinterest in morals, good taste in art, heroism in action, delicacy in customs . . .

While the crowd passes, I observe that although it does not look to the sky, the sky looks down upon it. Upon its indifferent and obscure mass, as upon plowed land, something descends from on high. The vibration of the stars is like the movements of the hands of a sower.

For its time *Ariel* was obviously very advanced. To use it as a model half a century later is of doubtful validity. A grateful *pastiche* of Comte, Carlyle, Nietzsche, humanism, Gallican Catholicism, and the Latin American cult of youth, Rodó's comments have their appealing side. But he is typical of the *Philosoph*, of the pensador, the man who could be inflamed, who could meld the ideas of others and propagate them, but who could not pass into the truly creative stage of putting systematized questions to his materials and thus proposing their possible answers within a system of method and not of yearning. Time has long since passed by much of his political commentary, but "Rodonism" and *arielismo* remain important parts of the mystique of Latin youth, whether they have read this work or not. The point is that Rodó still touches chords of sympathy and desire in Latin America.

There is something sad in the construction of a stereotype which doesn't quite come off. The essence of a stereotype is that it is partly true; therefore, it is also partly false. Rodó's belief that the Germans would help to solve the cultural deficiencies of the Americans demonstrates the wellsprings of his kind of idealism, as well as the pitfalls of stereotypical views.

An illustrious thinker who compared the slaves of ancient societies to particles undigested by the social organism might perhaps find a similar comparison to characterize the situation of that strong colony of German ancestry who, established in the states of the Mid- and the Far West, conserve intact in their nature, their sociability, and in their customs the imprint of the Germanic spirit which, in many of its most profound and vigorous characteristic conditions, must be considered a true antithesis of the American genius.

Rodó's half-truth is the Germany of Goethe, Hegel, Beethoven, and Schiller. How unfortunate it is that the half-falsity should have so well obscured for Rodó that Germany which gave rise to Hitler and Goebbels. But still his largely unrevised rendering of the United States remains the stock in trade of the Latin American idealistic and intellectual nationalist.

I do not deny the right of Latin American intellectuals to attack the United States or any other country as they will. But two things must be insisted on if their opinions are to be respected: accuracy of commentary and observation, and covert motives at the same level of generosity as their avowed ideals. My purpose is not to belabor Rodó for his generalizations or to point out the factual failings of other Latin Americans as they construct their views of the United States. Nor is it my purpose to accomplish the same attack through the back door, condemning Latin America's thinkers by making selective and invidious comparisons with their counterparts in the United States.

The tragedy of the Latin American intellectual is his necessary constriction by the context within which he lives. He desperately wants to be what he cannot be—a universalist—in societies just learning to be national. He complains about the United States from the posture of the Greek Stoic and not from that of the contemporary man trying to get at least some of his view of the present from forecast. The clamoring demands throughout Latin America for the useful and potentially liberating claptrap of modern civilization have made Rodó's Hellenic yearnings obsolete. The tragedy is that their contextual obsolescence is not even yet recognized by the Latin intellectuals who can support their yearnings for the contemplative and spiritual life *as they define it* only at the cost of a Greek-like social organization, slaves and all. And yet they are dedicating their lives—and some do so with great abnegation—precisely to combatting social inequities as they see them.

I am reminded here of a biting *New Yorker* cartoon showing an analyst jumping up and shouting at his patient, "Dammit, you *are* inferior!" My desire at this point is to jump up and say to the *arielistas*, "But dammit, señores, you *are* underdeveloped!" Americans overseas have been carefully taught that the term "underdeveloped area" refers only to economic matters and not at all to cultural and intellectual attainments. But of course the term has something at least inferential to say about intellectual and artistic matters. An economically poor country cannot support symphony orchestras, cannot provide competent university training to qualified persons, and cannot pay for the research necessary to the kind of contemplation this century demands.

Even more hampering to the Latin American intellectual is that to be economically underdeveloped is also almost invariably to be nonnational in culture. As a result the thinkers of underdeveloped areas find it difficult to compete on the international market of ideas and art, for their expressions often lack the limited kind of universality understandable within the universe of the citizen of the nation-state. The Latin American *pensador*, with his pull toward the great outer world, is an effective instrument for the absorption of European trends and their translation into the terms of his homeland. But when it comes time for him to return what he has borrowed with the interest of his country's special cultural point of view, he finds that nobody is listening because what he has to say is either not significant or not fresh in a different cultural context. It is not that "fault" lies with one side or the other; it is basically that there is a break in the complete circuit of communications. This is caused in part by the representative of the economically industrialized area, who—with his different outlook— finds it hard to understand what the man from the underdeveloped area is saying.

The major exceptions to my statements come out of Mexico and Brazil, where the nationalism which has seized on large parts of the population has been fed its distinctive flavor by a new ethnic amalgam expressed within intriguing (for the rest of the national world) physical surroundings. The other major area of exception is in the general field of literature, but again, the few Latin American novels, for example, which have had the widest circulation are of the genre of the novel of protest, an area of obvious universalistic appeal both in function and, usually, in description of the clash of cultures and of desires.

It hardly needs to be added that nation-state status will not automatically produce hordes of creative Ariels. The factors of the accident of the individual and then his training and his stimuli are still to be taken into account. There is little doubt that Uruguay has national attitudes in ample measure, but playing against it is its smallness, its overreadiness to ingest European ideas, and its physical isolation from the mainstreams.

It is very often said that anti-imperialist movements must not be confused with democratic ones, as witness so many cases in Africa, Asia, and Latin America. In the short run, I suppose the argument is correct; in the longer run, the usual way of looking at the matter has been to say that democracy cannot flourish except in conditions of national independence. But is it possible that misdirected anti-imperialism may not also make the development of broadening democratic institutions more remote? It is convenient and easy to direct frustrations to the outside, but one inevitable result is to create a climate of fear and impotence with respect to local problems truly subject to solution from within. If anti-imperialism serves to paralyze the will and thus reduces the area of possible action, it is at the very least antisocial. My feeling is that what I have seen of the Uruguayan anti-imperialists puts them into the category of the self-destructive ones, at least for the time being. They would be shocked to hear it said, but if their rationale is still *arielismo* and their effect is to limit choice, then they are, of course, reactionary in the truest sense of the word.

But Uruguay remains fortunate in the depth of its traditions and in the complexity of its society. And if we isolate and describe a certain kind of intellectual, it does not by any means follow that we have described the entire society. But even if it is true that a solid majority of Uruguayans objects to American society, objection is not enough. Anti-imperialism which is not mere *antiyanquismo*, Third Positionism which also is not mere *antiyanquismo*, attitudes with an affirmative content, selected and expressed with respect for data—these are what Latin American politics sorely need. The politicalized Latin American intellectual has his task clearly presented to him. If he is to justify the goodly measure of leadership and respect he now has, he must begin to speak in terms of *specific* wants, *specific* programs, and *specific* capabilities. To do so he must learn techniques of research to find out what is possible to satisfy what he thinks is desirable. He must leave his ivory tower and dirty his intellectual hands, finding solutions within himself and within his society.

In answer to this argument about the necessity for techniques and data in order to solve pressing public problems, an Argentine intellectual told me, "No, no, social knowledge reveals itself." Speaking of Greeks, I wonder what Aristotle would have replied to such a comment.

9

AMERICAN ACADEMIC ETHICS AND
SOCIAL RESEARCH ABROAD

American social science is in a crisis of ethics. Certainly, however, "American social science"—whatever that amorphous corporation may be—is not broadly aware of any particular problem or that its motives, techniques, and practitioners are falling into disrepute in many parts of the emergent world. Latin America, the most developed of the under-developed, is appropriately the scene of a confrontation putting into question the honesty, decency, and even simple competence not only of all of us engaged in that area but also of students of all our disciplines wherever they may work. The crisis, long recognized as latent by sensitive observers, has now passed into an acute stage. Throughout Latin America quantitative studies have halted or been impeded, and all scholars, whether in teaching or research, find their actions questioned in direct correlation with the sophistication of the persons with whom they deal.

These statements are not an exaggeration. Nor can they be dismissed by patronizing references to the sensitivity of Latin Americans, the harassment by leftist intellectuals, or the hostility of persons with inferiority feelings. The primary responsibility for the present state of affairs rests with Americans, despite the obvious complications induced by the nature of Latin Americans, who in this case are merely reacting to misbehavior. The immediate cause of the contretemps was the attempt in 1965 of the Special Operations Research Office of American University to launch a large-scale socio-political study of internal warfare in Latin America with funds provided by the Department of the

Army. The extremely noisy debacle which ensued almost immediately cannot be explained in the narrow terms of a few bungling individuals or even of misguided policy; the ground was well prepared by the ethical incomprehension, cavalier attitudes, and tolerance of ignorance manifested by American universities and scholars for many years. The sum of these saddening shortcomings bore heavily on Latin America as it became a lucrative and thus intellectually attractive field after the Cold War came to the Caribbean, producing a crisis far surpassing the immediate circumstances.

Such charges are serious indeed. They reflect on the personal work morality of scholars. They question the manner in which universities have chosen their priorities for foreign area studies. They raise doubts concerning foundation activities, the sponsorship of research, the proper relationship between government and the scientific community. These matters have been considered by two Chilean investigative committees and in the Congress of the United States. A reaction is beginning in academia, too, which will certainly lead eventually to changed university-government relations in the social sciences.

Let me make it entirely clear that in this matter I am what an anthropologist would call a participant observer. I was in Chile at the time the Camelot crisis erupted and discussed the matter with some, though not all, of the principal actors. One of my own research undertakings was paralyzed. I have an investment spanning twenty-five years, as student and professional, in Latin America. I have also been pained with the low prestige accorded scholarly work on Latin America and have both welcomed and been fearful of the present coming of the prestigious folk to the area. I make these statements, and put them in the first person singular, so that the reader may be fully aware that I consider myself an engaged scholar. By "engaged" I mean that I am personally concerned about the course of social events; by "scholar" I mean that I attempt not only to use objective procedures but also to take care that the specific questions I ask are theoretically determined and not the fruit of passion. I also presume that to be a scholar means to assume the rights and duties of freedom of inquiry and communication, accepting no covert sponsorship, being ridden by as few hidden motives as may be consistent with the dignity of personal privacy, and taking intellectual risks. Elementary as these remarks may be, they seem to need repetition at this particular time, and especially as prelude to my attempt to present a subject which makes so much personal difference to me.

PROJECT CAMELOT

The Special Operations Research Office labeled its proposed research Project Camelot. It was supported with an initial $6,000,000 for three to four years by the Department of the Army. These particular plans came to fruition in 1964, although for many years previously SORO worked under much smaller contracts involving secondary research largely carried out within the United States. But the unfortunately titled Camelot [1] projected an extremely broad look into at least half a dozen Latin American countries toward the end of isolating the conditions leading to internal revolt and deriving a set of conclusions indicating what could be done to contain or channel the effects of revolutionary disturbance. Historical as well as quantitative techniques were to be employed, and all sectors of society from schools to court systems and from paupers to presidents were to be analyzed. The directors of the undertaking sought advice from leading social scientists and attempted to recruit as stellar a force of scholars as would lend themselves to research so sponsored and focused.

The enthusiasm of the interested persons in the Defense Department and of the academicians involved is easy to understand, as are their administrative procedures. The military have become increasingly concerned with counter-insurgency and anti-guerrilla techniques because of the Southeast Asian situation, as well as because of the manner in which Castroism triumphed in Cuba. From counter-insurgency to the employment of soldiers in civic action programs is but a short step, for everyone knows that the sympathy of the peasant is a requirement of insurgents who seek to live off the land. A military force expecting to face many years of bush wars overseas has a legitimate interest in wanting to learn as much as it can about the conditions which spawn various types of revolution, the measures taken to combat "internal wars" in other countries, and in general the politics of modernization which are the backdrop for so much revolutionary disturbance. The question is not at all whether concerned military officers should know of these matters; it is instead how the knowledge should be accumulated and presented in the first place, and then what conclusions should be drawn and who should determine the action appropriate to these conclusions.

Likewise, the enthusiasm of the social scientists involved is easily understood. The opportunity existed for a massive, richly supported, highly detailed study into the conditions for social change in general as well as into the more specific subject of revolution. The study of modernization as well as of comparative societies has become of increasing academic concern in the past decade; indeed, there is probably more solid theorizing and competent field work going into these problem areas than into any others in the social sciences. In addition, the policy

[1] In colloquial Spanish, *camelo* means joke or jest; hence, Project Camelot is often spoken of as Project Camelo(t). *Camelo* is also close to *camello,* or "camel," a notoriously nasty beast.

implications of this work are clear and, for those intellectuals who "want to make a difference," the combination between heavily endowed academic research and immediate access to the instruments of powerful implementation can prove irresistible.

It should also be understood that Camelot represents no new departure, that the actors might well have felt no need to consult the academic community concerning the ethics of the matter because so much similar work has already been done and is still being done. A difference in scale is not necessarily a difference in type. In any event, to what formalized academic bodies could the Camelot directors have turned for an advisory opinion on the ethics of their undertaking? How many scholars who knew of this widely publicized project actually wrote to SORO questioning the wisdom and ethics of the matter? [2]

So Camelot began its short run. The person who made the first contact in Chile for Camelot was Dr. Hugo Nuttini,[3] an ex-Chilean, now an American citizen and an associate professor at the University of Pittsburgh, according to Chilean press reports. After making some initial contacts in December 1964, he returned to the United States, following up with letters and a second trip in April 1965. The report of the affair in *Ercilla,* a Chilean news magazine, contains details exactly as they were told to me by some of the major participants:

> He [Nuttini] spoke with Urzúa [a sociologist at the Catholic University who had studied with Nuttini at UCLA], explaining that [the study] would cover "a series of aspects of the Chilean social system," and that it would be backed by "several million dollars" granted by the National Science Foundation. He added, by way of bait, that among the directors of the project there figured distinguished North American social science personalities, citing names of such prestige as Kingsley Davis, Seymour Lipset, and Robert K. Merton. . . .

> In March he began the final offensive. He wrote exploratory letters to Raúl Urzúa and Alvaro Bunster, Secretary General of the University of Chile, dated the 22nd and 30th respectively, telling them of the matter in very similar terms.

> "The project in question," read the letter to Alvaro Bunster, "is a kind of pilot study in which will participate sociologists, anthropologists, economists, psychologists, geographers and other specialists in the social sciences, and which will be supported by various scientific and

[2] This question, though unanswerable fully by anyone outside American University, can be answered in tiny part here. The writer was requested to join in Project Camelot last year. He declined but raised no troubling questions.

[3] Ironically, in view of events, Dr. Nuttini was not a regular member of the Project Camelot staff. He was in Chile only for an informal survey into the suitability of the country as a case and was not authorized to make any commitments in the name of SORO.

governmental organizations in the United States. The researchers are all members of the most prestigious universities in this country, such as Pennsylvania, Yale, California, Columbia, Chicago, etc. . . ."

Not once—not during his later trip to Santiago, either—did he mention which were the "governmental institutions" supporting the project, nor did he again mention the names of the participating scientists.[4]

The April trip was the beginning of the end. Nuttini ran across a Norwegian sociologist, Dr. Johan Galtung, teaching at UNESCO's Latin American Faculty of Social Sciences, a two-year school attended by students from throughout Latin America. Galtung, deeply dedicated to his task and profoundly loyal to his students, had been invited to attend a Camelot planning session during the month of August in the Washington area. He was thus fully informed concerning the nature of the project, which was never handled with any duplicity at all in the United States. Nuttini, confronted by Galtung with documentary evidence (the completely open and frank letter of invitation to the conference), persisted in proclaiming his ignorance of the Department of the Army connection. In *Ercilla's* words, the same as those told me by Galtung, the end of Nuttini was as follows:

> The upshot of the story was the unmasking in both universities of the agent, and his simultaneous protestations of innocence, alleging that he "had been fooled," that he would "immediately abandon the project," that he would call Washington to settle accounts. The indignation of the Chilean scientists was rooted in a double reason: one of them patriotic, that of being used as tools in an espionage plan; and another professional, the betrayal to which their own North American colleagues wished to induce them.

Until this moment the affair had not gone far beyond university circles. But then came the American intervention in the Dominican Republic. This action was widely interpreted in Latin America as signaling the political end of the Alliance for Progress and a regression to support of right-wing military governments throughout Latin America as the best insurance against Castroism. This conclusion was reached not only by civilians but also by many military groups, which began immediate agitation of both an internal and external nature, leading to the mobilization of at least two armies in South America. Project Camelot then snapped into another focus; it became intimately laced in public opinion with interventionism and militarism, with the image of the United States as a power dedicated to the throttling of any revo-

[4] *Ercilla*, July 7, 1965, p. 20.

lutionary movement of whatever center-to-left stripe. The oft-repeated statements by very high American officials that Communists tend naturally to rise to the top in any conditions of social turmoil led to immediate charges that American foreign policy was, in effect, *macartista* or McCarthyite in refusing any longer to differentiate among progressive parties. Wrapped into already grave suspicions of anti-guerrilla programs, it was only natural that Camelot should be seen as part of a carefully planned policy instead of merely a project whose research design was still far from being complete.

Another circumstance not only increased the confusion but also deepened Chilean suspicions of the nature of the enterprise. Before the outburst the American Embassy knew nothing of Project Camelot or the coming of Nuttini. In addition, it became obvious with the passage of time that the State Department was most unhappy with the entire undertaking. It was the diplomatic protest of the Chilean government against Project Camelot that precipitated the revelation of these discrepancies among official American agencies. In answering the official protest of the government of President Eduardo Frei, the Embassy was forced to make clear its lack of prior knowledge and its embarrassment at the entire situation. This event served further to convince many Chileans that the United States' Latin American policy was really being made in "The Pentagon." The impression was not lightened when the Chilean Minister of the Interior goodheartedly but innocently absolved the American "government" from blame, making the standard Latin American discrimination between the armed forces and the civil authorities.

The Chilean government subsequently established a committee of the Ministry of the Interior to investigate the case, and the Congress launched its own investigation with a special *ad hoc* committee. *El Siglo*, the Communist daily, of course played the matter for all it was worth, running a long series featuring photostatic copies of Camelot's long and involved research plan. The terminology was allowed to slip, also: "Project Camelot" became "Plan Camelot," the word espionage was accepted by most political shades as appropriate to the incident (as *Ercilla's* ready acceptance indicates), and even such conservative papers as *El Mercurio* employed these words in description of the matter.

SOME IMMEDIATE IMPLICATIONS

Whether social-science research with large groups will soon again be freely possible in Chile and many other countries is not known. Even if survey work is officially permitted, and even if respondents agree to answer, it cannot be known whether the answers will be a reasonably valid statement of attitude. A friend from the Catholic University, writing to advise me to halt my own field work, said:

> With all this, our research at the School is halting all field interviewing until the "water passes." Not only for the problems which may arise, but very importantly because we feel that the validity of the studies is in peril due to the great "sensibilización" [sensitizing] that is taking place. To give just one example: one of our colleagues worked very hard and came forth with a very good research design for a study paid by the Chilean government, for the chilean government and intended to benefit all chileans. The field work is scheduled for next week, but even in this case it is problematic that it will take place.

After indicating some of the incognita in the situation, he concluded with the sober note, "One thing is already done: research in sociology has been hurt and what's more, this affair has severely damaged the future of chilean-american co-operation in scientific and other endeavors."

Certain easy excuses will undoubtedly be used to back away from the full implications of the incident, which in my opinion are more profound than friendly Chileans, hurt as they were, would themselves be willing to admit. One of these bromidic explanations I have already indicated: putting the blame on the emotionality or ideological bents of the Chileans. Another, even nastier and more demeaning, is of the type to be whispered about. It is that American University is really a low-grade institution, that the scientists employed in Camelot were just second-raters and not representative of the most honest of American intellectuals, and that even the Army itself has long played second fiddle to the Navy and Air Force with their long histories of support of academic research. This explanation is already being advanced by Chileans friendly to American social science. Alvaro Bunster, the University of Chile's secretary general mentioned in the *Ercilla* article, is quoted in the same source as saying, ". . . the entity charged with co-ordinating its [Camelot's] execution was the American University in Washington, with which I became acquainted during my visit to the United States in 1959, which enjoys no academic prestige either in the United States or abroad, and which is located in the same city as the national government. . . ."

It is true that American University is not Harvard; it is also true that Dr. Rex Hopper, academic director of Project Camelot, is not Max Weber; and it is also true that the Department of the Army does not have its prestige counterpart of the Navy's Office of Naval Research or the Air Force's Rand Corporation. But it is not true that other universities and other scholars have not crossed into the same shadowy area of ethics entered into by Camelot, that other universities and other scholars have not committed grave tactical errors in Latin America, or that other militarily sponsored social research has not been carried out in Latin America.

The academic problems sharpened, but not invented, by Project Camelot can be expressed in three relationships: the first, between social science and the government; the second, between professional competence and integrity; and the third, between Latin American studies as such and the general performance of the American academic community.

The least difficult to discuss is the nature of the proper ties between the political and academic worlds. The trail has already been blazed by the physical scientists, and formalized procedures and institutions exist in all fields clearly defining the relationship of the scientist to his task, to the public, and to his profession. Legitimate differences of opinion exist, of course, concerning whether a scientist working on The Bomb has a special citizenship duty, for example. But the public identification of interest is plain, and the set relationships to the policy process into which any physical scientist may wish to place himself are also evident.

No such clarity exists in the social sciences. We have no National Science Foundation discharging a brokerage function between the two worlds. We have had no such consistent public debates on academic objectivity and public commitment as have, say, the atomic physicists. No broadly accepted statement of ethics has come from our professional associations, and very few university administrations have concerned themselves with the problem.[5] The result has been that social scientists have generally crossed and recrossed the lines separating their functions from governmental policy making, the only inhibitions being their personally held standards of conduct.

No problem of integrity exists for two polar groups of social scientists: those who work inside government on a long-term basis, and those who because of their disciplines, research interests, or convictions stay entirely inside the university world. (A third group, the commercial contract scholar, sells his services where he wishes. His product is sometimes of very high quality. In any event, he does not concern us here because he has neither the pretensions nor the security of the academic scholar.) It is the social scientist working both fields who is in danger of betraying both of his masters through the loss of his powers of independent analysis. And he adds to his other academic difficulties a partial silence imposed by his access to classified materials, so that paradoxically he is often able to muster fewer data for his students than his uncompromised colleagues.

[5] There are a few exceptions, of course, among them Harvard University. The AUFS has always been highly sensitive to the problem and throughout its existence has exercised extreme caution to remain entirely private and unencumbered.

A serious question exists whether social scientists under certain kinds of government contract should continue to have the protection of academic tenure. As is well known, the purpose of tenure provisions is to assure academic freedom. But sometimes the exercise of such freedom is in conflict with necessary security provisions. More subtly, how does a scholar under contract know that he is adopting one hypothesis instead of another for truly scientific reasons, rather than because of a particular applied interest or even political prejudice? How can the persons reading the published work of this scholar know that he may have a personal, nonacademic involvement in the research? Recently many academicians have been pronouncing themselves on the international politics of Southeast Asia. A letter to the editor of a major newspaper signed by a series of university professors may lead the unwary reader to think that a neutral, objective, academic opinion is being expressed. The wary reader, and the uncommonly informed one, will note that many of these letters are signed by persons who have been deeply involved in making the very policies they pretend to defend as objective scholars. Do these scholars think themselves beyond the lures of money, prestige, and personal political passion? If so, do they seriously expect the public at large to accept this self-estimation unquestioningly?

By no means am I suggesting that social scientists should turn their backs on policy questions, that governments should refrain from employing social scientists or using social-science materials. What I am suggesting is that the peculiar attribute and unique scientific virtue of the university-affiliated social scientist is his freedom. Once abridged, for whatever reason, then the people relying on his objectivity are in serious danger of accepting a misrepresented product, as many government agencies have learned.

I am fully aware that individual personality factors may prevent a professor from benefiting from the security given him by tenure. I suggest, however, that institutionalized temptation to the voluntary relinquishment of freedom be avoided, in the expectation that personal idiosyncracy will be canceled out of the final product by the numbers of persons engaged in the social sciences, as well as by the free exchanges in our increasingly numerous journals.

Let me add, too, that I do not believe that our present state of ethical disarray has created a Frankenstein's monster rapidly conducing us to the socially engineered society. It is this possibility which has frightened some Chileans inordinately. *Ercilla* concludes the article from which I have been citing as follows:

> In spite of the scant publicity which the "affaire" has received, in Latin America various conjectures are being spun about the discovery. It is being seen that many at times incomprehensible speeches made

by President Johnson himself as well as by other American officials have a firm theoretical basis, translated into a well defined international policy which, with the passage of time, will be made concrete in very real measures tending to reinforce "tranquillity"—that is to say, North American superiority—in the underdeveloped countries of the world.

In this way the North American and Brazilian pronouncement that now there are no national wars, only international ones, can eventuate in the death of the concept of sovereignty. The social sciences put at the service of intervention in the internal affairs of a country would do the rest.

The writer of the article need not be so pessimistic/optimistic about the social sciences. American economists do not know how to halt inflation in Latin American countries. American political scientists do not know how to help Latin American governments collect taxes. American anthropologists do not know what to do about the swamping of Indian cultures by national communities. Few American psychologists know that Latin America exists outside the pages of the *Times* or the *Monitor*. American sociologists have no theory of social change adequate to explain Latin American cases. Social scientists working in the government cannot protect the image of the United States in Latin America and even the election pollsters have been surpassed by some of their Latin American colleagues.

Latin Americans can relax on the issue of the magical effectiveness of the social sciences. But when they say they can no longer accept individual American social scientists at face value, they are correct. The solution for Latin America, however, is not to close the doors to all foreign-conducted or -sponsored research and teaching. It is rather to insist upon clean credentials and academic competence—just as should we.

SCHOLARLY COMPETENCE AND INTEGRITY

The statements I have made about what social science cannot do anywhere, let alone in Latin America, are not to be taken to mean that I think we are in a hopelessly low estate. To the contrary, we are increasingly masters of our disciplines; our grossest failures stem from our being willing to try what we are not peculiarly competent to do. The economists cannot effectively stop inflation in Latin America because some of the measures necessary to the task are political. Public administration men cannot make income tax collection easy because certain legitimacy and consensus patterns are necessary before the payment of such imposts becomes in large part a voluntary, individual act. The protection of certain segments of Indian culture before the tidal wave of national society is much more a function of ideological choice and public will than of anthropological writings about acculturation. To expect such macrosocial problems to submit themselves to mere social scientific manipulation, or to think that the policy advice of social scientists is magically efficacious, is a denial of the statesman's art and a burdening of the social scientist with what he is incompetent to handle.

Under the very best of conditions, the social scientist with his special skills can do the following for governments:

a. He can generate and make available new data.
b. He can order these data to permit informed guessing about the nature of the lacunae.
c. He can indicate relevant theoretical patterns for the interpretation of the data.
d. He can—explaining himself carefully—indicate the probabilities of effectiveness of various selected courses of action.
e. He can indicate which choices are foreclosed by the adoption of given courses of action.
f. He can indicate which new choices will be made available by the adoption of given courses of action.

Needless to say, very few, if any, scholarly documents submitted to any government have satisfied these difficult requirements. The temptation to take the easy path straight from description to prescription is great. But to go past these limits is to assume a vested interest in the ensuing policy itself, thereby rendering the scholar suspect in further objective analysis. Of course, I also continue to insist he is not peculiarly competent to make such value judgments. There is, however, always one overriding value decision the social scientist must make; that is, whether he will lend his talents to any government seeking them. I should suggest that if the government asking assistance is likely to use its powers to restrict that very freedom of inquiry essential to the academic task, then the social scientist is committing professional suicide, not to speak of what else he may be helping to do to existing or possible democratic institutions.

The point I am seeking to underline is that the social scientist should be given deference only when he is working in the peculiar area of his competence. To the extent to which he is incompetent but pretends to competence, he fails of professional integrity. Most unhappily, incompetence has manifested itself not only when academicians get out of their fields but even within them. Recent academic research and teaching by Americans in Latin America is heavily studded by examples of persons simply unequipped to do that to which they pretend. The Camelot fiasco, for example, could at least have been mitigated—if not totally avoided—if greater skill had been used in organization and administration. Professor Nuttini's conduct in Chile is a lesson in how not to do such things; the inattention in Washington to timing and to other people's views is a product of faulty technique as well as insensitivity, and the carelessness in the wording of documents and their distribution reveals methodological innocence as well as lack of regard for one's research subjects. Once again, however, the Camelot directors are not alone.

On my recent visit to Chile I was asked if I, too, was "an exporter of data," a kind of academic copper company engaged in mining attitudes and carrying away the profits, never to be seen again in the country. Puzzled, I asked the why of the question. It seems that a very prestigious American professor, a faculty member of one of this country's most prestigious universities, had recently finished a study with the assistance of a local UNESCO agency. Asked to leave his code books and IBM cards, he refused, clearly wanting to publish before letting anyone else in on his act. My guess is that in the future he will certainly send the materials. But the reaction in Chile among local scholars as well as international civil servants was that this person had violated the essential conditions of his agreement as well as the canons of academic openness. This kind of misunderstanding is needless and of course disturbs the work of everyone else. Unhappily, this particular professor had had no previous Latin American experience, and although he valiantly learned the language quite well, he still did not succeed in leaving the field clean after his departure so that his American colleagues would not be forced into easily avoided difficulties.

A full awareness of the terms of the responsibilities one accepts in a foreign area can also be included as part of the baggage of the competent scholar. Another internationally famous scholar, one of those allegedly named by Nuttini as an adviser to Camelot, dispatched a letter of denial to the Communist newspaper which had named him as a participant. In strict fact the letter was, of course, entirely honest. The trouble is that this person is working in Latin America supported by funds from other government agencies. Because there is no secret about the matter, interested professionals throughout the area are fully aware of these financial ties. If his letter of denial was to be honest in broad as well as strict fact, should it not have mentioned this connection and sought to inform Latin Americans as to the difference between, say, AID money and Department of Defense money for the social sciences? If social scientific research is to have a cumulative history in Latin America, instead of being the casual and accidental fruit of scholars of widely varying skills tapping funds which gush and dry up with the political seasons, then we had better start worrying immediately about the fate of our colleagues of the moment and of the future.

The first step toward rebuilding the consciously extended confidence of Latin American scholars and governments is to be willing to reveal the sources of our funds, the premises of our studies, the nature of our data, and the bases of our conclusions. We should also make every effort to go beyond making data and findings available; we must help to make effective the ability of trained Latin Americans to use those materials, for clearly simple revelation is not enough. The skill to understand is also required.

The incrusted mistakes of a decade of amateurism are behind the disgust directed at Camelot. That ten-year period is the one of mounting United States interest in Latin American affairs, of an increasing flow of Fulbright scholars as well as otherwise highly trained and mature specialists, many of whom have not bothered to learn the specific conditions pertaining to Latin America. Some have never learned the requisite languages; hardly any one has studied the cultures in depth. How they expect to teach well or to analyze their data with subtlety, let alone design appropriate research instruments in the first instance, I cannot say. But now the entire world knows that their technical shortcomings have an effect beyond their articles and books: they prevent other articles and books from being written, they bring disrepute on American academic life in general, and they mislead policy makers thirsty for reliable information and imaginative analysis.

The most pathetic result, however, is political. Many independent but sympathetic Latin Americans who have been distinguishing between United States policy and other sectors of American life are now becoming convinced that they were wrong. In effect, they understand American scholars as refusing to accept the responsibilities of a plural, democratic society.

COMPETENCE, THE ACADEMIC WORLD, AND INTEGRITY

The academic slippage which has become so apparent in our Latin American activities is one of the possible (though not necessary) costs of a free and largely self-regulating academic community. As I have said before, truly professional research is the return legitimately to be expected by the society at large for respecting academic freedom. The full assumption of professional responsibility also involves projection and prediction in order to create a stock of ideas for future choice as well as to provide a test of present ideas. Institutionalized anticipation is the fruit of the relatively sanctionless risk-taking made possible by real academic freedom. Our present frenetic concern with "catching up" in Latin America is an unmistakable indication that American higher education, seen as a total institution, has not paid for its freedom by anticipating need in this respect, at least. The lack of ethical definition can also be taken as a failure to build into our several social-science disciplines those standards which, carried by individuals, would have obviated the mistakes now a national concern in Latin America.

My point now transcends the individuals of whom I have been so far speaking and poses the question of whether there has been a lack of integrity at the institutional level, the product of the failure to assume a patent obligation. For long it has been the conventional wisdom—repeated *ad nauseum* without ever an attempt at careful empirical demonstration—that the quality of Latin American studies is the lowest of all area scholarship. This judgment is clearly false for anthropology, history, and language and literature. How true is it for political science, one of the most maligned of the disciplines?

Merle Kling, in a devastating analysis of the shortcomings of American political scientists specializing in Latin America, writes:

> Little capital (funds, talent, or organizational experience) has been invested in political studies of Latin America, and as a result the returns have been relatively meager. Personnel with adequate training and appropriate technical competence have been in scarce supply, research techniques adapted to Latin American studies have been of a relatively primitive nature, and the level of productivity has been low. Political scientists conducting research on Latin America, like some landowners, have been reluctant to introduce advanced tools and machinery and to extend the intellectual acreage under cultivation—that is, to acquire new skills, to accept technical assistance, to encourage methods designed to diversify the crop of research findings, and to consider a redistribution of disciplinary properties. Political scientists specializing in Latin America have not reached, to borrow Rostow's familiar metaphor, the take-off stage. . . .[6]

Let us accept this evaluation just for the sake of argument. Is the prestige of this field so low because the practitioners are so poor? Or are the practitioners so poor because the prestige is so low? These factors certainly interact to ratify the continued existence of an unhappy situation. I am afraid that no beginning of an explanation of this phenomenon is possible without turning to the disagreeable question of academic stratification—the professorial class system, if you will. Here is a list of the universities having the eleven top prestige departments of political science, in order, chosen by a recent nationwide poll of political scientists.[7] I will add statements concerning their politics and government professors who also are engaged in Latin American studies:

[6] "The State of Research on Latin America," in Charles Wagley, ed., *Social Science Research on Latin America*, New York: Columbia University Press, 1964, p. 168.
[7] Albert Somit and Joseph Tanenhaus, "Trends in American Political Science:

Harvard	None.
Yale	A junior professor.
California (Berk.)	Junior professors in a state of turnover.
Chicago	No regular professor.
Princeton	None.
Columbia	Nontenure associate professor.
Michigan	Nontenure junior professor; a long history of course offerings.
Wisconsin	Tenured associate professor.
Stanford	Nontenure junior professor.
California (UCLA)	Searching, using *ad hoc* professors.
Cornell	None. Searching.

In sum, there is only one senior professor of Latin American politics in any one of the major departments, and his tenure dates from 1965. If this list were to be published as of ten years ago, we would find only two or three of these institutions even as far along the road as they are now. A little over half of all American doctorates in political science are produced by these departments; but, "Taking the latest (1962–63) faculty rosters, we find that perhaps four per cent of the political scientists teaching at the leading eleven schools come from non-prestige institutions—and that these exceptions are found largely in the lower half of the group." [8] Aside from the basic academic question of whether Latin America offers any intrinsically important data for political science, ambitious students have not studied Latin American politics in the past because, among other possible reasons, it was simply impossible to do so in most of the academically politic institutions. Worse, top job opportunities were nonexistent. Thus the best Latin American offerings are generally in universities such as Texas and North Carolina which do not attract the best graduate students—or at least those destined for the prestige departments.

Kling, in the article to which I have already referred, states that few Latin American examples are used in comparative government texts. He is correct. But is his implication that it is the fault of the Latin Americanist correct? The evidence is that scholars outside of the area have not bothered to read what literature is available. Their absolute certainty that they are dealing with an intellectual desert is another element in the massive self-fulfilling prophecy of which we have been speaking. Let us take some examples. Because I shall have to cite, thus

Some Analytical Notes," *The American Political Science Review*, Vol. LVII, No. 4, December, 1963, p. 936.
  [8] *Ibid.*, p. 937.

revealing names, I will quote only two persons, both of whom have reputations so secure that nothing I might say could damage them.

Bibliographies and bibliographical articles would seem an apt place to look for an answer to the question of whether anybody is reading. Hans J. Morgenthau, in an article, "International Relations, 1960–1964," [9] assesses the current state of his field. Of 135 footnotes, 48 refer to specific countries or regions; two of this number are books on Latin America. "The literature on foreign policy," writes Professor Morgenthau in this section, "especially that of the United States, is, of course, particularly abundant and unequal in quality. Here are some books which are likely to have a more than ephemeral importance." His Latin American listings are Adolf A. Berle, *Latin America: Diplomacy and Reality,* New York: Harper & Row, 1962; and Salvador de Madariaga, *Latin America Between the Eagle and the Bear,* New York: Frederick A. Praeger, 1962. These choices are incredible, as I am sure the two authors would agree. The Berle book is a short and glittering statement of his personal appreciations of Latin America, suggestive of policy premises and applications. The Madariaga book does no credit to its author's distinguished life; it is an often inaccurate survey of Latin America, informed by a Hispanophile racism of no analytical value and in questionable taste. At least half a dozen journalistic surveys are much more reliable, better informed, and even better written.

If Dr. Morgenthau wanted to cite just two or three books on inter-American policy, he might have mentioned such works as Bryce Wood, *The Making of the Good Neighbor Policy,* New York: Columbia University Press, 1961; J. Lloyd Mecham, *The United States and Inter-American Security: 1889–1960,* Austin: University of Texas Press, 1961; or perhaps even a historical work with contemporary relevance like Dana G. Munro, *Intervention and Dollar Diplomacy in the Caribbean, 1900–1921,* Princeton: Princeton University Press, 1964. Certainly anyone taking Dr. Morgenthau's suggestions about Latin American readings would find his every prejudice about the field confirmed if he thought those two the best available.

Dr. Morgenthau is not alone in his disregard. For many years journals have listed Latin American materials out of alphabetical order, invariably at the end. Until the January 1964 issue of *Foreign Affairs,* for example, "Latin America and the Caribbean" was the last bibliographical entry. Since that issue, Latin America has moved into a section entitled "The Western Hemisphere," immediately following "The United States." Poor Africa has been relegated to the caboose. Alphabetical order may mean little. But when the Ford Foundation

[9] *The Annals of the American Academy of Political and Social Science,* July, 1965, pp. 163–71.

gets to Latin America only after Asia, the Middle East, and Africa, we have the operationalization of the *Foreign Affairs* bibliography.

Even when Latin America gets out of the book citation stage and into the analytical reference level, the specialist may feel it had been better neglected. Consider the following rather subtle reference by sociologist Edward Shils: "In Latin America, the armed forces histori- cally have played a role similar to that of the military in many of the new states of Asia and Africa." [10] It may take a moment to recognize that that sentence is backwards and should read, "In many of the new states of Asia and Africa, the armed forces are playing a role histori- cally similar to that of the military in Latin America." After all, the Latin Americans have been at it since 1810 and the military of the "new states" only during the past twenty years. It is more than passing strange to attempt to draw a base line from twenty years of historical experience when a variegated set of experiences in twenty republics exists for periods of up to 155 years.

There is no need to belabor this point with multiple examples. I sug- gest merely that it is time for rigorous and realistic thinking about Latin American studies, instead of the unprofessional surrender to stereotypes and status which has helped to hinder the growth of re- search as well as the reading and evaluation of what already exists.

The present state of emergency is a direct product of the insufficien- cies of our major universities and scholars, just as it is of the persons in the field, as well as all the other factors I have mentioned. This back- ground to the situation should not be neglected, lest we expend our ex- piatory energies in beating only on the scapegoat in Washington.

SOME PERSPECTIVE

To put an analysis into perspective is all too often to dilute it with the tepid water of sweet reasonableness. If the chances are that the punishment for our academic sins will not be overly harsh, the reasons are implicit in the general conditions and not in the promise of any dramatic change toward virtuous behavior. It is very probable that, after the passage of a little time, American social scientists will once again be able to work with relative ease in Latin America. Greater care will be taken to maintain respectable appearances on our side; Latin American social scientists and government officials will be more cau- tious in extending us their assistance, and that small part of the public which is informed will maintain a reserve affecting the nature of their participation in ways nobody will ever measure. Camelot has dis-

[10] "The Military in the Political Development of the New States," in John J. Johnson, ed., *The Role of the Military in Underdeveloped Countries*, Princeton: Princeton University Press, 1962, p. 8.

solved; a few other projects sponsored by agencies of the armed forces will be cancelled or camouflaged, and greater care will be exercised to inform American ambassadors in Latin American countries of academic activities in their bailiwicks.

Matters will follow this slow course because in neither Latin America nor the United States can radical change occur. The Latin Americans may extend their gaze to include a sharper perception of Europe, but they cannot blind themselves to the United States. The reasons are not by any means only political or economic. The enormous cultural weight of the United States in Latin America is a fact as obvious as the Andes. More pointedly, the contemporary revolution in the social sciences is a North American product, and whether Latin Americans go to Great Britain, France, Germany, or Italy, they will still return with one or another version of modern American social-scientific empiricism. They can also put to good use foundation assistance and interchanges with American educational institutions. It is not that they could not get along somehow without us, but rather that most Latin American intellectuals—including highly nationalistic ones—would prefer not to be forced to so long as their continued collaboration with American scientific institutions does not imply a narrow political subservience. What Camelot surely has done is to speed the Latin American desire to diversify academic contacts. As there is already Soviet university work stirring in such countries as Chile and El Salvador, we may expect more elsewhere in the normal course of events. It is for the French and British, however, that major room will have to be made, a tendency being promoted for the past several years by the Department of State and American foundations as well as by some Latin American universities.

American reactions inside the universities will be even slower and more difficult to recognize. The reason is that professors and professorships cannot be made overnight, that good research takes time to produce, and that the decentralized nature of American higher education creates subtle eddies among the stimuli of communications, the sorting of responses, and the flexing of implementation. We may expect a bit more care in the foundations and some discussion, as I have said, but we shall still have to wait for the maturing of the current vastly expanded crop of scholars in training. We shall also have to wait for the social-science "community" to attend seriously to the idea that there are ethical questions involved in policy studies, that ethics and technique are not to be separated under certain conditions, and that institutional snobbery is as testable for its validity as are election predictions.

For a while it was thought—and is still thought by some—that "retooling" was the answer to the problem of Latin American studies. All we had to do was take an expert from another field, let him turn the Cyclopean eye of his genius on Latin America, and the deficiencies of the field would rapidly be dissipated. The grotesque mistakes already made by some of these persons shows that, even in Latin American studies, the price of admission has to be paid. A highly trained specialist in Indian politics will find his Hindi—if he has any—of rather little use in Quito. And unless he is more theoretically gifted than most persons writing in the field of development, he will also find that his hypotheses may have little relevance to the only major underdeveloped part of the Western cultural world. It really will not do to have an internationally famous American scholar declare at an international meeting that it is a shame that there is so much more documentary material available on Africa than on Latin America. It really will not do to have as the only political scientist sitting on a major committee dispensing fellowships for Latin American studies an excellent scholar in another area who has never done research in Latin America, cannot speak either Spanish or Portuguese, and has so far made only academic touristic trips to the region. To be a violin virtuoso is not to be a concert pianist.

The reasons for a past lack of interest in Latin American politics are now fairly clear: the countries have little power; they pose—or until recently posed—no Cold War threat; they are Catholic countries traditionally looked down on by Protestant ones; they have little prestige among the ivied universities who have followed the area leads of Oxbridge, the Sorbonne, and Berlin first into Africa, Egypt, the Middle East, and China, and then the Realpolitik leads of international affairs into Soviet studies. I should like to suggest a reason now, not for the lack of interest, but for the lack of success in most of what political research has been done. It is that Latin America is a very difficult area to fit into extant theory. The range of cases is immense: twenty different republics with increasingly different histories are also characterized by vastly varied internal conditions. We must study migratory Indians and megalopolis, village economies and machine-tool industries, constitutional democracies and populist falangisms and mercantilistic dictatorships as well as village gerontocracies and institutionalized lawlessness. Latin America is the graveyard of simplistic and deterministic theories, of those schemes which hold that a nation which has "taken off" will automatically reach self-sustaining flight. It will not submit to simple notions derived without an adequate knowledge of the area's amazing store of data.

Let all who can revel in this potential richness. El Dorado can become real for the talented and dedicated social scientist. The mine will contain only fool's gold for the lazy and the self-seeking. But, as usual, the fool's gold will drive out the good metal if we are thoughtless enough to allow it currency in the market place.

PART FOUR

THE DIMENSIONS
OF INDIVIDUAL
ACCOMMODATION

The turbulence of social life in developing countries is not an unrelieved drain on the emotional resources of the people who live in those lands. After all, even in Latin America revolutions are not the order of the day, and the style of ordinary life—personal and civil alike—is important to a realization of the full meaning of the rapid change through which those countries are passing.

The essays in this section all deal with the tenuous contacts between government and the individual at the farthermost reaches of organized power, where personal choice and diluted institutional power meet. This twilight area is an excellent measure of the real freedom of the individual; it is the easiest place truly to understand the difference between a mere authoritarianism and a totalitarianism. The substantive meaning of liberty cannot be sought merely in bills of rights and in judicial procedures. The search must extend itself to all those human relationships involving the ability of the individual to make meaningful choices not only as to whether he will vote right or left but also concerning his education, his food, and whether he is free to take a walk in the park after midnight and buy a postage stamp without being barked at by the clerk.

10

ON STRAINING THE NATURE

OF LIBERTY

Buenos Aires' river front is a selvage edge of miles of docks and parkways. Anyone can wander freely among the cranes and piles of lumber and wet cordage of the river port down in the Boca, the flavorsome Italian quarter, Bohemia, site of good restaurants, tango writers, and hard-working Anarchists. Or he can ramble among the ocean-going vessels, docked where the central city streets touch the river front. And then, does the ambition exist, he can work his way to the shoreside parks of the elegant northern part of town to fish, or promenade, or set up a tent and drink beer. None will say him nay, although an occasional bored guard may glance at him as he leaves the international zones. He can stand still, and hot coffee, ice cream, and pop will come to him. Should he walk or take a bus to the appropriate trailer stands, he can get steaks, grilled udder, or whatever other intimate parts of a cow he may fancy

One day, at the foot of a fishing pier, a coffee vendor stopped to chat. We had talked of many things before he asked, "Tell me, in the United States, can a person walk around the streets as freely as we do here?" At the time I could not understand quite what the question was getting at. Several friends with whom I discussed the matter said they thought the vendor was simply being foolish. But the matter bothered me. The moment the question was put, an errant memory slipped through me which since has been difficult to down. On the day Japan capitulated, I was dining in a Washington, D.C., restaurant when a glass of beer arrived unasked. It had been sent by another G.I., unknown, also in uniform, as a kind of tacit expression of fraternal greetings of celebration. I reciprocated, saving a little in my glass for a toast. When his beer arrived, I stood up with my glass in hand to walk to his table to exchange a word. Like an eagle (and not the kind on a quarter, I hope), the waitress swooped, took the glass from my hand, shoved me physically back in my chair, and departed without a word. I was so astounded there was nothing to do but let the thing happen. Then I learned that it seems it was (and maybe still is) illegal to walk from one table to another in the nation's capital with a glass of beer in hand.

This occurrence, and all in its family, are simply unthinkable in Argentina.

I am not concerned here with big conceptions like *Liberté, Egalité, Fraternité,* nor yet mid-ocean declarations about Fear. Nor am I discussing knights-errant from Wisconsin as opposed to beribboned saviors of democracy from Venezuela or Colombia. The matter under discussion is an intimate one of freedom from restraint in the daily details of living which has to do with custom and not with jurisprudence. Whatever the law may say about the matter, the coffee vendor was implicitly right: the Argentine has in abundant measure the Sixth Freedom, the Freedom to Walk the Streets.

I wonder whether part of the charm of some Latin American capitals for the person of Anglo-Saxon culture is not precisely this Freedom of the Streets, tasted like a heady elixir, without name or recognition, but subtly there and violently stimulating. Argentine streets are made to be lived in. They are an extension of the home. They amplify the city, giving room for ambling, the satisfaction of aesthetic pleasures, courting, eating, conversing, and sometimes even sleeping. They are for walking off rages, for walking into compromises, for making politics and unmaking governments. What an American will do in the Elks, the Rotary Club, or the corner saloon the Argentine will do on the streets, the scenes of his public private life.

The social concept of vagrancy simply does not exist. In Buenos Aires no one cares what or how or where anyone does anything on the public ways at any hour—short of the commission of murder and mayhem, of course.

There is even a strange sort of extra freedom—license?—about driving a car here. Greater Buenos Aires is a city of six million. But five short years ago it had only three traffic lights and not one stop sign. Again I am not interested in explanations or rationalizations or in opposing the traffic system of a city like Chicago to that of Buenos Aires. It is just that the Argentines have an informal instead of formal set of rules which works pretty well and which implies an elasticity making for a sense of liberty. Of course the accident rate is higher than it "should" be. Until ten o'clock at night the street lights are dim and most store windows blacked out because of a shortage of electricity. Despite the lack of lights and the innumerable holes and other hazards in the streets, the *porteño* drives only with his parking lights. You would have to be an owl to see as much as you should for minimum safety. But recently an attempt was made to switch to head lamps, and a storm of protest went up about it. They like it this way, and if they're willing to pay for it in shattered cars, more wrecks than necessary, and fabulous insurance rates, well, I suppose it's theirs to decide. And so long as one escapes the wreck, the rate of "freedom income" is high.

In the past I have often spoken of this kind of liberty as "negative freedom." Some of the ways Argentines manifest it are by stopping a car in the middle of the street to gossip with a friend, or vociferously arguing politics when it is public knowledge that "it" is all settled anyway, or flouting a policeman to his face, or making a sport of evading all government regulations and taxes possible. I called these things "negative freedom" in the sense that they happen because government is not strong enough to stop the practices and because they are nothing which has ever been fought for in political contest. I'm no longer so sure that "negative" is precisely the correct adjective. I don't recommend these things to my own country, in lieu, at least, of mass psychoanalysis before the corset strings are cut, but let us not deny that these attributes can have their attractive side, if exasperating to the tax collector and the otherwise meticulous.

In two ways the Argentine is worse off in the street than the American: in what he carries on his back and in his pockets. In his dress he can be stiflingly formal. Jackets and neckties are worn even for many intimate gatherings despite the sticky steam of a Buenos Aires summer. And what he carries in his pockets are his identification papers, his ever necessary *documentos*.

And here we have a neat point of intercultural emotional comparison. I become indignant at the thought of being forced to carry a special little booklet issued by the police with photo and fingerprints and all the rest of it just to show that I am who I say I am. After all, what's a driver's license or a social-security card for? But why not the same reaction to a policeman who objects to one's "loitering" on a street corner talking with friends? What kind of a concept is this "street-corner bum" thing? To an Argentine, it is incomprehensible that one should *not* carry his *carnet* and equally incomprehensible that a policeman would stop him from chatting with his friends, whether they were plotting a bank job or not.

Maybe it is that an American worries about his rights in a strictly individual sense, while the Argentine preoccupies himself with his to a greater extent in terms of dignity and thus in a more public manner. Since there is a question of human dignity quite possibly at play here, then, there may be strong elements of positiveness in this kind of freedom. And in Buenos Aires it is affirmative for a second reason: because the city street has been made deserving of attention, inviting, warm, interesting, and varied to please all tastes and literally tickle all palates. The city is generously dotted with parks and plazas for the nature lovers. Tree-lined streets abound. Sidewalk cafés are omnipresent. They all offer chairs and friendly service and the passing crowd and traffic noises. The store windows are carefully and artistically dressed, more often than not leading to disappointment should one pass through the door. The city children have corrected the ways of their city fathers and pushed broad streets in all directions, making sure that the sidewalk is wide to accommodate the cafés and the constant crowds of window shoppers. And where it has not been possible to broaden the streets, as in the heart of the downtown area, two have simply been roped off to car traffic to form a gigantic "X" for the walker. It is as though Philadelphia decided to close off Chestnut Street between Sixth and Eighteenth, and Thirteenth Street between Market and South. And as though both the muggers and the police declared Fairmount Park a neutral area, leaving it to all the rest to enjoy in peace and anonymity in the protection of mutual self-respect. And as though every fifth street leading out of the downtown area were broadened into a boulevard, and Philadelphians slowed down at the end of day to look at the ugly urban creation around them, to savor it and play with it and use it to give the *Lebensraum* which even a huge city like Buenos Aires can afford if it is wanted enough by sufficient people.

11

ON THE COMPARATIVE MERITS OF
CORN-FEEDING AND MEAT-FEEDING

The mark of the skilled traveler is that, away from the Hilton Hotels and the American Grilles, he can manage to feed himself and still not commit a concomitant suicide. In Guatemala, for example, the basic dish that the hungry can consume anywhere is black beans scooped up with corn tortillas. The omnipresent hygienic menu in Argentina is a huge charcoal-broiled steak with salad and French bread and a glass of wine.

The relationship between what a man eats and the way he behaves is a favorite topic of folk sayings, but the aphorisms do not indicate the true depth of the Argentine-Guatemala cultural dichotomy. The former are literally "red-blooded meat eaters," while the latter are just as literally "full of beans." Unhappily, scientific observation denies these judgments a figurative extension.

Guatemalans have been known to choose pitch-black nights on which to have gang machete fights out in the public square. The thought of inimical naked steel whistling in the inky, thin mountain air is just as shuddersome to the gallant Argentine as to a New Jersey chicken farmer, say. Now take the opposed case of a bank employees' work stoppage in Argentina. One afternoon a couple of hundred strikers were milling about in front of the imposing façade of the *Banco de la Provincia de Buenos Aires,* when up sauntered a few policemen and told them to move along. And they did! A newspaperman friend of mine, whom I had met in more exciting times in Central America, shook his head in contrition at the sight and said, "This they could never get away with in Guatemala." No policeman with normal mental gear in that land of bean eaters would even think of trying to tell a gang of bitter strikers to move along on the strength of the color of his uniform. Do not be misled by the verbal savagery of Argentine politics during the past fifteen years or so. Political killing has never been either widespread or popular in that country.

Is an Argentine so gentle, at least as compared with a Guatemalan, because he eats so much meat, or in spite of it? Perhaps we should shift to another bit of folk wisdom: the word "beefeater" as applied to a Britisher implies a certain coldness, a contained quality, an aloofness. These characteristics could never be applied to the Argentine, who when he says *"inglés"* means a rigid and punctilious, unexpressive person. Maybe it is that all the South American meat the Englishman eats gets to him only after being chilled throughout the long ocean voyage, while the Argentine takes his fresh.

It is safer to retreat to yet another folkism and suggest that a full belly, no matter the stuffing, is the best antidote to revolution. If so, the Argentines are grimly determined to prevent violence, for their capital city is an eating place with a few office buildings and apartment houses scattered about to give persons an excuse for being so close to a little snack. Steak houses, coffee shops, *confiterías, pizzarías,* cafeterias, French and Italian and Chinese and Spanish restaurants stipple the city air with their smells. One of them, the Petit Café, has managed to give its name to an entire social class—the "fancy boys," or *petiteros,* favorite object of the disdain of the populist *muchachos peronistas,* who twice raided and completely wrecked the café. Anyone wearing sharp clothes is now a *petitero.* In a more generic political sense, there is common recognition of the sedative effect of eating in the term *pancista,* "bellyist," to signify the person whose politics are in rhythm with his peristalsis.

No Argentine has a "hamlike fist"; his punch is a *bife.* To make someone do something for another without being aware of it is "to swallow him." (*"Se le está tragando."*) The Italianism *morfar,* "to eat," is also widely used in slang, as in, literally, "I ate him up alive," meaning, "I sucked him in." There is too, as may be expected, a long string of expressions concerning the more carnal aspects of meat.

If Argentines know how to eat, it does not follow that they know how to cook. On the contrary, the local kitchen is distressingly simplistic, built around grilling meat, frying potatoes, and boiling *pasta.* It would be gilding the lily to own a cookbook here, for the raw materials are so good that Argentines don't have to bother with *haute cuisine* to make stringy yearling chewable or glamorize tuna fish in a casserole by adding canned mushrooms. Culinary simplicity reaches its height among working persons, whose diet is reputedly built around only five or six dishes. And yet labor-union leaders, when asked the extent of their economic ambitions, do not include any improvement in their members' board. I asked some workers in the union controlling the employees of the electric generating plants in Buenos Aires what their typical day's menu would be, and here is what they all more or less agreed on:

BREAKFAST: *Yerba mate* (a bitter herblike tea), much less often *café con leche;* sometimes bread and butter.

DINNER: *Puchero,* something like a New England boiled dinner, with great chunks of meat and rice. Sometimes an egg or two will also be eaten. Bread and butter again, soda and wine. Often men working out-of-doors will build an open fire on the job and buy meats at a local butcher shop for an *asado,* or mixed grill. This dinner is very common among construction workers.

TEA: *Mate* again, sometimes with bread and butter.

SUPPER: Grilled meat of some variety, a salad, bread and butter, wine, soda water, and coffee.

It is not uncommon for Argentines traveling abroad to go into fits of depression because they are away from their beloved meat. They complain about starving to death in the United States, and one of their favorite attacks against Anglo-Saxon culture is that Americans do not know how to eat. In a recent speech the rector of the University of Buenos Aires made a special point of U.S. eating habits in emphasizing the difference between the "epic" nature of North Americans and the "romantic" soul of the Latin Americans. What happens in the U.S. is often dismissed with a Gallic, "Well, what can you expect of people who don't drink wine?"

With respect to the taste of food, the Argentine is correct in his unhappiness. The raw materials in his land are exquisite in their flavor and freshness. Meat just cut from a huge slab tastes better than meat displayed for several days in cardboard and cellophane wrappings. Slowly cured bacon is a higher compliment to the palate than bacon cured with embalming needles. The apples here may not be so blushingly beautiful and uniform, but they have the self-respect to continue to taste like apples. Noodles and spaghetti and ravioli and other *pastas,* when made in the early hours of the morning and sold fresh, like bread, are simply not to be compared with their supermarket cousins, all taste long since subdued by dietitians and desiccation.

The bounty and the quality of Argentina's food has its price. Entertainment is built around the trencher, and woe the poor traveler, honored day after day with the traditional *asado,* where he must cope with tremendous helpings of meat of all cuts and organs. The first price is boredom, although the monomaniacal steak-and-salad eater will be in his seventh heaven. The other major cost is paid by the liver, seat of the humors. Offer an Argentine a rich chocolate dessert, and chances are that with a characteristic gesture (hand flat against the bottom of the ribs on the right side, wryly twisted mouth) he will say, "I cannot—my *hígado*." When office boys take off to go to the ball game, they don't plead a deceased aunt. It's their *hígado*. This excuse is one everybody honors, the best possible evidence that democracy of the gullet is universal. Maybe it is this organic identification, this national caloric loyalty, which restrains the Argentine political hand so that the threatened may live to eat yet another day.

But still there seems to be an unconscious attempt going on to change these gustatory facts of life. Little real, systematic thought is given to the problems of the farm, far and away Argentina's major producer of foreign exchange and domestic pleasure. The romantics talk of agrarian reform, but in terms of social justice in a crude ownership-distribution sense, rather than in terms of the enjoyment of a higher level of productivity for all. A labor leader who once accompanied me on a trip into the *pampa* set to expounding his economic beliefs over lunch. In between bites on the usual succulent mixed grill he told me all about the urgent need to industrialize Argentina into autarchy, not recognizing that the strength to talk he was deriving from his meat is threatened by an overenthusiastic, underplanned, and shapelessly xenophobic industrialization. It would be pleasurable to see Argentina think its way into enjoying the best of both worlds, instead of selling its pottage for a mess of machinery.

12

ON CUSTOMS

It was seven o'clock in the morning, and I had just been awakened by the turning on of the bed lamp; my roommate was reading *Economic Panorama,* a Chilean review. My companion, M.S.G., is a highly placed official of the Chilean government who had accompanied me to Valparaíso as a friendly gesture in order to help me through the customs, notoriously labyrinthine and inhabited by appropriately taurine officials.

We were staying at the Hotel Miramar, overlooking the sea of course, in the famous resort town of Viña del Mar, a continuation of the port city of Valparaíso along the Pacific coast to the north. But it was off-season. The Venetian blinds in our room were twisted; there was no soap in the bathroom, and only the smallest of bulbs were provided in the one overhead light and the one tiny bed lamp which disturbed my sleep in the first paragraph. There is a chronic electric shortage in Chile, whose industrialization program has outstripped its energy requirements. In 1947, during my first Chilean tour, the current was turned off for two nights a week in the capital, Santiago de Chile. On two other nights the gas was turned low, so that for four nights a week everyone knew what it meant to be either blind or hungry. Now a rationing system is in effect, involving fines if the monthly quota of electric consumption is exceeded, with the threat of cutting off the power completely if the allowance is exceeded during three consecutive months. Certain astringent critics assure me that the latter threat never is carried out and that the fines add up to a kind of Robin Hood maneuver of making the well-to-do pay at a high rate for luxury consumption. The electricity shortage in Santiago was finally solved in 1960 with the tying of a new plant into the system.

Outside it was murky and cold. Sea gulls and pelicans were wheeling under the dirty clouds, a year-round phenomenon in those coastal areas affected by the Humboldt Current, deglamorized by the geographers into the South Pacific Current. In Santiago, at 1,500 feet, there are nights in which the temperature drops to freezing, but the coastal areas are always a little warmer. Although there was no heat in the radiators, getting up was helped by the wooden floors—as distinguished from the tile to be found in almost all other Latin American countries, no matter how cold it may be in the highland cities. Chile is reputed to possess the largest uncut stand of temperate hardwoods left in the world, and certain it is that the parquet-type flooring almost universal in all but the poorest housing is handsome to the eye and hospitable to the bare feet. The upkeep, however, is difficult. In the United States we can put in hardwood floors and then shellac them, wax them, and carefully cover them with a pad and carpeting, relying thereafter on a vacuum cleaner. But in Chile rugs are prohibitively expensive. The floors instead are waxed and polished for public viewing, a heavy job which most maids refuse to do, so that the services of a man are required once or twice a month for floor maintenance. But this happy solution, which has led to a nation of expert balancers on slippery surfaces, is doomed by progress. Day labor is becoming expensive, just as maids are becoming scarce, because of the demands of the new industries, such as steel, tires, refrigerators, plastics, and even vacuum cleaners. In the long run, rugs and carpet sweepers will have to become less expensive than they now are, or the man of the house will have to do the work on the naked floors. Either course implies profound revolution.

Breakfast was the usual *café con leche,* bread, butter, and jam. Most Chileans who have maids—that is, the lower middle class and up, although there are cases of maids who have maids—take their breakfast in bed. But we ate downstairs in the restaurant, to the contemptuous annoyance of the waiters.

We were on time for the nine-o'clock opening of customs, after motoring the five miles or so to Valparaíso through a driving rain. I have always liked the port immensely, and seeing it through a heavy downpour added a new dimension. My companion vowed that in his previous six years' residence on the coast he had never seen more than a drizzle. The cold waters of the current pouring out of the Antarctic chill the air, of course, and thus condensation and precipitation usually do not take place until the clouds have been forced well up into the Andes—at this point some ninety miles inland. It is for this reason that the coastal areas from San Antonio south of Valparaíso all the way to the southern border of Ecuador range from dry to desert conditions.

The wet emphasized the European feel of Valparaíso. Most of the streets are narrow, winding sharply up and down steep inclines on which the city of some 300,000 persons is built. (This number includes the entire metropolitan area, embracing Viña and Concón to the north, as well as intermediate spots.) Funicular railways obviate the worst climbs for pedestrians. Streets join at sharp angles, promoting flatiron-type buildings, their porticoes embellished with highly polished brass signs announcing the Bank of London and South America or a shipping agent here and a chandler there. The deep British influence in Chile, whose national liberator was O'Higgins, and which has streets named Llewellyn-Jones, McIver, Príncipe de Gales (Prince of Wales), and Queen Victoria, is felt nowhere so strongly as in Valparaíso, a proud Pacific port until the opening of the Panama Canal. The new growth of an internal-looking economy has mixed with the old cosmopolitan stream to produce stores whose signs still proclaim them in English to be "Gents' Stores," while the proprietors are listed as Contreras or Eyzaguirre.

This extra-Iberian, non-Indian Europeanization is by no means confined to the ports, although it is nowhere so striking as in the southern part of the central valley, near Valdivia, where the German influence is universal. Santiago, with approximately one-fifth of the country's total population, has always struck me as being concocted in equal parts of any Latin American city and of Philadelphia, with a soupçon of Paris on top. It's a dirty city, especially in the wintertime when much soft coal is burned. Most of its streets are narrow, and the arcade is increasingly important in extending effective shopping area in the downtown section. And further reminiscent of Philadelphia, aside from the soot and the narrow streets, is also the fact that Santiago is a city of strongly marked neighborhoods which reduce the commercial importance of the center.

Beauty returns to Santiago with the change of seasons. Spring sees an outburst of flowers on all sides, delicately controlled until the next winter by careful irrigation. Few things are as pleasant to me as the gurgling rush of water through the city's irrigation ditches on a mid-summer's night, a sound evoking the smell of new-mown grass or a recently fallen rain. But none of this leavening is here now: Santiago is a dirty, gray city—but a city in the full sense of the word, not a country town distinguished only by a starred circle on the maps.

I think it is just because of this atmosphere that I miss a certain inspiration to be found in other Latin American countries. Red-haired women, blond youths, and pale-faced men are strange to the eyes of someone fresh from Indian Guatemala or *mestizo* Mexico. This clearly Northern European air makes Santiago homelike to someone from northeastern America. But it also makes Chile seem imitative, lacking in the excitement attending the birth of that new self-awareness and self-discovery so characteristic of the heady Mexican or Brazilian developments. Only in Chile, I think, of all Latin American countries, can a major part of the new housing be a sorry imitation of Tudor or two-story white boxes with columns and gaudy capitals.

But let's return to the thread of the story. Our first stop in Valparaíso was at the office of the broker specializing in automobiles. Here the problem was simple, for our troubles had arisen and been resolved several days earlier. It appeared that I had the right kind of visa for heavy baggage and a radio, a washing machine, and a refrigerator, but the wrong kind for an automobile. In the latter case, despite an international *carnet* issued by the American Automobile Association, as demanded by Chilean customs, and a monetary guarantee deposited in New York, I also was in need of tourist status. The latter can be gained by a tourist visa or by simply entering the country with an American passport bearing no visa, under the terms of a United States-Chilean accord. The contradiction was resolved by a letter from the Ministry of Foreign Affairs testifying to my occupation (all invoices from New Orleans had already been stamped by the Chilean consul there, "Purpose of Trip: Academic Research") and also giving its understanding, but not its guarantee, that I would leave the country with the car within a year. In effect, the Ministry was admitting to having given me the wrong kind of visa, a confession to the particular liking of the customs people, who seem to bear a special grudge against all consuls. And so ends the story of the car: it was delivered in good condition within an hour.

The next stop was at the office of a friend of my friend, a man who is an official of the customs service. It should be clearly understood that no question of undue influence or subornation was involved. In Chile it is commonly said, "Everything can be arranged." But not with bribes. In only Costa Rica and Chile, of the twelve Latin American countries in which I have had even a little experience, have I found consistent official probity. Chilean Spanish does not even have a current slang word for bribe equal to the Mexican *mordida* ("bite") or the more general *coima*. The Chileans use *propina*, whose gentle meaning is to be inferred from the fact that it is the general word, also, for "tip." What distinguishes Chile is the necessity for friends. In my own experience this need was best exemplified by the Chilean consul in New Orleans, who advised me it would be easiest to secure what is called an ordinary visa simply by writing to friends in Santiago. Annoyed, I took the matter up with the consul in New York. After half an hour or so he asked, "Have you any friends in Santiago?"

The necessary courtesy call made, then, we went along to the office of the agent specializing in baggage and used refrigerators. Under Chilean law, anyone dealing with customs must do so through a licensed agent, presumably to avoid the state of nature which undoubtedly would result should anyone try to brave the numerous forms, functionaries, and little windows without first having special training. By 10:30 in the morning we arrived at the warehouse ready to locate the effects. At 11:30 we had them, but it was time for lunch. We took our leave, with promises that if we returned by 2:00 P.M. we should have everything settled and be on the road back to Santiago by late afternoon.

Our midday meal was excellent, a not unusual thing in a country deservedly famed for its wines, sea food, and fruits. We ordered tiny ocean shrimps and a small filet apiece. The shrimps were nutty in flavor and crisp in texture and overwhelming in number. Although I should normally have preferred to accompany them with a mustardy mayonnaise, we decided to see what this restaurant's so-called American dressing might be. Upon arrival, it turned out to be what we call Russian dressing in the United States. After discussion, we decided that there was no political significance to this switch in nomenclature.

Chileans who can afford it usually take their eating very seriously. The daily schedule is quite similar to that followed in Madrid and, as everyone knows, what schedule there is in Madrid revolves about the dining table and the café. Again the caveat is added, "For those who can afford it." As has been indicated, breakfast is light, the prelude to a workday beginning at nine or ten o'clock in the morning. Some persons take a coffee break at 11:30, to hold them over until dinner, which comes at one or two o'clock in the afternoon. At a minimum this meal consists of a heavy soup, a main dish, dessert, and coffee. More often it starts with a fish dish, an egg salad, or some such preparation. Invariably wine is served. It is only in the last few years that some government offices and private businesses have attempted to institute a one-hour lunch period, leading to a curtailment of food intake at this meal. But most persons manage at least two hours for lunch. As a matter of practice, the important customs gentlemen in Valparaíso took three hours on the day we are discussing.

Some people in the city still take a siesta after dinner, although the practice is dying out. Around five in the afternoon comes the *once*—the "elevenses," which, given the British influence mentioned earlier, seem to have suffered a six-hour loss in translation. Chileans solemnly assure me, however, that the expression comes from a clerical habit of referring to *aguardiente* delicately as the *once,* the eleven-letter word. This refresher period may involve only coffee or tea, or it may be the highest of high teas, with sandwiches, cookies, a beverage, and a sweet. At

6:30 or 7:00 o'clock there begins the hour of vermouth. More women than men take tea; more men than women indulge in the vermouth hour. The institution is so solid a part of the daily itinerary that the movie showings at this hour are called vermouth performances. This is also the time for concerts, recitals, and plays. At 9:00 P.M. the supper hour begins, hits its full stride at 10:00, and then slowly tapers off. I have been served this meal at well past midnight on festive evenings. Most persons cannot keep up this eating with unbroken consistency, you know. Eight years ago I dyspeptically asked my friend M.S.G. about it, and he insisted that Chileans can eat so much and not become stout because the food is deficient in caloric value. I don't really believe it, but I suppose it is a matter I shall have to ask about.

Given the importance of eating, and especially of the midday dinner, it was only fitting that the most important business of the day should have taken place at the restaurant. There we met one of the officials with whom we had dealt in the morning. He was celebrating the birthday of one of his children at the bar with one of his friends. There was no recourse before his courteous insistence but to accept several *pisco* sours (*pisco* is a king of grape vodka) and to discuss the events of the day. He turned out to be an interesting and charming gentleman engaged in the collection of antiquities and especially of old clocks.

With the assurance of our customs-official acquaintance that all would go smoothly and that there was no need for hurry, since he intended to be a little late, we returned content to the warehouse a few minutes before three o'clock in the afternoon. By 4:30 the crates had been opened, everything had been inspected, papers were filled out, and we were ready to pay what we were assured was to be a low duty and to retire the baggage. I was a little embarrassed by the obvious disapproval of the customs people, even the handlers, at my bringing in a used refrigerator and washing machine instead of the gaudiest new ones to be found, but consoled myself with the thought that I was not really in Chile to engage in profiteering. A new American refrigerator can bring as high as $1,600, although commercial importation is forbidden. Automatic washing machines are even rarer than new American refrigerators and also highly desirable. Used machines, however, sit strangely on the market, for anyone who can afford to buy one at all can usually go all the way. The fact that my washing machine had accumulated a little rust was also met with disapproving headshakes. The wonders of the mechanical age must at all times be maintained in the glossiest of conditions, especially on the outside.

Content with our day, seeing the end in sight, we went to the office of the inspector, the next to the last step. In a matter of seconds he brusquely and uncompromisingly rejected the entire inspection and evaluation. He did not believe that these appliances were used; he thought their evaluation was much too low; he implied we were all engaged in a monstrous conspiracy to defraud the customs. After bitter argument we challenged him to make his own inspection. It was now 5:00 P.M.; everything was due to close down in thirty minutes. The party of six which we had accumulated by this time then dashed across town to the warehouse, and the crates came open again. The inspector was appalled: not only were the artifacts used, as we had said, but someone had driven a nail through the top of the radio in crating it. He blushed, reduced all the evaluations by a blanket 15 per cent, and asked to be taken back to his office.

My companion decided that he had better stay in the warehouse to make sure we were not locked out while I raced over to the finance office to make settlement. Too late: they had stopped taking money at 3:30. But in order to see how much I should leave for the agent, we figured out the multifarious taxes which applied. The process was literally carried out on a calculator and took half an hour. The duty only came to $214,000 plus other fees, for a total of about $250,000. The dollar sign is, of course, also the peso sign. In United States dollars the amount was still appreciable—US$500. Then an argument arose between the agent and a customs official as to why two separate sets of papers had not been filled out, so that I might at least have withdrawn the clothing, leaving the other things for the obviously necessary further discussion and deliberation. I interrupted with the decision to return the refrigerator, washing machine, and radio to the United States. This announcement brought an appalled silence. I wasn't playing the game. But I remained adamant, since it was economically silly to pay such a high duty; I was being charged at least twice as much as the value of the refrigerator and washing machine in the United States bringing their total cost to more even than they could possibly be worth in Chile, adding freight, crating, and insurance. Further, I had no intention of extracting large sums for used appliances from an unsuspecting *chileno*. After all, how much life is built into a washing machine?

Sadly we brought the negotiations to an end. I protested my undying love for Latin culture; the officials assured me they were only doing their duty. The requiem sung, we shook hands and I left for the warehouse, the clothing still impounded, awaiting a new set of papers to separate the allowable from the rejected.

Let me confess at this point that the taste of ashes and harsh cigarettes lingered in my mouth. The victory over the inspector was not sweet and left me wondering about the Latin *dignidad* I have heard so much about. On the other hand, the economic angles of the case are more pardonable, representing much more deprivation for the Chilean than for the visitor. Since my stay in 1948, when the peso was at fifty to one dollar, the Chilean currency steadily dropped until it reached a nadir of eight hundred to one. A drastic attempt to stabilize brought the peso back by 1957 to five hundred to one, leaving the cost of living expensive in both peso and dollar terms. (It has subsequently risen to over four thousand to one, uncertainly following the cost-of-living index.) This is not the place for an attempt to analyze the causes of the devaluation and the inflation, which at one stage saw an increase in prices of 75 per cent in one year. For the time being it is enough to say that high tariffs and the inflation are certainly both related intimately to Chile's industrialization program and to its international economic position. The tariffs are not only protective but are also designed to save scarce dollars, seeking preferentially to channel them into the purchase of capital goods.

The industrialization program has been seriously and intensely under way since 1939 and the establishment of the national Chilean Production Development Corporation. This country now not only assembles radios but also manufactures the tubes. Records are pressed, ping-pong balls produced, steel rolled and used for a wide variety of products, and on and on. M.S.G. told me one day with pardonable pride (he works in the Development Corporation) that there was not a single thing in his living room which had not been made in Chile. The price for this autarchy is not low. Most of these articles are produced inefficiently, measured against world market prices, and for a small effective market, so that their cost is high—sometimes 300 per cent of U.S. prices, and in a few cases even more. Imported goods are always horridly expensive. I can understand $6,000 for a Chevrolet. But one store wanted $195 for a tiny German electric train. I am referring only to the train—one locomotive and two passenger cars—and no track, transformer, or anything else. An imported musical top in the same shop had been reduced to only $16. So the second price the Chileans are paying for an elaborated economy is an inability to pick and choose among the world's supplies of manufactured goods. A third punishment is, in my opinion, aesthetic. Countries like Chile cannot afford to hire good designers; they cannot have enough producers of each individual article to allow for a wide range of style distinction. As a result, much of the locally produced consumers' goods are, to my eyes at least, ugly.

In any event, some Chileans now have refrigerators; there were practically none in the country in 1948. They make more electric waxers at higher prices than ever before, but they have more than they could possibly have imported with their scarce dollars. It may never be that Chilean industry as a whole will be able to compete with world markets, but so long as these markets remain in the kind of maladjustment which prevents such a country as Chile from satisfying its thirst for mechanical contrivances, then they are winning in the sense that they are consuming more of them than before.

For these reasons I could not be overly bitter about the duties asked of me. Of course, I had a semi-official letter in my pocket assuring me I would have to pay none, but the letter also warned that everything was in such a state of confusion that a prediction might not hold good through the time necessary for shipment. I had had the misfortune of being caught by a new set of regulations. But all was not lost.

Tired, wet, and defeated, I drove back to the warehouse to pick up my companion and call it a day. There he was, with our luncheon benefactor, the two trunks full of clothing in the middle of the street. Waving aside all explanations, the customs official ordered the trunks put in the car, everybody smiled happily and joked, I said good-by to all, and we left. The supervising inspector had so insulted the warehouse superintendent that the latter had, on his own initiative, revised the papers and released the clothing forthwith. A week later I received word from the agent that a reassessment had taken place of the value of the remaining articles and that the duty had been lowered to US$228.

We drove the hundred or so miles back to the capital in pouring rain all the way. We were now in two cars, so I drove behind the 1941 Chrysler my companion had bought several years before. His car was still worth about $2,000, but it was really not in very good condition. The switch controlling the overdrive went out after a few miles, serving to slow us even beyond the point demanded by the weather. Five hours after our departure, and a few miles out of Santiago, the generator also gave up. As we were creeping along together, my car close behind and to the right to shed light for both cars, a *carabinero,* one of Chile's national police force, waved us down. A hit-and-run victim was lying by the side of the road, the policeman trying ineffectually to shield him from the rain with his cloak. A taxi driver in a well-maintained Model A was standing by but refused to dirty his car by picking up the injured person, who quite clearly was suffering from a skull fracture behind the left ear. I audibly wondered whether it was wise to move him without a physician, but the *carabinero* overruled me by asking what physician would venture out in the rain to look. So we picked the injured person up as best we could and took him into Santiago to a hospital.

I was home by 2:00 A.M., dried myself out, ate two pieces of chocolate, and went to bed.

13

ON A MATTER OF BUSINESS

The home of the Argentine industrialist I am going to talk about is indicative of his character and way of life. The house is middle-aged, in a quietly respectable residential district of Buenos Aires. Little luxury is evident inside. The furniture is good, comfortable, stylistically undistinguished; there are plenty of records, but there is no hi-fi, and the many books are tucked away in their cases here and there with no attempt made to impress their number on the visitor. The second floor of the large house is devoted to business offices and a woodworking shop for the husband, a painting studio for the wife, a sculptor's corner for the daughter. The son plays the cello, kept in a small downstairs room where there is also an upright piano for the mother of the house and the violin which the father no longer plays. The most ostentatious of the family's material possessions are two quite new, middle-sized European cars.

The wife and the two children speak fluent English; the *pater familias* can make himself understood in the language. They count as friends many of Argentina's best known artists; in the family are several of the country's well-established academic intellectuals. Their air is one of active domesticity, not of Bohemianism, or self-conscious sophistication, or "artiness." Relaxation, friendliness, an utter lack of feverishness, is the tone imposed by the father, although rather more restlessness is noted in the other members of the tightly knit family circle, but not to the extent of rebellion. In politics, for example, the children are somewhat mildly leftist Radicals, while the parents are somewhat mildly rightist Radicals. It is not a strain to visit them, because they are neither hypertensive nor boring. The parents listen as well as talk, and their interests are wide enough to accommodate a diversity of friendships.

Not even when he speaks about the loss of his factory to an American combine does the father become violent in expression, although it is evident that the experience has been extremely distressing to him and that the entire family treats the subject with respect for his feelings. He chooses to discuss the matter as an example of culture clash and seeks to understand what it was that brought him to the point of being unable to accept further relations with his American peers. No financial privation disturbs the family because of the loss of the company. The father is for the moment the regional distributor for the plant he and his family used to own, and he is also the owner of another factory, as well as of sundry stocks and bonds. The distress is primarily one of feelings, not of pocketbook.

The establishment and growth of the factory is not an unusual story. When Sr. V. was thirteen years of age, he went to work for his uncle selling a certain American product, manufactured by four U.S companies, but marketed overseas at uniform prices through a commercial subsidiary of the four. In 1930, when V. was twenty-one years old and just concluding work toward a notary public's license from the faculty of Law of the University of Buenos Aires, the family decided to establish a small factory in Argentina to elaborate the product concerned, using imported raw materials available through the same American companies. With US$7,500 gathered from family members, V. bought out a bankrupt factory established by German interests; all the equipment was German, as was the technician who remained through the transfer of ownership. During the first two years the going was difficult, after which profit margins began to build up, and the factory thereafter went through World War II and the Peronist dictatorship without going into the red again until 1956. Annual returns ranged from 8 to 30 per cent of invested capital in the period, the average being between 18 and 20 per cent.

In 1939 the United States Supreme Court ordered the dissolution as a monopoly of the trading company representing the big four. Two of the four then merged, leaving three companies which continued to export individually to Argentina until after the war.

Technical "know-how" was one of V.'s major problems from the start. He states that U.S. technicians are by far the most advanced in his line of production and that it is almost useless to try to go for help to other areas of the world, for even in Europe the major producers are affiliates of the American parent companies or otherwise dependent upon them for patents. As early as 1935 he bought his first American machinery and says he has been most satisfied with the purchases: all the equipment bought then is still operating with only relatively minor modifications. The problem of technical knowledge grew acute after

1945, not only because great advances were made in the postwar period, but also because of changes in the competitive and political situations in Argentina. Since the industry concerned is almost totally dependent on the importation of raw materials, the exchange and foreign commerce controls imposed by the Perón government made honest importations increasingly difficult. Foreign investors were given preference in the importation of raw materials, so two of the three American companies involved entered Argentina as direct producers by affiliating with already-established Argentine firms. V. managed to continue to hold out as an independent through this period, his suffering heightened because he objected to paying under the table for import licenses. In 1949 he made a trip to Europe, where he found the raw materials to be as good as those available from North America, but he remained skeptical of technical advances there and so chose not to affiliate with a small European producer. The inevitable result was a constant dropping-off of profits. This trend did not end with the collapse of Perón because V.'s competitors were still gaining an increasing edge as a result of their constantly advancing techniques.

The one American company which had remained out of Argentina had done so in expectation of a clarification of the political situation. This enterprise, which we shall call Dashblank Overseas, Inc., had sent two vice-presidents to Argentina in 1954 to see whether there was a company into which they could buy. At that time conversations had been held with Sr. V., seemingly leaving both parties mutually satisfied. Perón finally fell in June of 1955, and V. then wrote a letter to Dashblank suggesting that serious negotiations could be opened. To repeat, V. really had no choice, for the matter of "know-how" was all-important, and obviously a small Argentine company was in no position to maintain the research department necessary for adequate competition with at least one U.S. company whose name is almost a household word in the United States.

Preliminary conversations opened in December of 1955, when V. was invited to visit New York. In February 1956 eight officials of the Dashblank enterprise traveled to Argentina and the merger was then concluded. V. and the other members of his family (including his mother, an uncle, a brother, and others) proportionately sold out 51 per cent of their holdings as of the value of a given day, in accordance with a mutually accepted inventory which put the value of the capital assets of the company at US$75,000, or three million Argentine pesos. The deal was carried through by the president of Dashblank Overseas, the president of Dashblank U.S., the treasurers of the two companies, two technicians, and the person who had been brought in from the company's Peruvian operations to serve as V.'s new assistant. V. himself was named a vice-president of Dashblank Overseas, in charge of the Argentine company. His understanding was that he would retain a large measure of control over commercial operations and that the technical side would be left strictly in the hands of the new parent company. Nothing at all was put in writing, the matter being handled simply as a sale of private stock.

At the same time of the agreement, functions were divided between V. and the incoming officials and technicians, new salary levels were established (with substantial raises across the board), two company cars were provided and paid for by Dashblank, and the new regime began.

Dashblank initiated little action during the remainder of 1956. Several engineers were sent from the U.S. when V. complained that nothing seemed to be happening, and in September Dashblank's president came through on a general swing around the company's installations, which include manufacturing units in Australia, France, Germany, Italy, the Republic of South Africa, Canada, the United Kingdom, Brazil, and Argentina. A raw-materials producing center was also being projected for Argentina, and has now gone into operation, liberating the entire local industry from the necessity of importing their most important raw material.

In early 1957 Dashblank began to raise the capitalization of the Argentine branch drastically, quintupling the plant's value in little over a year. But V. was increasingly restive, not only because of a year's delay in getting started, but also because little attention was being paid to maintaining the accounts on which the firm had been living, and so business was falling off sharply, causing the first losses since the first two years of operations. No dividends were declared in 1956, there being a deficit for the year equivalent to about US$40,000. The balance for the 1957 fiscal year was even more unfavorable. (These figures do not take into account the cost of the new machinery and the building expansion being paid for by Dashblank Overseas directly.) V. felt that these losses were unnecessary and that his advice was not being heeded. Increasingly restless, he came to the end of his tether on a question of the purchase of supplies. V. had found an opportunity to buy materials at a very advantageous price but discovered that before placing an order he had to inform the U.S. headquarters and argue the matter out, by which time the bargain was gone. Feeling that his last vestige of autonomy had disappeared, in August of 1957 he and the other members of his family offered to sell out a large percentage of the stock remaining in their hands. Dashblank Overseas accepted; a price was agreed upon in negotiation, and V. resigned to become a company distributor, his erstwhile assistant moving up to replace him.

The purchasing incident was only a last straw, of course. V. quit because of simple personality and culture clash with his new American partners. Neither side appears to have adjusted to the other. The difference lies not only between individual Americans and individual Argentines; it is also the difference between how a man thinks when he is running a comparatively important factory, on a family basis, in a country with a limited market, and how other men think when they are operating comparatively huge enterprises on an international basis. It is not that V. necessarily wanted his business to remain small. On the contrary, he quite clearly recognized that he had to expand and modernize or die. But as he himself puts it, he does not understand why expansion and technical improvement must necessarily mean impersonality and "bigness" in an attitudinal sense. His plaint is not an unfamiliar one in the United States, either.

V. does not think he was cheated of anything, and he attributes a great amount of the trouble to himself for having misgauged the personalities of the individuals with whom he was to work. In the word "personality" is the crux of the entire matter, as V. explains his own case. He says, with pity and his only touch of bitterness, "The Dash-blank executives remind me of Radio City Rockettes—all the same. Each does his own work very well but will not accept more than what is within his speciality. In Argentina the president of a company identifies himself with everything. The Americans have no sense of responsibility for the job as *owners*. They are just high-level employees." This criticism is especially harsh in Spanish, where the word *empleado* not only connotes job status but also low-level social and cultural standing, at least as compared to the *patrón*, or owner.

Pursuing the point that his American business peers were his intellectual inferiors, V. calls them "spiritually poor." He argues that it was difficult to be with them socially, that outside of work topics there was little to discuss. (The two exceptions were an engineer who had an interest in Mayan art and one of the company lawyers whose horizons went beyond corporate affairs.) He cites the case of a vice-president with a beautiful house, no children, and two dogs. On the occasion of one of this person's trips to Argentina, he left his wife at home because one of the dogs was ill. V.'s Argentine pride was visibly affected as he complained that his visitors from the United States were not interested in Buenos Aires, that they asked only to be allowed to work hard, sleep well, eat steaks, and go shopping. He states positively that the only other diversion on which he accompanied one of the company's missions was to the race track, incidentally his first and last trip to the Jockey Club.

He detailed his criticisms to me. It is striking how few of them have anything to do with business matters as such.

1. *Politicking.* The Americans talked about one another. Company politics and company gossip seemed a major preoccupation, causing V. much discomfiture both in Argentina and the United States. He asserts that every single officer with whom he came in contact sought an opportunity to talk with him privately and to speak ill of others and to describe the circles of influence in the company, in effect soliciting his membership in one or another group.

2. *Going by the book.* Much too restrictive rules were established for purchases, sales, and accounting. The regulations made necessary a constant communication with the United States and caused a great loss in flexibility. Local requirements and business practices were often ignored. V. says that he paid little attention to many of these rules but always kept within the strict bounds of accounting policy.

3. *Too many visitors.* Perhaps because of the tendency toward specialization, great numbers of persons seemed always to be coming to inspect the Argentine operations. In 1956 almost thirty persons, almost all accompanied by their wives, made the long trip to Argentina. V. estimates that the company spent at least as much on the travel expenses of these persons as had been originally paid for the interest in the plant. This rhythm of visits was maintained throughout 1957, occasioning an important loss of time on the part of the persons in Argentina.

4. *Conspicuous consumption.* One of the first acts after Dashblank assumed control was to provide V. and his new assistant with company cars. These were Chevrolet Bel-Air sedans, each worth upwards of US$12,000 in Argentina. New American cars are extremely visible here, whereas comparable European cars are not nearly so noticeable. V. felt the money should better have been spent on machinery and advertising and that the action was but another instance of employee- as opposed to owner-mentality. His pride was also damaged when the president of Dashblank Overseas, after concluding the purchase, asked V. whether he was in need of any ready cash. The Argentine interpreted the attitude as being most patronizing, and the question most personal, as well as again indicative of a boyish delight in dividing up the spoils of a corporate industrial giant.

5. *Simple misunderstanding.* V. had not fully understood the difference between being entirely his own boss and tying into an international company. He had thought that the administrative and sales experience he brought to the combination would be valued, and so he would have a large measure of autonomy in conducting this side of the enterprise. He would have had to change his total attitude toward his role in the company as well as his approach to business to have been able to adjust himself to the necessity for clearing all but routine decisions with New York.

6. *Personal distaste.* V. felt he had little or nothing in common, on a personal basis, with the persons with whom he had to deal.

7. *Distaff involvement.* The corporation wife became an issue because so many company officials traveled with their mates. This habit forced V.'s wife into the matter, not only on a simple entertainment level, but also in matters of shopping and company politics. Sra. V. is a busy woman, occupied with her painting and the running of a house. She has no interest in business doings, and her participation in such affairs would have violated Argentine custom.

8. *Dividend failure.* The fact that the company was allowed to suffer losses during the change-over period did not affect V. personally, for his very comfortable salary was certainly enough to tide him over this period, even should it have persisted for many years. But V.'s mother and other members of the family were not in the same position and saw themselves being affected in regard to their standard of living. V. argues that the divorce between management and ownership obviously taking place is but further proof of employee-mentality on the part of the Americans. He is also of the strong opinion that the losses were not necessary, or at least need not have been so great. If there had been a slower rate of investment and if money had not been spent on such frills as automobiles and needless travel, the plant change-over would have been a less painful process for the Argentine owners, to whom the marginal value of a dollar is much greater than to the Americans with their greater reserves and contempt for relatively small figures.

In summary, V. broke with the company because of an irreconcilable difference of attitude concerning the style of business, and because he would have had to change his mode of personal life to conform to the new demands. V. was fortunate in being financially able to make the break, whatever the emotional cost may have been.

SOME IMPLICATIONS OF THE INCIDENT

The assignment of "guilt" for the occurrence is not the purpose of this study; on the contrary, it may well be argued that the most distressing part of it is that no one at all is "guilty." V. obviously is not all in the right, and Dashblank is not all in the wrong. A manager *is* different from a manager-owner, and an American *per se* is also different from an Argentine *per se*. Certainly V. erred in bringing an undeniably "small-time" view to the merger, and unquestionably the Americans did not take local conditions and practice into consideration enough to cushion V.'s shock. And who can tell but that chance was a major factor in the sense that V. may have done well with another company and Dashblank might have done well with another Argentine? There need

be no breast-beating, either, over the thought that the U.S. may have
gained another enemy, for V. is not one to make easy political generalizations out of his personal troubles and quite as plainly is not an
antiyanqui. The question raised is better explored in another, and less
personal, sense.

Dashblank Overseas has much more power than V. and had much
more throughout the entire negotiations. V. could not continue in the
face of competition. And he had to go to the only major American
company that still was not represented in Argentina. On the other
hand, the Americans had the choice of tying up with V., the last of the
available Argentine entrepreneurs in the field, or they could have continued to wait in order to establish themselves independently, meanwhile continuing to inform themselves about the general market in,
and the economy of, the country. Dashblank had time; V. did not. In
addition, Dashblank had no necessity for immediate, short-run returns
and can still afford to wait a few years in the expectation of maximized
returns thereafter. V.'s family could not wait. The bargaining conditions, then, were unequal. If one assumes raw Social Darwinism as an
adequate business ethic, then "Good for Dashblank" must be the only
comment. Conversely it may be held that he who has more power also
has more responsibility. Slice the moral cake as you will, there are
political factors involved whether one likes that fact or not. But such
political factors must always come up against the further "given" that
Dashblank is a business and must offer returns to its investors.

Given the pattern of behavior of the persons involved on both sides,
V. might very well have become so bothersome as to be a positive lia-
bility to the company and actually cause it to lose money as prepara-
tions advanced for the mass marketing of the new products. Or he may
have caused the company to earn less than it was capable of doing.
These statements are purely speculative, of course, but the company
must have taken these possibilities into account. The question: should
Dashblank have been willing to string along with V. for a much longer
time, not for economic reasons, but in the simple desire to keep the undertaking as Argentine as possible for the very indirect political benefits which might have flowed therefrom? These "indirect political benefits" would not include avoidance of any immediate threats of expropriation or the solution of problems with governmental administrative
agencies, or the answer might be easier.

Latin America's major dependence on a few selected exports for satisfying foreign exchange needs is well known. Tin in Bolivia, copper in
Chile, coffee in Brazil, meat and wheat in Argentina were all major
subjects for worry when the American economic recession of 1957–58
threw markets into turmoil and disrupted the economic development

plans as well as the day-to-day budgets of Latin countries. But direct American investments in Latin industrial development, such as is the case with Dashblank, are also vitally important, if not as spectacular to watch as the tidal waves in monopolistic-monopsonistic relations brought on by domestic readjustments in the American economy. It is precisely such investments as Dashblank's which can help to complicate national Latin economies sufficiently to permit at least some blunting of the effects of foreign trade storms. The usual presumption is also that such direct investments contribute to building entrepreneurial and skilled labor groups within the under- and intermediately-developed nations, and that this social development may help to prevent political excess. In this sense Dashblank was contributing to Argentina's sociopolitical health as well as to its own business interests. This implication cannot be escaped.

But the Dashblank experience added up to depriving Argentina of one industrialist. Increased employment in the industry will develop some new skilled labor, it is true, but there is still one entrepreneur less. It is not that V. was replaced in this social sense, for the acting head of the company here is not now an Argentine, nor has he the owner-manager mentality which so strongly characterizes V. and which has certain implications for the country as a whole. The Argentine might have contributed to the building of a responsible and reasonable industrial leadership group. Now he, as an individual, cannot.

As more and more economic competition from the Iron Curtain bloc can be expected throughout the world, a greater weight falls on American business to defend itself, not from simple commericial attack which can be handled directly, but rather from the combined political-economic maneuverings that are possible to directed economies. Willy-nilly, then, American enterprises operating overseas, whatever their size, will be called upon to measure the political as well as the business results of their operations. Some of these effects may very well be supremely subtle, as is the case of V., for he represents the first point on the scale, the lowest audible note of protest, so to speak. His leaving Dashblank, as was said, made no enemy for the U.S.; it made for no personal bitterness by the fact of his losing social status, and it probably caused no economic harm to the company. But it did lessen Argentine participation in industry and so contributed to what supernationalists of left and right both call "cosmopolitan internationalism." In a very tiny way the incident may serve to aggravate anti-imperialist attitudes in Argentina.

The matter is, of course, very small. But after all, big numbers are made up of little ones.

PART FIVE

FORCE AND FREEDOM

"Remember that there is no happiness without freedom and that the basis of freedom is courage." Pericles' equation of freedom and courage is simple and admirable as aphorism, but most difficult as political prescription. The tensions between order and freedom, and haste and freedom, have tempted many Latin American leaders into a disdain for the dignity of liberty and a shortsighted acceptance of personalism and militarism. The proper mix of authority and freedom is the subject matter of all ideological dispute. The solution most adequate to the needs of the developing lands will be found when intelligence is put at the service of a freedom courageously espoused and practiced.

14

THE MILITARY: A HANDBOOK FOR
THEIR CONTROL

A Fourth of July speech can be a very important document for the understanding of American folkways. A foreigner might find it difficult, however, to understand the allusions without close guidance. The date itself, "Our Founding Fathers," "The Sage of Monticello," "Our Boys," "United we stand, divided we fall," are all references which demand impregnation with American values and symbols for an appreciation of their full emotional richness. Some nations are wealthier than others in the number and essence of these triggers to the connotative; others are scrabbling about to construct themselves a suitable set. Argentina falls into the first category, its history replete with hero figures, battles, philosopher-statesmen, and gentlemen historians.

This chapter presents the annotated translation of a long, rambling, and philosophically misty speech concerning the development and comportment of the modern Argentine army. It is a housekeeping document, intimate and filled with family slang. Certain portions of the statement, then, will be almost totally without meaning for Americans. The entire speech will appear inane to anybody who mistakenly regards the Argentine army as a subject for mockery. It may be a plaything, but it is not a toy. At this moment there are some 220,000 persons in the three branches of the armed services of Argentina, most of them, of course, complying with the requirements of the universal conscription law that calls for one year's service in the army or air force, or two years in the navy, for all male citizens when they are more or less twenty years old. This number constitutes 1.1 per cent of the country's population, if we accept the official figure of almost twenty million inhabitants. Compare this percentage with that of a world power of 170,-000,000 which has 2,500,000 under arms (a percentage of about 1.5) to answer the demands of global operations. About 40 per cent of Argentina's total budget goes to the military. The army, the most important branch, is trained to think in terms of international war in the halls of a set of training institutes that are elaborate despite the largely second-hand equipment employed. The fact that its only bellicose actions since the end of the Indian wars in the latter part of the nineteenth century have been for political ends is important to an understanding of the stress caused among Argentine military personnel by a vast difference between ideal action and real conduct.

The general view of a Latin American army is that it is woefully lacking in professionalism but abundantly endowed with social climbers, aspiring politicians, and brilliant grafters. Military academies are often jokingly referred to as schools of political science, and the officer himself arouses combined scorn and fright among intellectuals and civilian political figures. Whatever the degree of its professional competence may be (and I am no judge of such matters), the consistently active role of the Argentine armed forces in politics since 1930 has undoubtedly reduced their prestige and given rise to the same general depreciation of "brass hats" heard in all other Latin American countries. The problem is complicated not only because of the arguments concerning military interventions *per se* but also because the officers themselves are divided in political belief across a very wide range of ideologies. Strong Nazi and Fascist influence is unmistakable in varying degree throughout the entire period from the revolutionary ascendancy of General José F. Uriburu in 1930 to the fall of Juan Domingo Perón in 1955. The bitter fact that the latter was overthrown by dissidents within the armed forces with very little direct aid from civilians has created a debt of gratitude which anti-militarist democrats are not attitudinally well-equipped to handle.* From late 1955 to early 1958 the political affairs of the nation were guided by military men, the dominant groups among them determined to rebuild constitutional government. The civilian debt has become larger rather than smaller.

The retirement of the military from political administration did not automatically remove them from politics. But there are many different kinds of political intromission. In Chapter II above there is a discussion of the historical range of relationships in Latin America between government and the military. Briefly restated, I posited six sets of possible

---

* I do not mean to minimize the great risks taken by many civilians in opposing Perón or the many cases of heroic sacrifice which might be cited. But the fact remains that the job of his deposition was done at firsthand by the military.

relationships: first, that in which the military simply govern in caudillistic form; second, the modern variant, a military trustee government; third, the military as general orienters of policy; fourth, the situation in which no government can continue to exist without at least the tacit consent of the military; fifth, the military as a professionalized group exercising veto power only in those matters affecting the immediate interests of the armed forces; and last, the Costa Rican situation in which the military has ceded its functions to the police. The expressed hope of many Argentine officers is that they will be able to maintain their position as a guaranteeing and orienting group, the third possibility mentioned above. This role of tacit gray eminence with bandoliers will not be a simple one, the temptation to greater power being so ever-present. In truth, however, the Argentine armed forces have consistently contained all Argentine governments since 1955. The task has not been an easy one, punctuated as it has been with many serious military incidents whose cost in national pride is not to be ignored.

The Argentine political disasters of the last thirty-five years in which the military men have acted out so decisive a part have given rise to much discussion as to the formal role of the military, as distinct from what may develop as its functional status as discussed above. The strong German influence in the development of the modern Argentine army has favored the view that an army should be composed of professionals who simply obey orders. But the belief is now growing that the military rather should be bound intimately to those parts of the citizenry which propose democratic procedures, thus breaking the armed forces' social quarantine. The former entirely professionally oriented army has been called one submitted to "objective control," the latter one held in "subjective control." * If "objective control" is gained by isolating the armed forces from the currents of national opinion, "subjective control" is maintained in the opposite manner through seeing that officers are closely identified with daily life by reducing emphasis on professionalism and cutting down the contrast between military and civilian.

These designations are of only partial analytical use; they serve best to tell us what the ideal of service may be at any given time. What is wrong with these categories is that armed forces can never be divorced from the societies in which they develop, their influence and their power being always relative to that displayed by other social institutions in terms of the values of the time. For example, it may be a social value that the military be completely "objectively" controlled. But that value depends for its maintenance on how much it is believed by all

* See Samuel P. Huntington, *The Soldier and the State,* Cambridge: Harvard University Press, 1957.

groups (not only by the military but also by those who are tempted to manipulate the military) as well as on the amount of power other political groups display. It is obvious that if political parties lose themselves in factionalism and irrationality, the military gains power without the purchase of a single new rifle. And conversely, a complex and healthy set of democratic institutions creates a system of checks within which the armed forces can remain most legitimately professional.

To content oneself with the statement that military interventionism is *the* sickness of Argentine—and also of Latin American—politics is really to make little contribution beyond feeling the patient's forehead. Let us take an example. In 1955 when the Peronist regime was terminated, the Mexican press was almost unanimously anti-Perón and at the same time severely opposed to the manner in which he was overthrown; i.e., by a *cuartelazo,* or barracks revolt. The Argentines reacted so strongly to the Mexican opinion that a special emissary was sent to explain the case. In truth, it *is* unhappy that Perón fell not because of the *brazos caídos* (literally, fallen arms, a picturesque way of saying "sitdown strike") of the citizenry engaged in a withdrawal of their tacit consent to be governed, or even of a more active struggle against tyranny. But the fact that the dictator fell because of a military movement does not automatically mean that evil ends were being served. What it does mean is that the normal play of politics before Perón was not complex and healthy enough to insure against the rise of a demagogue promising to respond to the demands of major segments of the population theretofore falling on the deaf ears of those guarding the "normal" channels of access to the political institution. And it also means that during Perón's decade it was impossible to organize the means to wean away the strong popular support for the *caudillo* in the unions and limited parts of the middle class. The military, then, truly *represented* differing sections of the body politic at differing times, once to support Perón and once to overthrow him. In general the same individuals were not concerned in both movements, but the manner in which the power was employed was similar.

The good intentions of military and civilians are not enough, then, to prevent further direct use of military force in governing, despite the general belief among many current leaders of the armed services that they are not really very good at government and that the job should be left to civilians. It is sometimes said, even by officers, that "any civilian government is better than any military government." Such beautiful sentiments can be made to come true only when the political machine functions for all power groups and remains responsive to the legitimate desires of just about everybody concerned.

There have been many polemics in Argentina about this matter, perhaps none of greater interest than that provoked in September of 1956 with the publication of a speech by General Luis Rodolfo González, the one which is presented here in translation. General González is an old professional soldier who had survived the first years of Peronism. But he participated in the badly organized military plot of September 28, 1951, and so was of course retired and made the object of political persecution. But Perón took pains not to subject his military opponents to torture or death, so many of his earlier antagonists could wait for better days, either within Argentina or in exile. At the time of the speech General González was the "interventor" in the chain of official newspapers established by the successor regime to the Perón government. Other military figures attacked the general for his views, and the polemic still continues to a certain extent. Mention of these objections will be made in the footnotes when fitting.

The speech and the annotations necessary to make it understandable follow. The reading of it will become easier after the first few pages.

IDEAS CONTRARY TO THE SPIRIT OF MAY AND THEIR REPERCUSSION IN ARGENTINE POLITICAL LIFE
A MILITARY OPINION AT THE SERVICE
OF DEFINITIVE PACIFICATION[*]

The day after the May Revolution, the Argentines who had carried it out divided themselves into Morenistas and Saavedristas.[1]

[*] *Note:* This speech was delivered informally and so is not a highly polished document. I have attempted to retain this character in the translation. In addition, I have done no editing. What is clumsy in English was clumsy in Spanish; I tried to make a few passages clearer in English than in Spanish, but it is natural that in a talk in some part impromptu there will be places of confusion. I tampered little with the punctuation, broke down no sentences, combined no sentences, and even attempted to maintain Spanish idioms where possible. My reason for sacrificing style to content is that there is intrinsic interest in the speech as an instrument of cultural expression, as I indicated in my introduction. It is also for this reason that I resisted the temptation to omit certain passages.

It should go without saying that the fact that I have translated this speech indicates nothing concerning my agreement or disagreement with its contents. Its connotative wealth is enough to justify its translation.

In these notes I will offer explanatory material concerning only Argentine matters. The reader will have to supply his own judgments in regard to General González's references to Europe.

[1] The first Argentine government as such was organized on May 25, 1810, after the deposition of the Spanish viceroy. The imprisonment of the Spanish king, Ferdinand VII, by the French was seized upon by Argentine rebels to wrest authority from the powerless viceroy, an action taken presumably not in the name of national independence but rather to protect true Spanish interests against the French. The date is celebrated as one of Argentina's two independence days. Definitive Argentine independence from Spain was proclaimed in 1816 at Tucumán.

The "government" of May 25 was in reality a governing *junta*, or council, presided over by Cornelio Saavedra. The two secretaries of the first junta were Mariano Moreno and Juan José Paso; the other members were Juan José Castelli, Manuel Belgrano, Miguel de Azcuénaga, Domingo Matheu, Juan Larrea, and

The Morenistas, says Luís V. Varela in his *Constitutional History of the Argentine Republic*,[2] embodied the central idea of the thinking of the May Revolution; that is, of the independent fatherland, institutionally organized under a form of government whose regimen would permit a regular turnover of elected officials, the responsibility of public officers, and the real exercise of the collective and individual political and civil rights of the people and of the citizenry; while the Saavedristas, ". . . DISCIPLINED [all upper case and emphasis are the General's throughout] within the Government Junta,"[3] persisted in their determination to stay in power because at that time they did not have "full confidence in the people," as they themselves later confessed. It is what induced the officers of Patricios to deny Moreno entry into the headquarters where a banquet celebrating the victory of Suipacha was being served, and what convinced Lieutenant Duarte to ask that Saavedra should occupy a throne and wear a crown.[4]

Manuel Alberti—the first of a large group of *próceres,* or founding fathers. Saavedra and Moreno were politically the two most important members. The former was inclined toward a continuation of Iberian politics; *i.e.,* authoritarian and centralized control. The latter was a firebrand who also wanted centralization, but in addition stood for the full gamut of French Revolutionary ideals, thus earning himself the title of Jacobin. Both, of course, favored independence from Spain.

The "Spirit of May," then, is a term used to signify popular social change: the sovereignty of the people, civil liberties, "popular culture," public education, and so on. Belgrano, for example, in pursuit of these ideals, contributed from his own funds to help establish public schools, and Moreno inaugurated a public library and founded an official organ, *La Gaceta de Buenos Aires,* to publicize these political views and give an example of freedom of the press.

[2] *La Historia Constitucional de la República Argentina,* Buenos Aires, 1910.

[3] The first junta did not succeed by any means in assuming control over the entire viceroyalty of the Plata. Within less than a month of its establishment, for example, Córdoba and Montevideo both refused to extend their recognition, despite the fact that at this time the junta was still governing in the name of the king. Paraguay and Upper Peru (now Bolivia) also soon refused recognition. Thus began the tug of war between Buenos Aires and the interior which tones all Argentine political history.

[4] Resistance from the provinces to the rule of the Buenos Aires junta was obviously based on a realistic appraisal of the municipal nature of the new government and a belief in the centralizing tendencies especially of the Morenistas. Delegates elected to the junta began to arrive from the interior toward the end of June, 1810, and most of them grouped themselves with the conservative Saavedristas.

In order to subdue the separatist movements in Upper Peru, Paraguay, and Uruguay, three armies were sent out almost immediately after the news of the resistance of these areas reached Buenos Aires. Some trained military persons were available, for after the repelling of a British invasion of Buenos Aires in 1806 a civil militia had been formed. These units were organized on a democratic basis, electing their own officers who in turn named their own over-all commanding generals. There were five battalions of creoles (persons of Spanish descent born in the New World) and four of Patricios, composed of persons from Buenos Aires and answerable to the Assembly of the city, and another called the Arribeños,

Later, after Moreno was dead,[5] that same anti-democratic sentiment induced a Saavedrista, member of the First Junta, to solicit the dissolution by force of the Patriotic Society, the first Argentine political organization of popular origin and republican procedures, formed by the Morenistas.[6]

These two occurrences, following the mutiny of April 6, 1811,[7] were the first blows against the spirit of May which, after long vicissitudes, ended by disappearing from the scene under the attacks of the first tyranny.[8]

composed of natives of the interior. One of the battalions of Patricios was made up of Negroes and Indians; of the total strength of 8,151 of the Patricios in 1806, some 3,000 were Spaniards.

The Battle of Suipacha was the first victory of Argentine rebel arms against the Spaniards, accomplished by the column sent to Upper Peru. It took place on November 7, 1810, but on May 13 of the following year victory in the Battle of Huaqui fell to the Spaniards, who succeeded in dispersing the rebel troops completely and in nullifying for the time being the victory at Suipacha.

On December 13, 1810, when the victory at Suipacha was being celebrated in the headquarters of the regiment of Patricios in the capital, Moreno was refused entry either by a guard who did not recognize him (according to one account) or on the express orders of the officers of the regiment (according to other versions). In the course of the banquet Lieutenant of Hussars Anastasio Duarte gained his only historical fame by a drunken toast to Saavedra, head of Patricios. Duarte proposed that his chief be crowned emperor of America! When Moreno learned of the toast, he became infuriated and forced a measure through the junta prohibiting any honors for individual members of the government, obviously a direct attack on Saavedra.

[5] The showdown between Saavedra and Moreno came in late December, immediately after the banquet and its sequel mentioned above. Moreno was in favor of calling a constitutional assembly for the establishment of a formally independent government; the Saavedristas opposed the action as premature and, reinforced by the representatives of the interior, succeeded in voting down Moreno's proposal and also in censuring him for an earlier decree closing public posts to native Spaniards. Moreno resigned from the junta, but the resignation was not formally accepted, he instead being sent on a diplomatic mission to England. He left Argentina on January 24, 1811, and died on the high seas March 4. He was thirty-two years old.

[6] The Patriotic Society (also called the Club de Marcos, because its headquarters was in the Café de Marcos just off the central square in Buenos Aires) was composed of Morenistas in opposition to the judgments of the "big junta" (the *Junta Grande*); i.e., the original junta as enlarged by the provincial delegates allied with the Saavedristas. The Society was denominated a literary club to disguise its purposes, but its design was, of course, entirely political.

[7] This is the date of the Saavedrista coup, after which the Patriotic Society was disbanded and the Morenistas purged from the big junta. *La Gaceta,* now in the hands of the Saavedristas, defended the action by saying it was taken against a group of "fanatics" who wanted to establish a "furious democracy" and subvert religion and the social order.

[8] The term "the first tyranny" refers to the period of the government of Juan Manuel Rosas from 1829 to 1852. Ricardo Levene, one of Argentina's most prolific contemporary historians, divides the history of his country into the following periods: from 1810 to 1820—the organization of independence; from 1820 to

Found again after Caseros,[9] it survived until 1930 through the period of the struggles inflamed by the continuing organization of the Republic; then, with the revolution of September 6 crippled,[10] it received another blow and, *wavering thereafter,* again disappeared from the surface with the second tyranny.[11]

Now, thanks to the Liberating Revolution,[12] we hope to embrace it again forever.

In the desire of contributing my grain of sand to such a praiseworthy end, I have accepted the invitation to give this speech, *which I am directing especially to my comrades in the Army.* They also come from the people and for that reason they carry with them from their origins the various tendencies into which the people are divided. WE MAY SAY, TO CONTINUE THE SAME THREAD TAKEN UP TO BEGIN WITH, THAT THEY JOIN THE RANKS ALSO DIVIDED INTO MORENISTAS AND SAAVEDRISTAS. In other words, men consciously and subconsciously democratic, and men who, at best, think themselves democratic but who are not because their subconscious is blocked by appreciations incompatible with the true republican feeling of our authentic tradition.

The integral democrat (I am referring to one who is so both con-

---

1829—caudillistic anarchy; from 1829 to 1852—centralistic caudillistic tyranny in the name of federalism; from 1852 to 1880—the fall of Rosas and the struggle to achieve a national state; and from 1880 on, modern Argentina. Rosas is the Ivan the Terrible of Argentine history, governing in the name of federalism, but in reality the *caudillo* of *caudillos,* not a peer but an overlord.

[9] The Battle of Monte Caseros, February 3, 1852, in which the forces of Rosas were defeated by a combined army of Brazilians, Uruguayans, and Argentines from Entre Ríos, Corrientes, and Buenos Aires.

[10] The revolution of September 6, 1930, when the military under Lt. General José Félix Uriburu overthrew the constitutionally elected president, Radical Hipólito Yrigoyen. The latter, famous leader of his party and for the second time president of his country, was old and weak by this time, and there was much popular discontent before the inability of the Radicals to carry out their program. I presume General González uses the word "crippled" because it was hoped that the army would put into practice the democratic reforms promised by the impotent Radicals. Instead Uriburu early demonstrated himself a neo-Fascist and even went so far as to design a new, corporative constitution for Argentina. Uriburu ceded to a conservative government in 1931 after fraudulent elections, initating a period of so-called "patriotic fraud" which finally came to an end in 1943 with the open assumption of power by the military.

[11] The reference here is to Perón, whose period may be dated either from June 4, 1943, when Perón was one of a group of army officers which seized the government, or from October 17, 1945, when Perón emerged unmistakably as the country's central political figure. On September 19, 1955, Perón fell.

[12] The "Liberating Revolution" was proclaimed in the city of Córdoba on September 16, 1955; victory was gained on September 19, and General Eduardo Lonardi moved into Buenos Aires as provisional president on September 23. In turn, Lonardi was ousted on November 13 by military men who considered him too prone to forgive Peronists and too pro-Church. He was replaced by General

sciously and subconsciously) is an *impersonalist;* he believes little in men and much in institutions, WHICH HE RESPECTS MORE IN THEIR SUBSTANCE than in their form; he believes in the legitimate succession of elected officials, because he does not believe any public servant irreplaceable and he has faith in the succession which the electorate may decide; he does not fear ideas contrary to his or public acts so opposed and therefore rejoices before the spectacle offered by the genuine exercise of individual and collective liberties; he is absolutely lacking in social and religious prejudice because within a democracy no one may gain pre-eminence because of his title, his fortune, or his beliefs.

For all of these reasons he thinks that political adversaries should not be cast into jail, that the government should not dedicate itself to favoring religious beliefs, and that ideas are not quieted by choking off their free expression but rather by opposing them with new and better ideas.

He who is NOT an integral democrat (although he thinks that he is and proclaims it to the four winds) is a *personalist,* and therefore when he finds a man he considers appropriate to satisfy the achievement of his aspirations, "that person becomes transformed into an indispensable condition for governing," and from then on "he looks only for the means of perpetuating that person's presence in office," and of assuring him a maximum of power, even though to do so may damage and even destroy fundamental institutions. It is that he has no faith in the citizenry, unless it demonstrates itself to be tractable and submissive. If not, one must silence the ideas of the citizens, for they are always daring and turbulent, if not impious, when permitted to graze among their beliefs.

These factors so far analyzed, which conspire against the integrally democratic formation of the citizen who later is incorporated into the army, may be qualified as intrinsic conditions inherent to the nature of everyone. But there are others which undoubtedly weigh with greater force and which in my opinion are:

a) The high percentage of immigrants and the countries from which they come.[13]

Pedro Eugenio Aramburu, who headed the government at the time this speech was made. He turned over the office to his legally elected successor, Arturo Frondizi, on May 1, 1958. In representation of the navy, Admiral P. I. Rojas continued as provisional vice-president through the Lonardi episode and the Aramburu incumbency.

[13] In 1914 almost a third of the population was foreign born, and in certain areas, such as Greater Buenos Aires, the proportion was as high as 50 per cent. By the time of the 1947 census the picture had radically changed, the number of foreign born being 2,435,000, or 15.4 per cent of the population. Some 700,000 new immigrants arrived in the seven years following 1947 for which there are reliable

b) Colonialist propaganda.

c) Imperialist currents.

Countries distinguished by the firmness of their democratic institutions provide no, or very few, emigrants. Their people are too happy at home! [14]

Therefore, more important even than their great numbers, there weighs on the ideological formation of our people the origin of those immigrants who in their great majority come from states not exactly data, the total number of foreign born in Argentina rising to 2,830,000, but their proportion in the total population remaining more or less the same.

FOREIGN POPULATION OF ARGENTINA: 1869–1954

Year	Foreigners	Foreigners per 100 pop.	Foreigners per 100 Native Argentines
1869 (census)	210,300	12.1	13.8
1895 (census)	1,004,500	25.4	34.0
1914 (census)	2,358,000	29.9	42.7
1920 (estimated)	2,155,400	24.0	31.6
1930 (estimated)	2,834,300	23.5	30.8
1940 (estimated)	2,627,800	18.4	22.5
1947 (census)	2,435,900	15.4	18.1
1954 (estimated)	2,831,000	15.1	17.8

Source: Gino Germani, *Estructura social de la Argentina,* Buenos Aires, 1955, p. 81.

Because immigration slowed to a trickle for almost twenty years (from 1930 to 1948), the population has become somewhat more homogeneous. Some 83.5 per cent of the native-born population has at least one parent also born in the country.

FOREIGN BORN POPULATION BY COUNTRY OF ORIGIN, 1954

Italians	1,005,400
Spaniards	820,600
Paraguayans	127,700
Poles	114,800
Russians	87,300
Chileans	69,300
Germans	58,500
Uruguayans	56,000
Brazilians	52,000
Others	438,100
TOTAL	2,829,700

Source: Gino Germani, *op. cit.,* p. 89.

It is a popular interpretation in Argentina that the ranks of army officers are largely composed of middle-class persons and that it is further necessary to distinguish between those of established and traditional middle-class origins and the children of immigrants, reputed to be highly status-conscious social climbers. The latter are said to have formed the hard core of the Peronist military group. There is no statistical proof of this assumption.

[14] Although this statement is far from universally true, Argentine experience is not too far away from this opinion. See the second chart given in Note 13 above.

known for insuring those governed the full enjoyment of free institutions.[15]

Many Argentine citizens are thus born into homes where the parents do not emphasize and even deprecate our republican institutions, only to exalt in all their forms those of their country of origin; and outside the home relationships usually of the same origins, plus relatives who are also foreigners, contribute to making up the climate wherein the child and the adolescent nurtures his ideas.

It is also in these surroundings, dedicated ARDENTLY TO AMASSING A FORTUNE AND MUCH LESS TO BEING PATRIOTIC, here—as Ramos Mejía says in *Rosas and His Times*,[16] "the audacious imperialism of the men of the Assembly of 1813 is astounding." It is that hopes and aspirations, the regular change of elected officeholders, and innovations in the field of ideas DISTURB GOOD BUSINESS, and they therefore look for something "permanent, unmovable, whatever may be the form it may take."

And within this "foreignizing" medium there exists a current even more poisonous for democratic ideas. It is that fomented principally by Spanish clerics and proclericals of the same origin, very numerous among us and very influential among Argentine youth, some as heads of families and the others as educators and special pleaders. The former, availing themselves of the Hispanic glories of the discovery and the conquest, and the latter of the customs for which they feel nostalgia, SYSTEMATICALLY COMBAT ANY LIBERAL GOVERNMENT WHICH EVER HAS OR WILL EXIST; or, adding up to the same thing, all those which have governed the country since 1810 BEFORE AND AFTER ROSAS. And so, by putting their sentiments before all other reasoning, this clerical current is anti-democratic and, in consequence, does not wish to reconcile itself in any way with the liberal ideas which were the source of inspiration for our glorious May 25.[17]

[15] The author is, of course, referring to Italy and Spain.

[16] *Rosas y su tiempo*, Buenos Aires, 1952, 3 vols.
The constitutional assembly of 1813 was a convocation representing a temporary resurgence of the Morenistas. Ramos Mejía presumably calls it "imperialistic" because no residency requirements were demanded for the delegates representing the several provinces and because the assembly rejected a crucial set of election results which put the Morenista majority in jeopardy. The assembly never produced a constitution, but numerous laws were adopted, including the suppression of Spanish symbols, titles of nobility, and forced labor. They also adopted May 25 as independence day and commissioned the composition of the Argentine national anthem.

[17] Problems of church and state have agitated Argentine politics from the first moments of independence. Conservatism, the Church, large landholders, the Oligarchy have been the constant bugbears first of traditional Liberalism, and then later of the Radicals and in this century of the Socialists and other parties of the left. Freemasonry, too, early assumed importance among élite groups, many of the nation's most distinguished leaders (such as San Martín himself) having been Masons. The matter of church-state relations and political affiliation became con-

The task, then, consists in combating these ideas and the men who sustain them; and the best form of undertaking the task and the most effective for the inspiration of credulous youth is the one already mentioned. It is for that reason that those addicted to this current are fanatics, in the religious aspect as well as the Hispanic one. Because of this, also, in spite of their being Argentines, they yearn for the colonial epoch. And therefore, finally, they are called "Colonials."

To point out the fallacy of the paladins of this current, I shall limit myself to commenting succinctly on the best-known deeds of that Argentine personality that they hold as a standard-bearer.

The reference is to don Juan Manuel de Rosas, who in 1810 was of the same age as Lavalle.[18] The latter enrolled in the Regiment of Mounted Grenadiers of General San Martín and fought for fifteen years throughout Argentina, Chile, Peru, and Ecuador; meanwhile ROSAS, WHO HASTENED TO FIGHT AGAINST THE BRITISH DURING THE INVASIONS, PRETENDED THAT A WAR OF INDEPENDENCE WAS NOT GOING ON. It is that he was a "Colonialist" and therefore preferred the continuance of Spanish domination in America to the freedom of his fatherland.

Nevertheless, he served to foment anti-democracy, pointing to himself as the only guardian and the most jealous defender of the sovereignty of a fatherland to whose liberation from foreign domination he did not contribute.

It is that in this matter, too, they proceed propagandistically in order to proselytize, for while the "Colonials" were carrying out a confusionist campaign, combating with all their means the English who despoiled us of the Malvinas.[19] they forget to say that those islands were

fused under Perón, who maintained a close alliance with the Church while wooing labor groups, theretofore led largely by anti-clericals. The alliance began to fray after 1951 and finally broke altogether in the last year of the regime, when a divorce law was passed. The burning of churches brought chagrin to many of Perón's traditional enemies, for they too were largely anti-clericals and so approved the open battle going on between Church and State. Some commentators think Perón was overthrown primarily because of Church opposition and that the armed forces merely institutionalized a *coup* fundamentally accomplished by religious leaders. My personal opinion is that this interpretation is simplistic and, therefore, incorrect.

[18] Juan Lavalle was a general who led an insurrection against the governor of Buenos Aires Province in 1828. Initially successful, Lavalle was defeated in 1829 by Rosas, thereafter flying into exile. His fame among the "democrats" rests, of course, on his early opposition to the so-called "Bloody" Rosas. He is also known as impetuous and foolhardy. An act for which many do not forgive him is his having ordered the execution of a defeated governor of Buenos Aires, a deed which served to inflame the Federalists and aid them in their eventual victory. He was accidentally killed in 1841 after a decade of constant opposition to Rosas.

[19] Las Malvinas, better known in English as the Falkland Islands, have long been in dispute between Argentina and Great Britain. On January 3, 1830, the English frigate "Clio" came to the islands, dispossessed the Argentine government, and established the colony which still causes irredentist sentiments.

occupied during the political and military domination of the tyrant, who did not therefore estrange himself from the British minister, in whose house he lodged after the defeat of Caseros, then embarking in a British ship to sail to England and live there until the last day of his life. Nor do they remember, certainly, the case pointed out in *La Nación* for July eighth of this year [1956] where it is mentioned that on the night of the twenty-fourth to the twenty-fifth of May, 1839, there was a gala ball in the Fort,[20] not to commemorate the historic event of 1810, which passed unnoticed, but rather in homage to her Gracious Britannic Majesty, Queen Victoria of England.

And lastly, I shall go to the very bottom of the problem in referring to the influences which during the second half of the last century and up to the end of the last war reached us from several nations in full expansionism, the most forcefully pressing of these being Germany and Japan.

These currents are those which have most perturbed Argentine democratic life, in part coming through a certain sector of the populace, but more so from within the ranks of the army, where infiltration was facilitated for the reasons which soon we shall see. Even though, in civil as well as military circles—and similarly here as in the rest of Latin America and other parts of the underdeveloped world—these ideas have always been presented to the incautious under the very gracious mantle of anti-imperialism, when the proposition really was no other than that of the introduction of new imperialisms.[21]

I hasten to state that imperialisms do not alarm me so long as they are not imposed under the muzzles of cannon. Therefore I do not propose to censure nations which because of their demographic growth and notable progress need to expand and try to secure the best conditions possible in the countries most appropriate for the gaining of their ends, which are, generally, the least developed.

Because the fault in that case lies not exactly with the foreigner peacefully infiltrating, but rather with the nationals who do not see the game or lend themselves to it.

We all know that for a long time the great western democracies have been exercising a strong gravitational pull.

This obliged the major powers which developed in the second half of the last century to occupy themselves with displacing them to get room for their own expansion. To that end the most effective means is war. But so long as such war is not declared, the best conditions possible to

---

[20] Situated on the Plaza de Mayo, where the seat of the executive (the *Casa Rosada*) is still to be found.

[21] The author is referring to the Argentine nationalist movements and their obvious sympathy for Germany and Italy.

assure eventual success and then to exploit it must be prepared; that is, to get allies or at least to find sympathizers.

In consequence peaceful and friendly penetration and along with it propaganda constitute, as is known, the most effective weapons. For the rest, we also know that propaganda is that much more effective if, while it is conquering initiates for its own cause, it also succeeds in taking them from the other side, and for that it is necessary as well as indispensable that this task be in charge of nationals, because in any other way the game would be too gross and easily seen.

There is here to be found, so far as I am concerned, the origin of our *nazionalismo*, with a "z." [22] The same phenomenon which is often confused with colonialism, because both have a common denominator: the preachment against countries where liberty has its greatest hold, presented as damaging to our tradition. They then take advantage of a field in which it is easy to persuade: HATRED FOR THE FOREIGNERS. And one asks oneself, from whom did those "NATIVES" descend who don't have the names of "INDIANS"? The secret is this: for them the ones who directly or indirectly inspired the ideals of Moreno, the work of Rivadavia,[23] and the great institutional creations of the governments following Caseros are FOREIGNERS. This would not have to worry us if the matter ended there. But the worst is just beginning, because this anti-imperialism is nothing other than—as I have already said—a new Trojan horse, very practical for introducing into our midst other imperialisms NO LESS AMBITIOUS ALTHOUGH MUCH MORE VIOLENT WHEN THEY THINK THEY CAN ENJOY IMPUNITY. With "The Foreign" (difficult word, so often repeated in the last few years) the same thing occurs: THEY CALL EVERYTHING FOREIGN WHICH COMES FROM THE GREAT WESTERN DEMOCRACIES, ESPECIALLY DEMOCRACY ITSELF: because the more you succeed in weakening democracy, the greater are the probabilities of success for the opposing totalitarianism.

With capital coming from free nations something similar happens. If such capital comes here to stay, it is for the purpose of carrying off our riches and enslaving our sovereignty. As for the others, ON THE OTHER

[22] "Nationalism" is spelled with a "c" in Spanish (*nacionalismo*) and with a "z" in Italian.

[23] Bernardino Rivadavia was the secretary of the Executive Government (more commonly known as the "First Triumvirate") which took power after the dissolution of the "big junta" on September 16, 1811. Because the triumvirate is commonly held to be a liberal reaction against the conservative junta, Rivadavia is admired by partisans of Moreno. After a relatively long career, including the carrying out of diplomatic missions of some importance, Rivadavia was elected the first president of the United Provinces in 1826; he is thus the first president of the Argentine Republic as such. In the face of an unfortunate war with Brazil and the intransigence of the provincial *caudillos,* Rivadavia resigned his office in 1827. He has earned the dislike of nationalists who deplore the defeat in the war with Brazil and the respect of those who admire his legal and educational reforms.

HAND, THAT CAPITAL COMES AS CAPITAL GOODS; IT THUS ENJOYS SYM-
PATHY AND SOMETIMES EVEN PROTECTION.[24]

This is the tendentious and without doubt well-conducted preaching
of the "NAZIONALISTAS," because by hiding behind patriotism it is
easier for them to catechize young men with a vocation for the military
career. These then incorporate themselves into the army, bringing from
the street a sentiment of ill will toward the great democracies which—
according to them—"oppress us," and at the same time an enormous
dose of sympathy toward those other great foreign powers, because
propaganda has been designed to present them as victims of the same
oppression.

I have given this analysis to demonstrate that there are serious anti-
democratic tendencies within the Argentine people themselves BEFORE
they enter the ranks and make up our army. And if in the army there
exist currents opposed to the spirit of May, AND UNFORTUNATELY THERE
ARE, their reason for being does not pertain specifically to the army because in great measure they were picked up in the civilian circles from
which come our officers, that is to say, from all the social levels making
up the Argentine citizenry.

If we look at the matter in its origins, then, no country in the world
should have a corps of officers more democratic than ours, since all citizens have the same chance to enter and to be graduated from the Military College.

Nevertheless, looking at the ideology of the candidates who aspire to
go through it, I dare say that the immense majority is not identified
with Moreno and, therefore, with the historical periods in which he
succeeded in imposing the force of his spirit.

The reason is simple: the political life of those periods, as occurs in
all democracies, has been somewhat turbulent because of the agitation
of passions, free discussions, public demonstrations, and other characteristics which distinguish republican and representative life. This is
not very attractive for the young man of military vocation, for if he
feels attracted to a military career it is because he puts order and discipline before turbulence and freedom of will.

It was natural, then, that even at the dawn of our nation, Argentine
officers with Duarte at their head prohibited Moreno from entering the
military quarters while they were banqueting Saavedra inside, proposing to crown the latter to insure their indefinite stay in power, and that
many of our present officers prefer the disciplined regime imposed by
Rosas to the at times anarchic order which preceded it.

From the exclusively military point of view, that sentiment of order

---

[24] This is an obvious reference to the welcome extended during the Perón era
to many Italian and German firms. The case of Mercedes-Benz is notorious.

and discipline which characterizes the military profession, far from being undesirable, constitutes a guarantee for the entire nation, for an officer corps so trained always has a natural tendency toward obedience, and even in great crises they will maintain their unity, cohesion, and discipline, preventing themselves from falling into disorder and anarchy.

It is for these reasons that those civilian characteristics the aspirant brings with him when he joins the ranks are emphasized through all possible means and put to the test in tiring duties, under conditions which go to the limits of human endurance for long periods of time.

Thus is formed the personality of the cadet who learns blindly to obey the smallest insinuation of command without discussion, rapidly, in order and silence. On the other hand, if his spirit constantly rebels against this renouncing of his own will, the man has not the necessary attributes, he is a "Republican" in cadet jargon, and without further ado he is dismissed.

As you can appreciate from what has so far been said, it is difficult to take a citizen accustomed to a free life, convert him into a disciplined officer, and at the same time preserve the democratic sentiments with which he comes in off the streets; and how much more difficult to inculcate them when he comes in without them!

This problem does not exist under a totalitarian regime. The dictator saves himself the trouble by first converting the entire country into an enormous barracks where, someone has astutely said, "Everything not prohibited is obligatory."

But when the man comes from a civilian atmosphere of the kind we want for our people, where the citizen fully exercises the power of expressing his ideas and freely employing his will, the emotional training of the military man in the army has, from the disciplinary point of view, demands which are not so pressing in the other branches of the armed forces. For in the last few wars great physical demands or fatigue have not been demanded from the latter. In addition the individual acts as part of a team under the glance or the direct command of all his chiefs; and when he fights aboard ship, he necessarily goes where the commander of the ship or the airplane takes him.

On the other hand, on the battlefield THE SOLDIER WHO IS ALMOST TOTALLY IN HIS OWN HANDS CAN CONQUER FATIGUE AND DRAG HIMSELF FORWARD ACROSS MACHINE-GUNNED TERRITORY ONLY IF THE DISCIPLINE INCULCATED WITH AN IRON HAND MAKES HIM PUT OBEDIENCE ABOVE HIS OWN INSTINCT OF SELF-PRESERVATION. Nevertheless, officers of the highest ranks do not comply with their professional duty in a nation such as ours if within the units we establish we do not succeed—as I have already said—in containing those military virtues and reconciling them

WITH THE DEMOCRATIC SENTIMENT THAT THE MAN BRINGS TO THE RANKS, OR FORMING IT FOR HIM IF HE DOES NOT BRING IT. The point is TO MAKE AN OFFICER WITHOUT UNMAKING THE CITIZEN, OR IN KNOWING HOW TO DO THE TWO THINGS AT THE SAME TIME.

In summary, we can say that in our country there exist basically two factors which have a great deal of weight in preventing our officers from identifying themselves with Argentine democratic traditions:

1. Their popular origin which molds them among genuine men of the people, among whom exist those identified with the spirit of May and those not so. The latter are probably greater in number, because their predispositions toward order and obedience without discussion are constitutive elements of the military vocation.

2. Training within and immediately after the Military College which obliges them to develop those characteristics even more in MILITARY INSTRUCTION AS SUCH.

I have emphasized "MILITARY INSTRUCTION AS SUCH" because nothing forces anyone in the other kind of instruction—the intellectual—to do the same. On the contrary, in this kind of teaching carried out in the classroom, the cadet—save in externals—ceases to be a military person and converts himself into a student who reads, listens, reasons, and discusses, and therefore it is there where ONE MUST REMAKE THE CITIZEN WHO HOURS BEFORE WAS UNMADE ON THE PARADE GROUNDS.

And here begins, gentlemen, my big disagreement with the upper military levels of my fatherland, who (at least in the last forty years, the time I have spent in the army) never bothered themselves with this aspect I am pointing out with any of the zeal that its extreme gravity demands.

Worse, save for the orations and the ceremonies on the occasion of patriotic celebrations, one hears many times in the classroom—especially during classes in civil and military history—attacks against our democratic development, for in the analysis of our historical past it is usual for the professors consciously or subconsciously, "drunk or asleep," as Moreno said, to conspire overtly or covertly against our free institutions; THEY TEACH CIVIL HISTORY BY ACCUSING THE MOST REPRESENTATIVE MEN OF HAVING TOLERATED ALL THE EVIL WE SUFFER AND OF NOT GIVING US ALL THE GOOD WE NEED. This excites the impatient soul of the cadet, and his patriotism predisposes him against our system of constitutional government; at the same time he loses faith in parties and ends up denying the virtues of the majority of our public men.

Simultaneously the professor of military history awakens enthusiasm in an adverse sense by showing the great works and the expeditiousness and shining victories of successful dictators from the most remote times to the present. What they never get around to—BECAUSE THE

COURSES DO NOT DEMAND IT—is pointing out the ephemeral nature of their work and the poverty of their final balance. And when they do so, they study the consequences of his decline in the man himself, but not the state in which he left the country where he carried out his experiment.

If this last were done with seriousness but once, it would be sufficient to destroy the myth in many minds which dream of emulating impossible feats. For this purpose one must deal with the immediate as well as the long-run consequences—a panorama which only a true statesman can see—and not the immediate successes which blind the ingenuous and serve as fuel for demagogic plans.

This with respect to the Military College. But the instruction does not end there, for in reality that is where it only begins. As we all know, it continues during periods of assignment, to culminate finally in the Superior War School, PRINCIPALLY RESPONSIBLE FOR EVERYTHING I AM SAYING, since the teachings inculcated there form, definitively, the body of doctrine for the recruiting, equipping, instruction, and conduct of the whole army, from its nerve center (the General Staff) down to the last soldier who executes a simple order in the most remote post.

Well, then, the founders of the Superior War School—which opened its doors at the beginning of this century—undoubtedly inspired by the purest patriotism and their overwhelming love for the army, wanted it to have the highest military capacity possible. It was, then, natural and patriotic that its professors, its literature, and its doctrine should be imported from the nation which had demonstrated its great mastery in decisive battles of relatively recent wars and which, then, still distinguished itself, in addition, with its brilliant uniforms, its celebrated parades, and its grand maneuvers on the training fields. Even its geographical situation, constrained between two great powers, seemed to be the most indicated to teach us how militarily to resolve our own particular set of problems.[25]

As we shall see, there is no objection at all to any of this. On the contrary, there is nothing more logical than that our old and valiant soldiers, empirically forged in the Paraguayan War and in the desert campaigns,[26] should desire for their successors a scientific and artistic

---

[25] Argentina feels closed in between Chile and Brazil, or at least these are militarily considered the "potential enemy" in maneuvers.

[26] The Paraguayan War involved Brazil, Uruguay, and Argentina against Paraguay. Argentina was pulled into the conflict in April 1865 after having refused permission to the Paraguayan chief of state, López, to move troops across Argentine soil in order to engage the Brazilians with whom Paraguay had been in prior conflict. The war, a particularly bloody and vengeful one, was not over until 1870, leaving Paraguay a devastated country.

There were really two major military undertakings called the Desert Campaigns. The first one took place in 1833, a three-pronged attack against the Indians to

teaching not only superior to what they had received but also in tune with the military solutions of the hour.

From that intellectual point of view, and even in order to cement the highest form of military morale, the action was as unquestionable as it would be vain to attempt any sort of objection.

But what they did not see (it was not easy to see it then) were the far-reaching consequences of another type, because of the fact that war is an art which essentially depends on a state of mind; and therefore, in no way can one separate the intellectual from the spiritual from the ideological.

In this way the Superior War School—which in its first years (until 1914) had only foreign professors, at least in its basic fields, plus the complementary study trips taken by its graduates to the country from which the professors came—necessarily favored the training of General Staff officers spiritually more inclined toward the mentality of their teachers than toward the very reality of our own surroundings.

And so this inclination foreign to Argentine sentiments and at the same time identified with the characteristics of its brilliant teachers STARTED TO BEAR ADVERSE FRUITS some years after our Superior War School was founded and thus ORGANIZED.

At first these fruits were localized within the exclusively military sphere and were therefore without importance in civilian affairs; then they were extended past the ranks of the army and had repercussions in Argentine political life.

Although the first fruits seem divorced from our theme, the reality is not so, for they formed the climate propitious for the development of the second.

Before going deeper into the discussion, therefore, it is advisable to take a few minutes to cast a general glance at the influence of the imported school of thought within the army itself.

The beginning was the supplanting of the traditional Argentine uniforms, those which fill our souls when we see them in engravings or

drive them down to the line of the Río Negro and open up the area of the dry pampa across to the Andes. One prong was provided by the Chileans on their side of the mountains; another pushed south from Mendoza on the eastern slopes of the cordillera, and the third pressed southwestward from Buenos Aires Province, led by Rosas himself. For the time being the campaign was successful for the Argentines.

The second major expedition, and the last, took place in 1878, led by General Julio A. Roca, later elected president of the country. Within three months of the beginning of operations, all major Indian settlements down to the Río Negro were destroyed and occupation troops stationed to consolidate the victory. Because this part of Patagonia was in dispute with the Chileans, who reputedly were giving aid to the Indians for their forays, Roca waited until Chile was engaged in war with Peru and Bolivia to make his move. This second campaign, then, is also presumed to have major international implications.

photographs of the Paraguayan War and the desert campaigns. I should like to refer only to one detail, because a very significant fact has affected me profoundly: the abandonment of the comfortable, elegant, and by then traditional and Argentine-like kepi, in favor of an exotic helmet of patent leather and bronze which, when tried on for the first time by our conscripts, especially the little dark ones from the interior, moved them to HYSTERICAL LAUGHTER. It is that they felt themselves made ridiculous by a strange disguise not fitting to their physiques or their idiosyncrasies, and less even to the old traditions of the *patria*.

It will seem to many that I have paused over a simple detail in order to make a snide criticism. It is not really so, nevertheless, because among the imponderable elements which sustain the morale of armies historical factors play an important part, and among them is the uniform, which although it cannot always be the same in all epochs, because STYLE AND ORGANIC EVOLUTION have their demands, neither should it be made to suffer radical erasures of that which, because it is traditional, fits our customs and touches the hearts of all Argentines.

This first consequence of the new doctrine has been so lamentable that from then on (1911), forty-five years have passed without military personnel having been able to REDISCOVER the uniform which pleases all of us. The proof is that in almost half a century there has not been a single ministry which has not effected substantial changes in our uniforms; and never has one of them been satisfactory, I do not say to the majority of the officers who are still thinking of new changes, but also to the Argentine people, who impassively watch the changes in our dress while they become electrified with patriotic joy as soon as they spy weaving in the distance the historic steel helmets of our glorious grenadiers.

HERE WE HAVE, GENTLEMEN, THE FIRST DEFORMATION OF DEMOCRATIC ARGENTINE SENTIMENT, PRODUCED BY THE ALIENATING ENCUMBRANCE OF THE SITUATION WHICH MOST HONORS THE CITIZEN: THAT OF BEING A SOLDIER AND DISPLAYING THE INSIGNIA OF THE FATHERLAND.

The second aspect was the equipment, transplanted with the same misapprehension and which, thanks to the maneuvers of the year 1914, ordered by the then Minister of War, General D. Gregorio Vélez, could then—after those difficult exercises and the vast information gathered—be again changed for matériel fitting to our probable theater of operations.

Finally we see the gravest consequence, that affecting the mentality of the Argentine officer.

The influence gained in the classrooms of our Superior School by the foreign professors who imparted their teachings until they had to return to their land, because of the eruption of the First World War in 1914, is clearly seen in our officers at the end of the same conflagration as a consequence of the abundant and very well presented bibliography characterized:

a) by showing in masterly fashion—as is very natural and just—the great victories obtained on the eastern front against the armies of the Czar;

b) by pointing out the initial victories gained against the Belgian, English, and French armies during the first month of operations and in justifying the later failure;

c) by depreciating or ignoring the sucesses of the enemy side.

This is perfectly legitimate and nothing can be objected to in the authors or in even the governments which publish the official works.

The censurable is in ourselves. In effect, when any art or science is studied, one should follow the masters or, what amounts to the same thing, those who excel in the specialty and not those who fail in their attempts.

And in war this is even truer, since in this field the one who wins is right. Thus, for example, when we study the campaign of the Andes,[27] we analyze the details of the private life and even, when possible, the intimate thoughts of General San Martín, for nothing should be discarded in the study of the factors which contributed to the success. The study of the other side, on the other hand, is less profound, since the vanquished lacks the rich ores which the genius can offer us.

Well, then, the campaign of the Marne when I was a student was studied in such detailed fashion from the side of the beaten that, in addition to following the operations of all the armies from day to day, we studied not only the military personality of the commander and his immediately subordinate chiefs but also the psychology of low-ranking personnel such as is, in an army of millions, the case of the famous Lieutenant Colonel Hench.

It is that this kind of study, MADE BY THE VANQUISHED, NECESSARILY HAD TO BE PROPAGANDISTIC IN ORDER TO RAISE THEIR NATIONAL AND MILITARY MORALE AGAIN

And so it is that all of the bibliography produced by them after 1918

---

[27] The movement of an army of 5,200 men in 1817 across the Andes from Argentina to Chile to aid in the emancipation from Spanish rule of the west coast of Latin America. The operation was under the command of General José de San Martín, the liberator of the southern portion of South America, as Simón Bolívar gained fame for accomplishing the same task for the north.

tends to create the myth of a genius—Schlieffen—whose design, if followed in its full scale, would have led to complete victory.

On our part it is forgotten—and we don't have to justify anybody or anything—that in war no technician can be considered a great commander if he himself, at the front of his armies, does not demonstrate the truth of his propositions. If San Martín had failed in his undertaking of liberating Chile,[28] he would not be our Great Captain, in spite of the mastery with which he organized and planned the employment of the Army of the Andes. He would have been lacking the final decisive proof for that: triumph over the royalist armies on the battlefield.

In spite of this so simple truth, our General Staff officers are graduated thinking of a man who made plans but never conducted armies in the field as a crowning figure; and at the same time they do not even consider the capacity of the enemy general who finally destroyed those plans and triumphed over them on the field of battle, a neglect which is the consequence of the fact that in the campaign I am referring to, save for one or two glances, they never deepened their study of the side of the victor, not even the professors of transportation in spite of the fact that the movements of the army in the month running between the first days of August and September, 1914, constitute a masterful example of the value in war of well-planned and wisely used railroads. So the sensation I had on being graduated as a General Staff officer— and I believe that many must still think so today—was that the Battle of the Marne was not won by the victors but rather lost by their adversaries. All of this is what propaganda can do when it is developed in a propitious climate, like that of our first institute of superior education.

I will not extend myself further over the for me tendentious manner in which they studied the most important war yet, judging by the higher officers I have seen coming out of the Superior War School up to 1945. But allow me to say that, estranged from the school since that year, whenever I could I have followed this aspect closely through my students, for it is a preoccupation I have had since then. All my opinion is that up to 1954, at least, its graduates, just like the rest of us twenty years earlier, carried in their spiritual baggage a sickening admiration for the group which lost the war of '14 and a type of deprecation I shall call subconscious toward the democratic nations which won it only after four years of struggle, but WHICH KNEW HOW TO DEFINE IT FROM THE FIRST MONTH OF ITS OUTBREAK.

Another campaign also studied with the same anti-democratic tendency is the Paraguayan War. Speaking with students some few years

---

[28] The decisive Battle of Maipú on April 5, 1818, determined the independence of Chile.

ago, I found with real horror that admiration for the tyrant López [29] progressed as the course advanced. And running parallel, admiration diminished almost to deprecation for the moral, intellectual, and military appreciations of President Mitre.[30] And even more horrifying is that I began to see these same students begin suffering as the unhappy denouément of the enemy army approached. They seemed to wish that we had lost the war—perhaps unjustly declared, according to them—so that the man whom they had learned to love with devotion might have won.

I do not say that they twisted the facts, because the study itself is probably objective and true; but partiality to such a degree is possible only if the teaching is inculcated on the basis of the primary acts carried out and not through the distant mists which have clarity only for chosen minds.

As for the last war, then, I shall not relate the form in which it was studied during the past few years because I lack proof; but through conversations with ex-students I have come to the conclusion that nothing has changed from previous periods in the sense I am speaking of.

On the other hand, to finish this aspect, I shall tell the following anecdote, dated more or less fifteen years ago. One day I learned that they had changed the name of "General Headquarters" to "Command" in operational units. The former denomination has been employed for centuries in all the countries of the world, including Germany, from which in those same days there used to arrive communiqués from the "General Headquarters of the Fuehrer." So, since I did not understand the reason for this change, because for me Command (brain) is only one part of a General Headquarters, I occupied myself with learning what had been the cause for this measure, for at the time I was a professor of military organization and I had to explain it to my students. To this end I consulted a lofty high-ranking officer who, because of the nature of his duties, had taken part in the study concerned. The reply, then—and be astonished, gentlemen!—was as follows: he himself had proposed the change because the universal and extremely old designa-

[29] The Paraguayan leader, Solano López, mentioned in note 26 above. A standard argument of the pro-Rosas, pro-López, anti-Mitre school in Argentina is that entrance into the Triple Alliance (Argentina, Brazil, Uruguay) signified surrender to the country's real enemy, Brazil. Paraguay and Uruguay are looked upon by this group as being sister provinces which have strayed. Alliance with the truly foreign enemy against Paraguay, then, was sororicide. It should not be forgotten that Rosas was ousted with the aid of Brazilian troops.

[30] General Bartolomé Mitre, president from 1862 to 1868, and thus responsible for the major political decisions of the Paraguayan War from Argentina's point of view. Mitre was also one of Argentina's foremost historians, one of the first to dedicate himself to working with archival materials.

tion of General Headquarters "had had its origin in the French army and, therefore, it did NOT fit in with our Germanic configuration."

We should not be surprised then if, during those same years, a quite large group of officers, some of whose leaders were the gestators and the principal executors of the last tyranny, formed a secret society, GOU,[31] whose origins, organization, and functioning I do not know, since it is logical that I should not have belonged to it; but I do remember that the principal argument employed by those who wished to proselytize me was that its mystique—as they called it—had been taken from a sect dominant in the totalitarian and ultranationalistic Japan of those years.

With what I have narrated to this point I have scarcely sketched, as I cautioned you, the first adverse effects of that school within the ranks themselves—in other words, the "small causes" which in my opinion have led to the "great effects" beyond them. I now address myself to these, TO THE GREAT EFFECTS.

Let us say that until 1922 nothing happened, beyond the change of uniform, the organic errors evidenced in the great maneuvers of 1914, and other more or less important things, such as the anecdotes I have just told. All of that was the fruit of the education received in our Superior War School, with the orientation I have given above, as well as in consequence of the instruction imparted in all the units in light of the same doctrine because of the zeal and fervor so fitting to the officers in the faithful carrying out of their duties.

But in that year, if my memory serves me, there appeared in Europe the first dictator of totalitarian stripe [32] who, even if he did not really succeed, was able to awaken sympathy in many officers because of the military nature of his system of government and the expeditious form in which he succeeded in putting an end to the Moroccan War.

This sympathy then transformed itself into admiration for the man who in 1923 implanted the same kind of regime in Italy but with more theatricality; and that admiration increased among predisposed spirits until it reached a maximum with the ephemeral conquest of Ethiopia.

---

[31] GOU—*Grupo de Oficiales Unidos*, also sometimes erroneously called *Grupo de Oficiales Unificados*. "United Officers' Group" is the translation. Some say that Perón was the head of the group at the beginning of his rapid political climb, others that he was the secretary. In any event, the GOU, ostensibly copied after a Japanese model, was in reality but a group of pro-Nazi and pro-Fascist officers convinced of their ability to blackmail their superiors into silence or acquiescence by the very fact of their organizational strength, as well as persuaded of their ability to take over and run the national government. They succeeded in aiding in the implantation of military rule in 1943 and in the eventual full success of Perón, but the Group itself was soon subordinated to the personality and power of Perón, falling apart soon after Perón's assumption of the presidency.

[32] The reference is to Diego Primo de Rivera, Spanish dictator who took power in 1922.

And lastly, the supreme lesson of the Nazi dictator whose devotees formed a legion in our ranks and who had "his best student" in the person who until September of 1955 was "The First Worker" among us.[33]

With that mentality in many of our officers, especially those of high rank, THE GRAND EFFECTS make themselves felt after 1930.

We all know, of course, that the intention of General Uriburu, victor in the revolution of that year, was to re-establish the full weight of the Constitution of 1853 which he and with him the majority of the army considered trampled underfoot.[34] Therefore, as soon as the triumph was won, he hastened to be sworn in solemnly before the people, from the balconies of the Government House. We all also know how— unhappily—he saw himself obliged to forsake that thinking, reaching the point of aiding with almost the same solemnity the implanting in the country of a corporative regime, toward which end he proposed a new constitution which he delivered to his successor in the ceremony of transferral of power of February 20, 1932.[35]

The same thing occurred in the case of the high-ranking officers who on June 4, 1943, called out the troops in the Campo de Mayo.[36] At that time they were basically trying to avoid official continuism by means of a fraud already in preparation and to point the Republic again in the direction of a true democracy. The paladins of such patriotic inspiration were quite soon contained by the government and soon after also separated from the active ranks of the army. And the nation then remained in the hands of military men who immediately showed their admiration and their faith in the grand hierarchs of European and Asiatic totalitarianism, before whom they crowded to show what good students they were, with all the evil consequences then suffered, and with those which we still suffer despite the Liberating Revolution.

In spite of efforts to unify the thinking of all the officers in this respect, a reaction by young officers (and because they were very young not yet contaminated) carried with it the deposition of the then Minis-

[33] One of Perón's self-assumed titles, not only to gain favor with his *descamisado* ("shirt-sleeve," or working class) backers, but also to support his argument that the leader (the *conductor*) has the hardest job of all, and that all is simplicity for the remainder once policy has been "worked" into existence by the "orienter."

[34] General José F. Uriburu. The author is, of course, being sarcastic in this passage. As noted above, Uriburu took advantage of popular desires for a Radicalism with substance to overthrow Yrigoyen. In succeeding provincial elections in Buenos Aires, however, the Radicals won and Uriburu declared the elections void. He proceeded to hold other ones giving provincial and later national victory to the Conservatives. The period of 1932 to 1943 is thus called the era of the Patriotic Fraud, since the argument was that falsifying the elections was for the people's own good.

[35] Uriburu had had prepared the draft of a Fascist corporative constitution and handed it to his successor, General Agustín P. Justo.

[36] The *Campo de Mayo* is a major military encampment immediately outside Buenos Aires.

ter of War in October of 1946. The return to the democratic inspiration of the forgers of the uprising of 1943 in the Campo de Mayo appeared to be realized. It was a mere illusion soon dispelled, because the majority of the high-ranking officers with troop commands sympathized with totalitarian systems, which at that time were falling in all the rest of the world, and they tolerated if they did not actually stir up the movement of the regimented masses who swarmed to the Plaza de Mayo for the restoration of the seventeenth.[37]

What happened between September 23 and November 13, 1955, I do not need to point out again, because we all know very well that the INVISIBLE THREADS of those acts fitted and still fit the same totalitarian conception.[38]

Let us get on, then, with this simple narration, saying that from 1930 until now there exists among many chiefs of our army a current responding to the same anti-democratic line to which they are uniform in their fidelity.

In sum, it is the consequence of the education received and of the instruction given, settling in the manner of a doctrine, which has created in the spirit of many officers a manner of thinking characterized by three fundamental aspects:

1) Phobia against the essential forms characterizing political cooperation in the great Western democracies; that is to say, the free dis-

---

[37] On October 9, 1945, segments of the army moved to have their fellow officer, Colonel Perón, ousted from all his government positions. Perón was then Vice-President, Minister of War, and Secretary of Labor and Social Welfare, from which latter post he was beginning to make his bid for labor support. Perón was imprisoned aboard a vessel stationed in the river. On October 17 massive public demonstrations took place in favor of Perón, who was allowed to make his reappearance. From that time on his path was easy. And October 17 was celebrated as Loyalty Day, probably the most important Peronist holiday.

Turning on this point, there is much disagreement with General González's statement. From his post of Argentine ambassador in Peru, General Tomás Dalton, another confirmed anti-Peronist military man, argued that the events of October 17, 1945, demonstrate that the army was *not* guilty of the imposition of the Peronist regime. At that time he said, "The armed forces which had just manifested themselves as against and not in favor of that leader stayed quiet, doing so because there was an undeniable climate . . ." He added that it was the people and their "natural" leaders who permitted the development of the atmosphere "which made these events produce themselves." Thus the army has no more guilt than that which would normally accrue to it as an integral part of Argentine society.

The argument becomes even more complicated with the addition of the events of September 28, 1951, "The Menéndez Revolt," named after the general who led it, of course. In that case the uprising was suffocated in a day, proof of the Peronist nature of the army even at that late date, according to those who oppose Dalton's view.

[38] These are the dates of the short-lived provisional presidency of General Eduardo Lonardi, referred to above. General González's reference to "invisible threads" obviously has to do with the belief that Lonardi was controlled by Peronists who were still pro-Church.

cussion of ideas and, very especially, their diffusion by means of the press.

2) A lack of confidence in and a deprecation for every citizen who feels a vocation for problems of a public nature, whom they sneeringly call professional politicians, as though to concern oneself with the art of governing instead of being an obligation of every able patriot is something like a simple way of being a delinquent.

3) LACK OF FAITH IN THE CITIZENRY.

I shall start with this last point, although it may seem the least important, because in reality it includes the two previous ones.

The true democrat believes in the citizenry and does not fear that it will be fooled for long if it is permitted to know the facts and if their discussion is accepted. And he also believes that this is the only road which will bring him to discover the truth.

Further, he who has faith in the citizenry IS NOT FRIGHTENED BY THE POSSIBLE EXTRAVAGANCES OF THE VENAL PRESS NOR DOES HE FEAR THE CITIZENS' LOSS OF DIRECTION BECAUSE OF THE TEACHINGS OF UNSCRUPU-LOUS POLITICIANS.

If there was one military man in the last few years who could have had faith in the citizenry, it was that man who—for good or ill—was elected president by an immense majority in 1946. If he had had such faith, he was in a position which no other president has ever had of rejoicing in contemplating the use of all the liberties established by the Constitution; but because he did not have such faith, he choked off all the means of information which could teach the citizenry and he intoxicated them with the pestilences of official propaganda.[39]

In my opinion this is the fundamental difference between the true democrat and he who is not one.

The former believes that his duty is to ORIENT THE CITIZENRY and he does it by helping them to reason with the truth at hand. The latter feels the necessity of training them and he gives them every service: false information and propagandistic commentary, along with the sole solution to the problem. As for the people, the only thing left for them is to applaud. And that they must.

Therefore the first job of totalitarian organizations is to deprecate by all means available the public men who inform opinion. And in this re-

[39] Within Argentine practice, the two Perón elections were "honest." He won in 1951 by approximately 65 per cent of the vote. By that date, however, he had instituted a quite harsh censorship and established a chain of newspapers and radio stations to pump out official views. When he was elected for his first term, in 1946, the opposition grouped itself entirely against him, including parties from far right to far left. They seemed to feel themselves confident of victory and thus for a short time were pleased with the restoration of October 17 and the elections promised thereafter.

spect it is unfortunately much which has been done from the classrooms of our military institutes and even greater the successes obtained within the ranks of the army.

With the epithet of "professional politician" there is denied talent and capacity to persons who since their youth have distinguished themselves in party contests, in elective posts, and in the university chair, sometimes succeeding in gaining universal fame and renown.

So it is that on occasion it has been extremely difficult for me to make certain comrades understand that those men must necessarily be better trained to see, analyze, and resolve grand national problems than others not submitted to the same disciplines or obliged to discuss such problems in opposition to contrary opinions from all sides.

So it is that they are easily able to dazzle CERTAIN FOREIGNERS in their management of PUBLIC AFFAIRS, audaciously presenting them with miraculous plans for fantastic undertakings which were not done before because of the "incapacity" of the politicians as well as, according to them, the slowness and inability of the REPRESENTATIVE SYSTEM to legislate with acuity and in good time.

The ex-dictator therefore used to like to repeat very often from his chair, "If the world had had to be made by a Congress, we never would have had one."

THESE ARE THE APPEARANCES; the reality, messrs. officers, SHOWS US THAT THE COUNTRIES WHICH FOR CENTURIES HAVE BEEN MARCHING AT THE FOREFRONT OF THE WORLD IN PROGRESS, WELFARE, AND POWER HAVE ALWAYS BEEN GOVERNED BY PROFESSIONAL POLITICIANS WHO HAVE REACHED THEIR GREATNESS STEP BY STEP, and never by providentially sent persons to resolve all at one blow what can only be the labor of time, wisdom, and the efforts of all. In problems of state, history collects the names only of those who have served the Fatherland with far-reaching wisdom and a sense of the permanent.

Another criticism which my comrades advance against public men is that within as well as outside government, they aspire only to defend their political interests.

So far as I can see, this appears to me natural and fitting for political contest. So, IF THEY WERE POLITICAL INTERESTS which pushed Sarmiento [40] to combat barbarism and civilize the people, and Pellegrini [41]

---

[40] Domingo F. Sarmiento was one of a remarkable group of statesmen, writers, historians, essayists, and intellectuals which erupted after the defeat of Rosas. He was elected president in 1868, leaving as his major work the introduction of the first normal schools into Argentina and a body of fairly high-quality political theorizing. On a more violent front, his greatest contributions probably were in the direction of forcibly beating down various ambitious provincial *caudillos*, anxious to relive the glory that was Rosas'.

[41] Carlos Pellegrini assumed the presidency of the nation after the revolution of 1890, a popular protest against government corruption and unresponsive pol-

to establish the progressive bases still enjoyed by the Republic, to cite only two of our great figures, in their time they may well have served their political interests from the highest office.

Another danger attributed to politicians, according to many officers, is their lack of honor. There are no politicians, according to them, who are not prepared to sell out their country. The name of "country seller" [42] was made overly familiar to us in the years prior to 1955. I ask my companions in arms what civil president from Mitre to our times has ever been accused of having enriched himself in the exercise of public office or even came to give reason for suspecting such a thing?

And the same can be said of many other illustrious men, who without having managed to reach such high position served the Republic in extremely important affairs with honesty equal to their clear talent and their elevated patriotism.

Finally, and perhaps here is the key, the fear of many certainly quite patriotic officers is that the politicians neglect the military preparedness of their country, whether it be for electoral purposes, a failure to understand the problem, or by letting themselves be carried away by dreams of international peace and brotherhood.

Only apparently is this true. The reality is very different. In effect, the military history of all times teaches us that armed forces never have such a level of development as at the service of democracy. The most powerful nation of the world at present testifies to it; the British navy, which dominated the seas for centuries, confirms it. On the other hand, it is precisely in the hands of tyrants that armies are bled white. Thus in our country that wonderful war instrument which carried out the campaign of the Andes, conquered Peru, assured the liberty of America, and triumphed on the fields of Ituzaingó [43] was born under the sign of May and was definitively lost with the first tyranny, and the present army of Richieri was on the point of being dissolved with the second tyranny. [44]

icies. Pellegrini gained fame as an excellent economic administrator and, above all, as a conservative politician willing to recognize the need for free elections and the possible victory of opposition parties. Arthur P. Whitaker, in his *The United States and Argentina*, Cambridge, Mass., 1945, p. 57, writes of him, "Except that he rose to be president . . . Pellegrini was the Alexander Hamilton of Argentina, and he won enormous prestige by steering Argentina safely through the grave political and financial crisis of the early 1890's."

[42] *Vendepatria* in Spanish. The term applies to those willing to sign concessions with foreign companies in consideration of bribes or juicy jobs. Perón rejoiced in the term but himself made arrangements with European industrialists and an American oil company.

[43] The battle of Ituzaingó, February 20, 1827, was won by the Argentines, lost by the Brazilians. The issue was the longstanding one of possession of what is now Uruguay.

[44] Professional soldier, considered the major integrator of the modern Argentine army. The old provincial armies were all disbanded by 1875 in favor of a national

222 *The Conflict Society*

And now that I have named the purest Argentine military hero of the twentieth century, I shall repeat here, paying homage to his illustrious memory, what I had the honor to hear personally from his emotionally inspired lips the day of the inauguration of the monument to Mitre. General Richieri said then that he had that day returned from Salta and that he was leaving the following day for the same destination, where he was taking the cure, because on no account did he want to miss the inauguration of the monument to the founding father. And he added: when my comrades within and without Congress, with the prestigious General Capdevila at their head, combated the bill establishing obligatory military service, Mitre counseled the legislators who came to consult him with these words, "Vote for the project, for that 'Little Colonel' is looking far." [45] Think well, messrs. officers, over this fact that the modern conscript army which today is our pride owes itself to the patriotic beliefs of "professional politicians" in spite of the adverse vote cast from their congressional seats by the high-ranking military figures of the epoch.

And lastly, a fear very much graver than those expounded above, although based as they are on undemocratic elements interested in maintaining the officers in a state of alert against given men and parties, is that intention attributed to certain leaders who once installed in the government would proceed to disorganize the army in order to rule arbitrarily and assure themselves indefinite stays in office.

Such a danger would not present itself for the first time in this part of America. Consequently those who fear it are not lacking cause. What they are lacking is knowledge of the facts. For these facts demonstrate that armies have forgotten their mission and put their duty to one side in order to mix themselves into the party struggle and oppose themselves to popular currents of opinion. It is, then, from that precise moment that THEY BEGIN TO DISSOLVE BY THEMSELVES. WHAT THE OTHERS DID WAS TO TAKE ADVANTAGE OF THEIR OWN STATE OF DECOMPOSITION. And this the military could have avoided only by remembering that each mission imposes a duty, and the faithful accomplishment of that duty is what we call subordination and discipline.

The day in which we military men stop deluding ourselves with the fugitive scintillations of adventurers from other parts, we shall discover that our mission is to be at the service of democracy and our duty to accept the decisions of the citizenry, maintaining freely elected authorities without interference of any sort in the life and decisions of the parties.

And this is not for the benefit of those who think themselves in the

force, but it was Richieri who, after the turn of the century, professionalized the land forces in modern fashion.

[45] "Little Colonel" refers to Richieri and the rank he held at that time.

majority. It is, precisely, for our very own good. Because if we all comply with the duty I have indicated in the service of the common mission, we shall be united in subordination and discipline.

We shall then be as strong as we should be. And an army like that is a sword too sharp for anyone to try to wrest away with his bare hand.

In conclusion, so that the army may be respected in its rights—which it has—it should not have more than one kind of enemy: the enemies of our traditional system of government as it is described in the fundamental principles of the Constitution of 1853. ALL OTHER MEN AND PARTIES, EVEN THOUGH THEY MAY AT TIMES THINK DIFFERENTLY WE, THE MILITARY PEOPLE, should be our friends in conditions of equality, for we all together have the common mission of safeguarding those postulates in domestic affairs.

And the day that that happens, WE SHALL LEARN TO OUR ASTONISHMENT THAT IN SPITE OF POLITICAL RIVALRIES, NO LONGER ARE ARGENTINES ENEMIES TO THEMSELVES; not even will civilians be the enemies of the military to cover the suspicion that the former are conspiring against the existence of the Argentine army, to which at one time in their lives they have the honor to belong.

With what I have said and what still remains to be said, I do not hope to modify the thinking of the officers already trained, a matter which furthermore is not my task; but I do have the high proposal of collaborating with the military authorities to insure that the officers presently in training, and those who are prepared in the future, should be educated in a spiritual atmosphere free of foreign ideological currents to which can be attributed—as I believe I have demonstrated—the detours taken by our comrades who so disturbed the institutional life of the Republic from 1930 on.

These deviations had their origins in the highly patriotic proposition of converting the army into a great instrument of war. And the teachers contracted for that purpose created a military spirit pre-eminent over any other consideration, because so it behooved them and so it was in their country of origin.

Had our race and our political objectives been the same, the grasp of these ideas would have been total and no one could have objected.

But our race is not the same; our objectives are not at all similar and the majority of our people follows a different route because they are inspired by the inheritance of May and the brotherhood of America.

As a consequence we should agree, after this difficult experience, that the education given our army in the last fifty years, highly efficient from an exclusively military point of view, has not been equally so in the sense of guaranteeing the stability of Argentine institutions.

Because the ideological deviation of many officers did not carry them on roads parallel to those of the people themselves. And this is what should be done.

We hope now that this Revolution will be the last. The President of the Nation has so stated solemnly in a public ceremony, the most representative men say so, and every Argentine citizen who wants to live honestly from his work repeats it fervently.

The dilemma—the great dilemma—is what we must do to terminate the era of convulsions which for more than twenty-five years had slowed the progress of the Republic and defamed us as a Nation before the civilized world.

We all know that the guilt is ours; but we all also know that without the intervention of the armed forces no one can shake the stability of any government, even though the popular base on which it rests may be small. Lastly, we also know that of the three armed forces the decisive one is the army, because it is large in numbers, because it is distributed throughout all the Republic, and because it is the only one which can make the success of its arms effective with territorial occupation.

The remedy—it is often said—rests in discipline and respect for the hierarchy. AGREED, BUT THESE TWO THINGS ARE NOT ACHIEVED WITH TARDY HARANGUES, WHICH CONVINCE ONLY THE ALREADY CONVINCED.

The solution is in the education to be imparted: and so, in order to be effective (as the twig is bent, so is the tree inclined), one should start at the moment that the citizen enters the Military College and continue afterward at every propitious moment, especially in the advanced training institutions through which pass the graduates for the remainder of their professional careers.

Only thus, by common education in the civilian and military scenes, can the chiefs of the army and men of public affairs follow parallel paths.

Common education should convince everyone from his childhood that DEMOCRACY is not merely a form of government which can be changed for another one by taking advantage of the momentary popularity of a man or of transitory states of public opinion.

Because DEMOCRACY IS A WAY OF LIVING, the only way in which peoples WHO HAVE COME TO KNOW LIBERTY CAN LIVE.

Therefore democracy is something more than a form of government; it is above written constitutions, and its force is superior to that of all the powers of the State.

And because IT IS A WAY OF LIVING, it reigns alike in a kingdom as in a republican system. The forms do not disturb it. It is the essentials which prevail and the only thing indispensable to its vitality is that the people shall have known it.

Ours know it. Therefore any move to annul it—whatever may be the disguise—is an interruption in the progress of the Republic, and furthermore a vain one, because every deviation from its natural course is necessarily transitory, and it will not be stopped until it finally returns to its first course, that course indicated and detailed by the thinking of May.

Consequently our democracy must be defended, and in the first instance by military men, for that is the position in which the Argentine people have always wanted to see us.

This demands that we educate our cadets and officers and officer candidates and noncommissioned officers in the cult of the traditions WHICH GIVE FORM TO THE WAY OF LIVING of the Argentine people, as enunciated in 1810, fought for at Caseros, and debated during the course of the last few years.

No reasoning, not even that of the greatest technical or professional efficiency, should serve as a pretext to us for public or hidden interference with ideas which disorient or confound the young persons to be educated concerning this supreme ideal of our citizenry.

In consequence, so far as the army is concerned, it is my opinion:

1) The professors of our institutes, especially those of Civil and Military History, should be recruited from among those who suggest not the slightest doubts concerning their democratic sentiments, even though there may be others who apparently are more fitting to offer the courses. The difficult part is to make these sentiments known to higher authority. One manner might be the stimulation of Argentine literary production of a historical character . . .

2) The study plans should be modified in the sense that studies are not made of men, happenings, or campaigns, which tend to pile up in the souls of the officers sentiments of adoration for tyrants or which deprecate democratic regimes.

It should be remembered in this connection that if in the beginning dictators have succeeded in illuminating themselves with spectacular successes, these have always been transitory; and that the democracies, with all their defects, have always triumphed over them.

So, THE NATION WHICH FOR CENTURIES HAVE BEEN LEADING THE WORLD MAKE UP AT THE SAME TIME THE FIRMEST BULWARKS OF THIS FORM OF GOVERNMENT, PRECISELY THE BASIS FOR THEIR POWER, IN WHICH SOME DO NOT BELIEVE BECAUSE THESE NATIONS USE THEIR POWER WITHOUT OSTENTATION. The conclusions of the two great wars of this century confirm this in unquestionable manner.

3) Simultaneously with the revision of the study plans the bibliography to be consulted by the professors and students should be so selected as to make propagandistic texts disappear from the classroom. I

recognize that it is very difficult to uncover the texts, because historians always declare themselves impartial and write in such a fashion that they even seem to be so.

Certainly by studying campaigns from the viewpoint of the victor—the correct way, as I have already said—the danger is less because the victors do not have to lie to justify themselves or hide the truth in order not to make errors manifest. In addition, official documents should be consulted in preference to narrative accounts. And when the latter have to be used, they should be compared with the narrative accounts of the other side.

4) Another aspect is that of obliging the professors to cover the entire course program. In extension as well as in depth. I remember that in all the schools and colleges I went through, the study of Argentine history never went beyond the anarchy of the year 1820. Thus because the program was not completed in its full extension, the studies always ended in the most unfavorable period for Argentine democracy; and I also remember that once when we passed that date (this was in the Superior War School), from 1853 on we only looked at the territorial losses we had suffered as a result of arbitrations.

Here, because we had not completed the program in its depth, we discovered the "Achilles heel" of the governments which the country had in the second half of the last century. Of the good they did, not a word for lack of time.

Similar examples of even greater seriousness could be given of the way in which the programs of Military History were carried out.

5) Finally, I feel that officers should not be sent on study missions to countries where they can come to identify themselves with ideologies which in the long run can be dangerous in our midst, especially if those so assigned should on their return serve as professors in our military institutes.[46]

In the event that their being sent should be indispensable or highly fitting, the selection of the candidates on the basis of a firm character or of ideas well defined and clearly known to higher officials should be the rule.

6) Insofar as military attachés are concerned, I am of the opinion that with the exception of America these posts should not exist in nations where totalitarian regimes flourish. ON THE OTHER HAND, I THINK IT APPROPRIATE TO SEND SEVERAL ATTACHÉS THERE WHERE THEY CAN LEARN HOW THE ARMED FORCES KNOW HOW TO FIT PATRIOTICALLY INTO THE

---

[46] At the time of the outbreak of the Second World War, Perón was in Italy attached to the Argentine Embassy as a military attaché. He has often been quoted as having expressed a debt of gratitude to Mussolini as a political tutor. He also observed military procedures in Germany. It is said that most of the GOU officers had had similar experiences.

DESTINIES OF THE NATION WITHOUT THEREFORE MIXING THEMSELVES INTO
ITS POLITICAL LIFE OR INTO THE WORK OF ITS GOVERNMENT.

When all this has taken root among us military men, the people, the
politicians, the armed forces, and the government—each one reserving
its manner of thinking and its feelings—we shall march hand in hand
joyfully singing the patriotic songs learned as children; because then,
ONLY THEN, will we be on the path which will lead us forever toward
the so desired PACIFICATION OF OUR SPIRITS.[47]

LADIES AND GENTLEMEN:
I owe nothing to any politician and I expect nothing from them in
the future.

Were I to be born again, I should be a soldier again; I would enter
the Military College as soon as possible and again I would enter the
competition to win a chair in the classrooms of the Superior War College.

Thus do I define my highest honor and my most legitimate pride, in
spite of the criticism I have directed against the two institutes, the pillars of our military training, to which I am bound with ties of affectionate sentiment which only death can destroy.

Of the titles I am able to display, two are for me among the highest:
my duty as an officer instructor and as a company commander of
cadets in the Military College; and my having been for six years a professor of the Superior War School, where I taught three different
courses: military organization and mobilization, General Staff tactics
and service, and, finally, the last course in military history.

DO NOT TAKE IT ILL, THEN, if I have said things which damage the
affection which my colleagues may have for our Military College, a
model in the world; or for our Superior War School, on a level with its
counterparts in the great European powers.

Because it is precisely my love for these institutes which has brought
me here for this discussion: the desire to see them participate actively
in our DEFINITIVE PACIFICATION.

And let my last words be those of affectionate remembrance for
those who were my professors there: for the great amount which they
taught me, for the innumerable mistakes which they knew how to
pardon in me, and for the uncontainable vocation of their military
credo, always at the service of the Fatherland.

[47] This ugly term, "pacification," is in great vogue in Argentina now, as it was
in Perón's period. I have found no similar use of the word before. It is, of course,
taken from the political military lexicon and means exactly what it seems to, although of course the content of "pacification" now is not what it was in the period
1946–1955.

15

HEMISPHERIC RELATIONS IN THE
LIGHT OF CASTRO

Quetzalcoatl, Columbus, Bolívar, and Castro are the supreme myth figures of Latin America's major historical ventures. They represent not
only glory but also the sadness of failure in their inability to reach the
ideals of their grand aspirations. The major Indian civilizations were in
decay even before the arrival of the Spaniards. Columbus opened new
lands to the Hispanic search for the perfect order and stability of an
idealized medievalism, a yearning which must always reveal its anti-
human evilness when challenged by the heresy of modernism which
substitutes the probable for the absolute and uncertainty for dogma.
Bolívar lived the frustration of the revolutionary who in a traditional
world could impart only form but not substance. And Fidel Castro is
the first to lead an Iberian country into quasi-modern social organization, choosing the black path of charismatic totalitarianism for his
tempestuous passage. Whether even Cuba's way of storming the gates
of contemporary life is preferable to a continuance of the indignities
and uncertainties of the present political life of the Latin American republics is the question that most disturbs modernizers who also are of
democratic commitment. The mere fact that the question exists, however, gives scope for imaginative policy-making among the hemisphere's leaders to north and south. We can be "soberly optimistic," to
use A. A. Berle's assessment, so long as an effective choice of social
goals and means can still be exercised in almost all of Latin America.
    An analysis of the effect of the Cuba Revolution on hemispheric rela-
tions risks being a restatement of the trite. So many commentators have

handled the various aspects of the unfolding Cuban situation as to make yet another interpretation a challenge both to ingenuity and intellectual honor. The problem is to prevent the ingenuity from compromising the honor, the honor from being shaded by passion and the many already conventional schools of wisdom about the Cuban "case." We have a "Draper thesis" and a "Matthews thesis"; [1] we have been told countless times by proponents of all "theses" that the hemisphere is in crisis. There are those who propose immediate and drastic action as the only remedy, those who argue that nothing *can* be done, while still others say that nothing *should* be done. There are "realists" who want a Caribbean *détente* and "realists" who want a Cuban invasion; those who want to be "tough" and "turn Latin America loose," and those who want to be "tough" and get more involved than ever. The recital of positions need not be extended. This author's obligation is not to choose from the bulging shelves but to justify an addition to the literature by trying to use his profession to help others make whatever may be their choices in a mood of rationality and self-awareness.

The specific obligations of this analysis are: first, to present some of the "givens" of the international situation in this hemisphere; second, to discuss the nature of international relations both in general and with narrower focus on the Americas, at this point considering such applied policies as the Alliance for Progress; and lastly, to relate the analysis to the several kinds of social situations in Latin America, so that we may know who can be affected by *fidelismo*, who may potentially be so affected, and who are immune. These three elements—the hemispheric settings of Cuba, some of the policy responses, and how differing types of Latin American society may respond to Cuba—examined in detail, may lead us to some conclusions in which political taste may combine with analytical discipline toward the derivation of reasoned predictions.

THE MEANING OF CUBA IN THE HEMISPHERE.

Foreign relations are compacted of many layers. At the bottom, every nation and every culture group is interested profoundly in its own present and future integrity, in living in a secure and predictable and understandable world.[2] This basic foreign-policy aim tempts

[1] Herbert L. Matthews, *The Cuban Story*, New York: George Braziller, 1961, and Theodore Draper, *Castro's Revolution: Myths and Realities*, New York: Praeger, 1962.
[2] This statement is a truism. See, for example, Joseph E. Black and Kenneth W. Thompson, *Foreign Policies in a World of Change*, New York: Harper & Row, 1963, p. 710: "At minimum, the national interest as expressed by a long succession of changing governments has been protection of the security of a sovereign, independent state."

every nation to try to construct a world in its own image, one not confounded by conflicting views of reality. When the projection of self-image is frozen into policy, we have a second, more ideological layer of international events exemplified in this hemisphere by such benchmarks as the Monroe Doctrine, isolationism, and pan-Americanism on the American side, and non-interventionism, the rule of asylum, and a religiously strict adherence to narrow views of international law on the Latin American side. And third, to complete this temptingly trinitarian approach, we should also add the day-to-day events of international affairs, those immediate decisions of an often *ad hoc* nature which define the style of affairs and give immediate reality to the primary politico-military defense values congealed in the secondary policy statements. Pinning a medal on a dictator's jailer, celebrating a presidential visit, or breaking an embassy's windows are the hurly-burly of this essentially instrumental part of the conduct of foreign relations.

Another device for breaking international politics into manageable pieces is to look at happenings in the various ways in which they are "seen" and acted upon in differing countries and by differing groups within countries. In the case of the deposition of Guatemalan President Jacobo Arbenz in 1954, for instance, there was such a Rashōmon-like disparity of views as to put on record at least three quite different revolutions. To Americans at large the incident was a part of the Cold War, intimately related to defense posture and to internal politics, especially in the United States Senate. For Guatemalans the operation was understandable and expected, seen as reprehensible or not according to political views, with the whole matter ending in a series of unhappy, corrupt, and personalistic events by no means unusual in Central America; the solace of familiarity was theirs. Latin Americans in other countries took the incident to be an example of United States interventionist rejection of the politics of reform, the exercise of a colonialist *droit de seigneur*—a view widely shared in Europe. These differing interpretations lead to differing actions, which is what here concerns us, although certainly the moral "rightness" or "wrongness" of the actions are well worth discussing in other contexts.

The emergence of Cuba as a revolutionary Marxist socialist country, as those terms are commonly understood today, pulled all the stops on the organ of international affairs. The missile crisis as a specific incident raised the most profound questions of survival for the United States, Cuba, the Soviet Union, and indeed the world. The growth and elaboration of Cuban ideology as revealed by property confiscations, Messianic "revolutionism" with its accompanying subversion of neighbor's politics, and a "new look" within the Communist bloc has put under enormous strain all the programmatic designs for hemisphere organization a-building since 1889. The day-to-day problems, too, have been at flood levels since the Sierra Maestra, besetting us with such questions as whether Premier Castro should or should not have been invited to the White House by Mr. Eisenhower and which New York hotel Dr. Castro should have patronized.

As all these levels of international affairs began to interact furiously, selective perception beclouded interpretations everywhere. The American business community joined with conservative Latin American elements to see *fidelismo* as a total threat, leading many of its spokesmen to an early advocacy of force to destroy the Castro revolution in its home. The American intellectual community split into fragments, shifting from broad sympathy to overwhelming antagonism as time revealed ever more of the design of the new Cuban government. Behind these specific reactions was a mass, amorphous welling of enthusiasm for Castro. Even though part of this excitement was certainly "faddish," as in the Elvis Presley and Beatles crazes, this fascination at large and the particular sympathies even of some banking circles was an asset squandered by Castro, the victim of his own deterministic views of a United States ineluctably dominated by Wall Street.

Latin American nationalists passed through an early period of infatuation into a harsh polarization, as the march of events carried Cuba all the way to military, economic, and political alliance with the Soviet bloc, plus the added Chinese complications. As in the Guatemalan case, however, it was possible to predict what the different views would be and who would hold them. The United States interpreted a communized Cuba as a threat above all else to national security, then as an economic and ideological defeat, and lastly, as a nuisance in the conduct of foreign policy. In the early phases of the Castro regime the Latin American nations started at the second level, seeing Cuba as an ideological and legal problem which led to necessary but troublesome international negotiations; only much later did Cuba become a basic security matter to them. It was the missile crisis, perhaps more than any other single factor, which forced the issue of national integrity on Latin American policy planners, revealing a primary community of interest between North and Latin America which has as yet to be exploited.

The special relationship between the United States and Latin America had as its traditional basis the role of the former as the "protector nation" of the hemisphere.[3] The exercise of this security function has

[3] For an excellent and easily available debate on the issue of the "special" position of the U.S. in Latin America see "Ypsilon," "A Note on Inter-American Relations," and Lincoln Gordon's rejoinder, "Abrazo vs. Coexistence: Further Comments," in Albert O. Hirschman, ed., *Latin American Issues: Essays and Comments,* New York: The Twentieth Century Fund, 1961, pp. 53–68.

not been appreciated by many Latin Americans and, for geographical if for no other reasons, weakened with distance from the United States. For a short time after World War II, however, this relationship was at its peak, supported by the economic strength of the United States, literally almost monopolistic prior to the European recuperation. However, the atomic stalemate, the economic resurgence of Europe, and the growth of modern nationalistic ideologies in Latin America reinforced by the world-wide dismantling of colonialism have all served to change the meaning of United States power in the hemisphere. The missile crisis served to reveal that the bedrock layer of interest was still there.

The Latin American nations immediately were divided on the measures appropriate to their defense, the divisions being in frank accord with their estimates of their own domestic strength and their historical positions with respect to the United States. The troubled Caribbean nations, even before Cold War weaponry came to their area, favored decisive military action against Cuba, and some extended warm hospitality to Cuban rebel forces. But the stronger and more distant nations did not share these sentiments. The more political "play" that a given country enjoyed in internal affairs, the more difficult it was to persuade it into joint hemispheric security measures, as distinguished from the internal measures against *fidelista* movements that each might take. The government of Mexico, for example, has taken a strong international position against any measures implying interventionism [4] but domestically has adopted stringent laws against "social dissolution" to contain domestic *fidelista* subversion. Chile, Bolivia, and Brazil also reacted in direct response to their traditional foreign-policy lines and their own internal political arrangements, resisting United States "adventurism" in Cuba and striving to maintain normal relations. Temporarily weakened, Argentina vacillated and finally reacted with respect to foreign affairs in a way consistent with an internal disarray that made it necessary to find external support. First opposing Cuban expulsion from the Organization of American States, Argentina then fa-

---

[4] Francisco Cuevas Cancino, "The Foreign Policy of Mexico," in Joseph E. Black and Kenneth W. Thompson, *op. cit.*, p. 658, states: "Intimate geographical and strategic ties make it impossible for Mexico to maintain a position of onlooker with regard to what happens in Cuba. Toward the revolutionary government, she seeks refuge in her traditional policy of non-intervention. She believes that this government constitutes one more stage in the self-determination of the Cuban people. With this policy, she is trying to face the situation which changes assumptions which have existed since the Clayton-Bulwer Treaty (1850) which established Anglo-Saxon superiority in the 'American Mediterranean.' Leaning on her conscience of law and on the free determination of peoples, Mexico acts on the assumption that the Cuban Revolution will unfold without affecting her own development."

vored it after pressure was applied to ex-President Frondizi by his own military. Brazil, too, changed its policy as a direct result of the military revolt of 1964.

The result of this belated understanding of the breadth of the Cuban problem was to make a wide spectrum of Latin Americans potentially receptive to the North American point of view. The clear meaning of the missile crisis forced many believers out of an emotional support of Castro and into independence or neutrality, causing a renewal of interest in what might possibly be forthcoming from the United States in the way of ideological as well as material assistance toward fulfillment of their aspirations for modernization. Although the extensive Latin sympathy for the late President Kennedy provided a ready means for the expression of such American support, this opportunity for political discourse in the grand sense was never seized. Instead, the Alliance for Progress was advanced, and then tinkered with, as the due and entire response to a hunger that was larger than Washington knew it to be.

An aspect of the Cuban experience which has been little understood in the United States in its full practical and emotional strength is that socially and politically the little island is the Iberian cultural world's first almost modern state. Of course there are many most significant portions of political modernism in other Latin American countries, but the Cuban government seems to have been the first to evoke as well as to impose forcefully a kind of national coherence throughout what is left on the island of Cuban society. Latin American interest in Cuba thus is far beyond an understandable pride in "one of our boys making it" in standing up to the United States and still surviving. The matter probably goes even deeper than whether Cuba is attempting to demonstrate a Soviet as opposed to a Western path to modernization, for in social and political, if not economic, organization the island may well be already modern or almost so.[5] This statement must unfortunately be uninhibited by data, for there is little hard information concerning attitudes, values, and social structure on which firmly to judge the matter. Some speculation based on the behavior of the Castro government is required, however, for the notion that Cuba has broken out of traditional Latin American molds and into the early stages of modern nationhood is taken for granted in Latin America.

Definition here becomes imperative. Modern social organization, as the phrase is here employed, refers to a social system sufficiently open to permit broad interclass mobility and possessing communications and

[5] Throughout I have used political modernity to mean the existence of the secular nation-state and the correlative attitudes and ideologies required for its legitimation. See below in the text and for a fuller statement see my "Introduction" in K. H. Silvert, ed., *Expectant Peoples: Nationalism and Development*, New York: Random House, 1963.

attitude systems which transcend class lines. In its related political sense, modernization then implies the growth of the national community as the claimant of the citizen's primary loyalty. An open class structure, training and formal education to promote mobility, a reward system of status as well as economic nature, and the containment and channeling of class differences by the building of supra-class community-wide loyalties are necessary elements of the practice of modernism. These national phenomena open the society to citizens' armies, industrialization and industrial urbanization, and the devices of social control which when concentrated in a few hands can produce despotism, and when dispersed and controlled and rooted in an enlightened citizenry create the conditions for democratic processes.

Many bits of evidence suggest that Castro's Cuba is functioning in certain respects like a modern nation-state. The reduction in numbers of the middle groups by death, emigration, escape, and exile created a social vacuum which must perforce promote mobility for at least a limited time. The military as well as political confidence vested until very recently in the Cuban militia, and even the present process of military professionalization, all smack of modern ways of weaving the military into the social fabric. The power of the government to withstand blockade, cultural and political isolation, the work of exiles in sabotage and attempted invasion, drought, hurricane, and massive technical inefficacy coupled with uninformed political experimentation implies a strength which can only be based in important measure on a high degree of consensus from certain groups and a special kind of opposition from others. Although there can be no demonstration of this analysis,[6] as I have said, it is probable that Castro draws on several negative and positive sources of strength. First, in Cuba, as in all societies, many—perhaps most—people are politically apathetic. Second, the anti-Castro position within Cuba must be split between those willing to revolt

[6] Current sources on domestic affairs in Cuba are contradictory not only factually and interpretatively, but in the very essence of the understanding each author brings to his subject. For example, Jean Daniel in his "Boycotting Cuba: Whose Interest Does it Serve?" *The New Republic*, Dec. 28, 1963, pp. 19–22, as well as in his well-known interviews of Castro at the time of President Kennedy's assassination, is directly opposed to the "feel" of Theodore Draper's latest article, "Five Years of Castro's Cuba," *Commentary*, Vol. XXXVII, 1, January, 1964, pp. 25–37. The reader may also be interested in comparing such a recent book as that by Tad Szulc, *The Winds of Revolution: Latin America Today—And Tomorrow*, New York: Praeger, 1963, with the equally fresh and little-known Leslie Dewart, *Christianity and Revolution: The Lesson of Cuba*, New York: Herder & Herder, 1963. Again, in these two cases, we have a profound difference of focus. The only empirical data available can be found in Maurice Zeitlin, *Working Class Politics in Cuba: A Study in Political Sociology*, unpublished doctoral dissertation, University of California at Berkeley, 1964. This investigation, based on interviews of 210 workers in twenty-one plants in 1961 and 1962, cannot be definitive, but it is inferentially supportive of the national identification thesis I have been advancing.

with assistance from abroad and those who reject such action as treasonous. Indeed, this schism even affects the Cuban exiles. Perhaps the most important piece of evidence, however, is the totalitarian nature of government in today's Cuba. The government's power seems to be the product not only of extensive policing and saturation propaganda techniques, but also of the acceptance by most Cubans of state-fostered attitudes and actions. Distasteful as these procedures are to those of us committed to democratic process, we well know from recent experience that totalitarianism is not incompatible with high levels of educational achievement, mass communications, and industrial urbanization. (How viable such politics are for long-term dynamic development is another matter which is discussed in the following chapter.[7])

Whether in fact Cuba has or has not crossed the frontier from the last century to this one, most policy makers in the hemisphere act as though it has. The island is being dealt with, willy-nilly, as a national society and not as a banana republic—even though the latter treatment, too, was tried at the Bay of Pigs. The internal changes in Cuba, whatever their defects, seem to have been sufficiently effective to support these implicitly held external views.

The present situation of Cuba in the hemisphere may now be summarized:

1. Time has worked its usual wonders. Gone is the always unfounded fear that Castro and Khrushchev would or could combine to turn Cuba into a showcase of communism in a matter of months. The appeals of *fidelismo* have not disappeared, but with respect to the problems of development Castroism has become highly distasteful to most Latin Americans. The nationalistic component of the ideology has been weakened by Cuba's Cold War involvement but seems still to be strong. Time has also afforded reflection to the other nations of the hemisphere, with these results:

a. Almost all Latin American governments now agree with the United States that all levels of international affairs are involved in this dispute, that problems of fundamental sovereignty, long-range policy reformulation, and *ad hoc* difficulties are sure to continue. Tactical divergence still continues, however. The United States has seemingly eschewed unilateral armed action against Cuba unless Cold War military-security matters again arise, but would like effective multilateral isolation of Cuba on all fronts and with enthusiastic Latin American cooperation. The weaker states, with such exceptions as

---

[7] For a discussion of this question see George F. Kennan, "America and the Russian Future," *Foreign Affairs*, Vol. XXIX, No. 3, April, 1951, pp. 351-70. Also, K. H. Silvert, "Peace, Freedom and Stability," in William Manger, ed., *The Alliance for Progress: A Critical Appraisal*, Washington: Public Affairs Press, 1963, reprinted here as Ch. 16.

Haiti, would still like to see an inter-American invasion of the island, but failing that possibility, because of the opposition of the major Latin American powers, will follow the containment lead of the United States. Argentina, Mexico, and Chile, as seconded by Bolivia for special reasons, oppose any invasions of Cuban sovereignty and only reluctantly concede to some aspects of isolation. Although aware of Cuba's subversive intentions, they remain faithful to traditional forms of safeguarding sovereignty and presume that their internal situations afford them sufficient strength to avoid falling into *fidelismo*. These policies are pursued at the governmental level, of course; dissident groups in every Latin American country oppose those decisions from right as well as left.

b. The various perceptions of the significance of Castro Cuba have grown closer but still remain significantly apart. The fundamental reason is a divergence of interest: development remains Latin America's major problem, whereas security in a world of rapidly shifting power blocs as well as increasingly pressing domestic questions claims the primary political attention of North Americans. In an immediate sense, then, this need for security can only be met by the United States with policies designed to halt Cuba's attempts to subvert other Latin American political systems. Because the nature of political publics varies so widely among the nations of the hemisphere, as we shall see later, the matter of perception must in addition differ not only with ideology but also with social class and, in some Latin American countries, caste.

2. A broader spectrum of communications and policy has become available in the hemisphere. American political leaders have publicly stated that all forms of social and economic organization were acceptable in the hemisphere so long as affiliation with the Communist bloc was not implied. Military coups in Argentina, Peru, Ecuador, the Dominican Republic, Guatemala, and Honduras in the space of eighteen months put American political intentions to a severe test. Even though American intentions and deeds were not in full harmony in these cases, enough of the new liberality remained as the appeals of *fidelismo* sharply decreased so that broad areas of the Latin American national publics could be expected to continue to respond receptively to the United States policy.

3. New policies began to evolve, both in the United States and in Latin America. It is to these that we will now address ourselves.

THE ALLIANCE AND SOCIAL CHANGE AS ARMS OF
INTERNATIONAL RELATIONS

Containment has become the long-range element in American action against Cuba. Even though critics complain that containment is mere negativism, the policy had its very positive side and its ethical justification when applied earlier in the Cold War to the Sino-Soviet bloc, as well as later in its extension to Cuba. The "X Papers" of George Kennan argued that drawing firm international lines could assist in creating the conditions of security and thus in gaining the time necessary for the internal dynamics of the Soviet Union possibly to push that country into a more responsible internal as well as international posture. Kennan's theoretical commitment in making that prognostication was necessarily that self-sustaining development must create patterns of responsibility, if not of democracy. He also argued that the justification for saying nay to others must be the conviction that the Western system, although imperfect, is in greater harmony with the nature and dignity of man than totalitarianism. The only conclusion for a reasonable man, as he saw it, was that the Western democracies must strive for greater human freedom and dignity to serve as example and morally to justify containment, as well as for their humanistic sake alone.[8]

Immediate American aims in Cuba were at times mixed, of course. The initial economic sanctions and the invasion attempt were essays at the destruction of the Castro government. Short of that end, however, the recurrent policy has been to isolate Cuba from the hemisphere and to give an essentially negative policy an affirmative tone. American economic measures to harass the island, the military and intelligence moves to seal off the export of weapons and of trained revolutionaries, and the political means employed to counteract ideological affronts were all combined with affirmative justifications—the commitment to change in other countries those conditions inviting to *fidelista* sympathies, the promise that the United States would exert itself in favor of all brands of non-communist modernization, and even perhaps a hint (whether real or fancied is not publicly known) to Castro after the missile crisis that he would be free of the threat of invasion and permitted to work out his path toward political decency as best he might within the surrounding set of other political imperatives.[9]

[8] "Any message we may try to bring to others will be effective only if it is in accord with what we are to ourselves, and if this is something sufficiently impressive to compel the respect and confidence of a world which, despite all its material difficulties, is still more ready to recognize and respect spiritual distinction than material opulence." Quoted from George F. Kennan, *American Diplomacy: 1900–1950*, Chicago: The Univ. of Chicago Press, 1951, p. 154.

[9] This matter has, of course occasioned much debate. Some persons have purported to see in President Kennedy's television address to the nation during the missile crisis an implicit guarantee against United States invasion of Cuba if the island ceased to pose a Cold War military threat. The sentences are: "These new weapons are not in your interest. They contribute nothing to your peace and well being. They can only undermine it. *But this country has no wish to cause you to suffer or to impose any system upon you.* We know that your lives and your land are being used as pawns by those who deny you freedom." [Italics added.] The

The Alliance for Progress is the major instrument of these justifications for sealing off a neighboring state. Despite the bitterness of many of the criticisms of the Alliance, much can be said in its defense. Certainly the Alliance program was not merely more of the same in its original ideology. Old and persistent Latin American requests for their own Marshall Plan were manifestly unrealistic; to offer economic assistance to already developed states is different from aid to underdeveloped areas, as has been so often stated. The examples of Argentina, Uruguay, and Chile—Latin America's old economic leaders—have finally been seen in Washington as convincing demonstration that measures to promote economic development do not by themselves take effect quickly enough or massively enough to provide the social and political bases necessary to assure American security in the hemisphere and to promise self-sustaining development to the Latin American states. The Alliance undertook a combined program of social and economic development, with the overt political aspects once again underplayed in the largely unexamined hope that desirable politics follow in the wake of industrialization, literacy, decent housing, and so forth.

The social-development objectives of the Alliance are designed to chip away at the iron shield separating lower middle from upper lower groups in Latin America. The impermeability of this relationship impedes the "automatic" operation of the "trickle system" relied on by the economically orthodox to keep the capital investment cycle going; the "trickle" is simply not permitted to go all the way down, thus limiting effective demand, inhibiting labor availability and mobility, and creating the kind of resentments that make massive groups available for political extremism. The agrarian, tax, and other reforms proposed under the Alliance also have for their purpose a change in social structure and thus in the distribution of political power. Insofar as participation, mobility, and identification are necessary concomitants of development, the Alliance has not been pursuing illogical or irrational ends. On the contrary, these measures are imperative *no matter what the ideology of the modernizing groups may be.*[10]

To pass judgment on the success or failure of the Alliance at this time is entirely unjustified: five years are insufficient for the program to

President continued with an exhortation to the Cubans to throw off foreign domination, at which time they would be welcomed back "to the associations of this hemisphere."

[10] ". . . [N]o real economic development consistent with the goals we have set ourselves is possible without a social structure which permits the great mass of people to share in the benefits of progress, and affords each man a fair expectation of social justice. This often means basic, even revolutionary, changes in the structure of society." Dean Rusk, "The Alliance in the Context of World Affairs," in John C. Dreier, ed., *The Alliance for Progress: Problems and Perspectives,* Baltimore: The Johns Hopkins Press, 1962, p. 112.

"take." The problems which have arisen to harry the future development of the Alliance, however, are well know. They include the recalcitrance of some, although by no means all or even most, of the influential Latin American political leaders. More important, many Latin American leaders do not know how to go about forging the social change they desire, even when they have the power sufficient for some substantial reform, as may well be the case in Chile and Uruguay, for example. Other problems stem from the fact that social-development funds call for offshore purchases, inevitably implying a drain on dollar reserves in a time of exchange concern in the United States. Congressional difficulties are notorious in foreign-assistance matters, and all too often aid planning has been confounded by the exigencies of immediate political crisis. Another major problem, usually given too little emphasis, is that massive amounts of money for economic and social purposes are not being made available. Latin American capitalists have not rushed to stimulate their national economies; Congress has given the Alliance less money for nineteen countries than Soviet Russia extends to Cuba; and the American business community lacks confidence in Latin America and has alternative investment channels of greater attractiveness.

> Latin American politicians sometimes say—and others probably think—that the United States "cannot" withdraw her interest from Latin America. This is not the fact. She should not, if it can be maintained. But she "can." The United States does not need Latin America as a field of investment for her capital. There is, and increasingly will be, more than enough work for American capital at home. . . . Everything taken into account, American capital does not yearn to go abroad at all and does not go abroad easily. In recent years it has been difficult to induce it to go to Latin America. Nearly 80 per cent of the capital actually exported to the area has been expended for discovery and development of oil. . . .[11]

If the criteria for the granting of AID funds are to be wrapped more tightly into immediate political considerations, the amounts will have to be increased to bolster the power they are supposed to apply. Further, if the Alliance as such is to carry out its particular objectives, then the social-development aspects of its program cannot be neglected. In addition, if the hemisphere is also to proceed with all deliberate speed toward democratic as well as modern organization, then strong political persuasion wrapped into a programmatic knowledge of the essentials of total development is absolutely indispensable.

Observers have said time after time that the Alliance has no "magic"

[11] Adolf A. Berle, *Latin America: Diplomacy and Reality,* New York: Harper & Row for the Council on Foreign Relations, 1962, p. 8.

in Latin America. The blame is usually attached to the submergence of the myth factor, the absence of an appealing ideology in the program. Tad Szulc, among many others, writes, "Even as late as 1963, it was not fully understood in Washington that the success—even the acceptance —of the Alliance for Progress as a workable cooperative scheme hinged to an immense extent on its political impact on the Latin Americans." He continues by speaking of a *cansancio*, a tiredness, which has also subjectively influenced many others with deep experience in Latin America: "Among the many elusive and often contradictory feelings now rising in the hemisphere is an undefinable malaise that can only be described as a 'weariness of the West.'" [12]

A basic weakness of the Alliance is that it has commonly been seen and "sold" as everything, when in reality it is only a highly necessary part. Without an infusion of political spirit, it cannot hold out the promise which will excite acceptance of the principle that demands for immediate economic, social, and status gratification must be set aside in the expectation of improvement for the next generation and for the community. The administrators of the Alliance have never fooled themselves about the length and complexity of their task, but certainly at large the hope has been that machinery and houses can manufacture developed people. Like it or not, the Cuban approach has been the opposite—that participant individuals, or persons who can be fooled into thinking themselves effectively participant, are the first cause of national power. Involvement of the people in programs of the state, whether it is illusory or real, can be useful for such short periods as that of the present Cuban regime's experience.

A Latin American sociologist has put the matter very clearly:

> If it is of course true that in some countries of longer democratic tradition—such as Argentina, Chile, Uruguay, and others—the only way of obtaining legitimacy is through a proper election; in the majority of the less developed nations, *especially outside of the cities*, the vote lacks symbolic value or has it negatively. When Castro asserts that the Cubans have something more than the vote, for they have been given a rifle, he certainly does not express a conception of democracy acceptable to the urban workers or the middle classes of the more developed countries of Latin America, but indeed he does probably reflect an attitude which can be extended to a large part of a recently mobilized population or one in a rapid process of mobilization. . . .[13]

The Alliance's inability to generate political sex appeal stems in important part from Washington's discomfort with and suspicion of Latin America's nationalist movements. From the Mexican Revolution to the

[12] *Op. cit.*, the first quotation is from p. 185, the second from p. 186.
[13] Gino Germani, *Política y sociedad en una época de transición*, Buenos Aires: Ed. Paidós, 1962, p. 161.

moment every Latin nationalist movement has caused policy vacilla-
tion in the United States, even though very stable and fruitful accommodations always are eventually made. In nationalism lies warm,
human, earthy magic and not the chill of "sensible" and apolitical
moderation. The political appeals of Castroism must remain strong in
Latin American to the extent to which the Cuban evolution continues
to be seen as a success for nationalism. *Fidelismo,* however, is of
course not Latin America's only example of nationalism. Between the
right-wing neo-fascist nationalism of Argentina, the Christian Democratic nationalism of Chile, the Social Democratic nationalism of Venezuela, the pragmatic nationalism of Brazil, and the Marxist-Leninist
nationalism of Cuba lie broad ideological gulfs. Because all aspiring
nations must share some nationalistic foreign-policy commitments,
there is a community of interests and even of subtle understandings
among almost all the more advanced Latin American governments
(Uruguay, Argentina, Chile, Brazil, Peru, and Mexico). These implicit identifications have stayed their hand against Cuba and led them
into other international actions which overlap many of the less extreme
measures of the Castro administration. The only exception among
the more developed nations is Venezuela, which has been made a special target of *fidelista* Messianism and thus has a survival interest in the
destruction of the Castro government. Brazil's now defunct policy of
"neutralism benevolent to the West" is the best-known example in foreign policy of the new nationalism. Underestimation of the aspirations
of some Latin American political leaders and ideologists is all too common in a world so accustomed to thinking of that region as perma-
nently benighted.

In the rather blood-chilling exercise in *Realpolitik* which closes [a nationalistic treatise by the Brazilian intellectual, Helio Jaguaribe] . . .
the author outlines a policy in which, by judiciously playing all the
actual or potential major power blocs off against each other, Brazil will
eventually emerge as a major power in itself, completely equipped
with a store of advanced ballistic missiles and atomic weapons. There
is no reason to doubt that this kind of hardheaded analysis of future
possibilities is going on wherever such decisions are being made in
Brazil. The new outlook has recently been quite succinctly stated by a
former Minister of Finance in a newspaper defense of his dealings
with the International Monetary Fund: "Let us not create anew in
Brazil the impression that to deal with the Monetary Fund and other
credit agencies of friendly countries is an act of submission or *entre-
guismo. We are already too big and too powerful to feel shy about
contending with other nations.*" [Italics added.] [14]

[14] Frank Bonilla, "A National Ideology for Development: Brazil," in K. H. Silvert, ed., *op. cit.,* p. 253.

Brazil under Goulart was not the only state of Latin America ambitious for a kind of third-positionism. Argentina's dreams of having an A-bomb were not simply the maunderings of Perón. That country is now in the Chinese wheat trade. Uruguay has been quietly trading extensively with Soviet Russia, including massive petroleum imports, for the past five years. Chile has for long been threatening to expand contacts with Iron Country lands and has been an independent voice of non-interventionist conscience on Cuban affairs from the beginning. Mexico's political independence on the international scene has been amply demonstrated many times during the past three decades. Although the Cuban departure from the hemispheric comity is in its extreme character of a qualitatively different order from "neutralism," certain policy constituents are clearly similar.

Even though many official and semi-official spokesmen in the United States have begun to suggest that economic and social "orthodoxy" are not required for good standing in this hemisphere, "neutralism" in foreign affairs and such accompanying internal measures as the nationalization of industries strain the fabric of American policy. Latin foreign-policy independence inevitably means a weakening of the Organization of American States in favor of the United Nations and its subordinate agencies; but the United States is deeply committed to hemispheric agencies while maintaining a certain bilateralism in its dealings with Latin America. "Neutralism" also implies closer economic relations between Latin America and the Soviet bloc; but the United States remains unconvinced that pre-national states are sufficiently strong to resist the politics which accompany trade. Expropriations are often symbolically necessary to new nationalists and sometimes also have implications for the heavily *etatiste* planning for development which is characteristic of emergent lands everywhere; but such action is embarrassing to the U.S. Government when it faces its domestic business constituency and also hinders the development of the private-capital aspects of the Alliance. Independent foreign policies carry Latin American states closer to the United Nations and also drive them into an identification with Afro-Asian nations; but the ballooning of the United Nations with the recent birth of so many new states has already caused Great Power problems in that agency which have been only exacerbated by the hints of Latin American rebelliousness.

The United States will inevitably have to become accustomed to such tensions, for they are the price of the political nationalism which seemingly is a natural accompaniment of economic and social development. The Cuban experience drove the United States to much greater toleration of these stirrings than it had before, although it would be overly generous to say that as yet Washington has a fully rationalized program for the adjustments required as each Latin American country approaches the responsible exercise of power in the international community. Attempts by the United States to interest allied European nations more deeply in Latin American economic development, as well as in certain aspects of hemispheric security, indicate that the logic of multilateralism is slowly impregnating the style of hemispheric relations. The threat of the French style of international relations, however must cause worry in the United States, for its natural consequence must be an intensification of the "neutralism" and its corollaries we have noted. The debate as to whether the United States "should" have a special role in Latin America will continue, nevertheless, as will the slow emergence of Latin America into a less isolated and subordinate role—into participant membership in the Western world, instead of simply into the Western Hemisphere.[15]

In this scene of a generalized international response to the domestic processes of modernization, the role of Cuba has been extraordinarily instructive. For those whose perception is not blurred by their distance from understanding the modern world, Cuba has demonstrated the clear difference between neutralism and overt commitment to the Soviet bloc, between pragmatic statism and totalitarian *dirigisme,* between the ghetto of self-willed inferiority in which Latin America has for long wallowed and the real possibilities for emergence into the modern community of nations. Never again will we be able to say that Catholic Latin America is immune to Communism; but never again shall we be able to say, either, that Catholic Latin America is immune to modernism.

Modernization and Receptivity to Castroism: A Typology. Once again before us, then, is the central issue: how to find a modernization process containing implicit in it a minimization of the risks of totalitarian developmental procedures. Let us in the first instance note that to be receptive to modernization does not mean also an automatic receptivity to Castroism, which is by no means Latin America's only authoritarian alternative. Some of the area's scenes of high development are not very receptive to *fidelista* ideology, although they may be most hospitable to falangist authoritarianism. Others are so socially backward as to provide only meager promise of available "followership" publics. The distinction being drawn here between generic modernization and specifically *fidelista* totalitarian development is important if the Alliance on the American side and the varying approaches on the Latin American side are to create techniques for international assistance fitting to the particular circumstances of each Latin American country.

[15] See again Albert O. Hirschman, *op. cit.,* especially pp. 59–63.

In order to breathe some order into the many diverse Latin American cases, typology-building has become almost an obsession among specialists in comparative politics, as was pointed out in Chapter II. A typology—literally, the "study of types"—is simply a set of categories linked by certain common theoretical assumptions. There are, for example, typologies of Latin American countries by such criteria as their political systems, economic and social levels, their degree of national integration, and even categorizations according to what some American scholars think those republics are. Such constructions are useful in a double manner: they prevent us from thinking either that all Latin American countries are alike, or that there are no similarities among them. A "good" typology is one which guides predictions realistically and for certain purposes. In the case here being considered, a "good" typology would help to indicate where *fidelista* sentiment is most likely to occur, where urgent drives toward development exist, and how deeply into the social structure such attitudes may penetrate. Rational policy for specific groups of countries may then be developed in anticipation of crisis.

Some profound conceptual dangers attend the making of typologies, however. The figures ordinarily used, for example, are simple country averages. But the fallacy of averages is particularly to be guarded against in dealing with Latin America, where not only are intercountry differences enormous, but intra-societal variation can be so large as to make meaningless even a per capita income figure in such a country as Brazil, for example. What can be the meaning of an average which squashes into a single number the incomes of Amazonian Indian tribes, disaster-ridden farmers and villagers in the northeast, and such modern city types as the residents of São Paulo? Unhappily no typology of Latin American societies yet devised effectively mingles measures of differences among states with degrees of difference within each one. The result is that the classifications always afford higher predictive value to the cases at each end of the spread. The rudimentary countries at the bottom have such small upper groups and such massive lower ones that the averages are little affected by the few on top. In their turn the advanced lands at the top have relatively homogeneous populations (like "white" Argentina, Uruguay, Costa Rica, and Chile—the cases in point), so that the averages obscure little more than they do for such a nation as Italy. However, the countries in the middle, undergoing rapid change and with enormous social distances separating ethnic as well as class sectors, are the ones the statistics can handle least well. Obviously they are also the ones which are most politically unstable.

This warning is not meant to discourage the use of typologies, but rather to encourage their employment with caution and to suggest that more adequate categorizations are urgently needed—a task which will demand not only better statistics but, more difficult, better theory. Included as an appendix is perhaps the best typology yet devised by social stratification characteristics.[16] Some of the criteria used for the establishing of the types are literacy and higher education rates, the number of persons engaged in farming and mining and other primary activities, the percentage of persons in middle and upper social strata, the annual rate of urbanization, and so forth. These measures are very appropriate to finding those situations in which populations are mobilized and ready for admission to the modern sectors of society, but in which the channels for their reception into fully participant national life are lacking or insufficient. Such frustrated groups are presumably the ones most likely to seek extraordinary solutions to their aspirations and to be most receptive to the promises of demagoguery.

The typology set forth in the appendix divides the Latin American republics into the following categories according to figures of circa 1950, the last year for which relatively complete data are available for all the cases:

SUMMARY TYPOLOGY BY SOCIAL STRATIFICATION SYSTEMS

(In order of modernity)

Group I:	Argentina	Chile
	Uruguay	Costa Rica
Group II:	Mexico	Brazil
Group III:	Cuba	
	Venezuela	Colombia
Group IV:	Panama	
	Paraguay	Guatemala
	Peru	Nicaragua
	Ecuador	Dominican Republic
	El Salvador	Honduras
	Bolivia	Haiti

This distribution clearly is realistic in certain important ways. For instance, Costa Rica appears in the first group, despite its unindustrial and generally rural nature which in other typologies usually condemns

[16] Gino Germani, *op. cit.*, p. 168. For a related discussion of "stages" and an early version of this typology in English, see Gino Germani and K. H. Silvert, "Politics, Social Structure and Military Intervention in Latin America," *Archives Europeénes de Sociologie*, Vol. I, No. 2, 1961.

this advanced little state to a low position. The large rural populations of Mexico and Brazil do not so override their enormous modern sectors as to push them into statistical equivalence with much less developed states of more even economic characteristics. It is also fitting that as of 1950 Cuba, Venezuela, and Colombia should have occupied the same box. Even a scant six years ago the governments of all three countries were dedicated to the mutually untenable propositions of (a) maintaining unchanged social structures; (b) continuing industrialization; and (c) retaining military authoritarian rule. Since then Cuba has broken out into *fidelismo,* Venezuela has been making the hemisphere's most valiant and earnest attempt at institutional change toward the consciously chosen end of expanded democratic values, and Colombia has experienced only relatively superficial political shifts on top of an essentially unchanged social situation as the death toll from civil violence has risen past 200,000 since 1948.

The striking political changes in two of the three countries in that category of the typology containing the most rapidly transitional of the Latin American states underscores another element difficult to capture in such an instrument: velocity of social change. Dazzling is the only word for the rapidity with which Cuba moved into Communism and Venezuela passed from a horridly repressive military tyranny into Social Democratic developmental endeavors. These rapid changes are rooted in long preparatory periods, of course, but because they are most manifest in the political kingdom, a typology by political criteria would also be fitting. Although hard data are simply unavailable for such a construction, an arraying of the Latin American cases by their degree of integration into national polities may be essayed upon a subjective analysis of historical appreciations.

SUMMARY TYPOLOGY BY DEGREE OF NATIONAL INTEGRATION

GROUP I: Highest degree of homogeneity in social structure and polity:

Cuba	Uruguay
Argentina	Costa Rica

GROUP II: Strongly demarcated and homogeneous national sectors in coexistence with large groups alienated for class or ethnic reasons:

Chile	Brazil
Venezuela	Mexico

NOTE: The national sectors of these countries may exhibit a higher level of national integration than some of the lands in Group I, but their attaining full, integrated nationhood is impeded by the social differences alluded to.

GROUP III: Superordinate groups split by value disagreement concerning the desirability of national values and integration, again in coexistence with large groups alienated for class or ethnic reasons:

Bolivia   Panama

Colombia   Dominican Republic

Peru

GROUP IV: Little or no consensual acceptance of national integration among superordinate groups, with large subordinate groups alienated for class or ethnic reasons:

Guatemala   Nicaragua

Ecuador   Honduras

El Salvador   Haiti

Paraguay

This typology is open to much disagreement. Whether Bolivia fits comfortably into Group III is, for example, a matter for some debate with any definitive settlement rendered objectively impossible because of the unavailability of information concerning attitudes and values among Bolivians. This typology is informed guesswork, presented here as a sample of what is needed for articulated policy making. It suggests, for example, that even though there are few Indians in Chile, it might well be in the same functional category as Mexico because both countries possess strongly integrated sectors and functionally alienated ones, signifying that the former cannot count on consensus or the other attributes of national participation from the latter. Thus in both cases law will be less universally effective than, say, in Uruguay, where the polity has broader coverage. Whether or not this particular typology is accurate, this kind of approach is necessary to an order knowledge of the nature of Latin America's various political systems and thus, more pointedly, to a knowledge of the probabilities of given kinds of manifestations of possible significance in hemispheric relations.

This organization of materials permits suppositions concerning the relative calm of Argentina, Uruguay, Chile, and Costa Rica with respect to their internal *fidelistas.* They all have more or less powerful nationalistic movements of their own which have sopped up otherwise potential recruits to Castroism. Except for Venezuela, which has recently ascended rapidly in degree of national integration, the appeals of *fidelista* solutions are probably strongest among middle and upper social elements in whichever countries of Group III the channels of national identification are not clearly marked by domestic political ideologies.

But violence can be expected in the smallest and poorest countries, too, as the recent cases of Panama, Haiti, the Dominican Republic, Guatemala, and Honduras demonstrate with painful clearness. If *fidelismo* is to affect these republics, it can only be through leaders sufficiently cosmopolitan to understand and accept the idea system involved. Indian villagers and the alienated and suppressed peasantry of most of these countries are little susceptible to this kind of appeal in any depth, although they are often immediately available for short-term peasant revolts. If these traditional manifestations of violence among the peasantry are to be folded into continuing revolutionary activity, then it can only be through the efforts of leaders from higher in the social order acting in the name of an ideology having nothing whatever to do with peasant thought. This pattern was followed in Cuba, of course, where the revolution of the peasantry was not at all that of their middle- and upper-class coordinators.

Conclusions. The United States is most fortunate that it was Cuba and neither Venezuela nor Colombia that chose to march into the Soviet bloc. The absolute smallness and relative weakness of the defector has given the remainder of the hemisphere time to examine the case and also to inquire into the strange power ratio of the United States to Cuba, which has allowed the latter to survive—worried, it is true, but still there. The rationality of democratic discourse has not been our lot, however. A chorus of laments about the "erosion" of American power in the hemisphere has served as accompaniment to the swelling voices of desperation, their pitch going up as newspapers report revolution in Cuba, then Argentina, Peru, Ecuador, the Dominican Republic, Haiti, Guatemala, Honduras, Panama . . .

Perhaps American power is not being lessened; instead it may be that what is changing is the *nature* of the relationship between American power and that of other countries, and that what is required is simply recognition of what it now takes to achieve desired goals. Hans J. Morgenthau has recently written, "The United States has at its disposal the greatest concentration of material power existing in the world today . . . it is the most powerful nation on earth. Yet the government of that most powerful nation is incapable of making the actions of even the weakest of foreign governments conform to its desires." [17] Professor Morgenthau continues into statements most appropriate to the Cuban situation, writing:

> Some of these peoples [of the weak nations] have become active participants in the process of emancipation, and they now have governments that govern in their name and with their support. Thus, a strong nation intervening with military force may not accomplish its task by removing the government or even conquering the country. It may also

[17] "The Impotence of American Power," *Commentary*, Vol. XXXVI, No. 5, November, 1963, p. 384.

have to subdue the population at large, which may take up arms against it. While these possibilities do not rule out the use of force, they make a powerful nation think twice before resorting to it.[18]

The lesson is quite clear in the international market place of ideas that among other reasons, the United States does not wish to use unilaterally applied armed force against Cuba because of the probably high mortality figures which would result. A contained uprising of Cuban rebels with some limited American support is obviously one thing, a quasi-national war a very different thing. Castro's running defense against invasion rests, then, in the loyalty he can command though his charisma; his *ultimate* defense against invasion, however, is that the United States does not *choose* to destroy him under these conditions. Is this impasse the result of a lack of American power? If we are speaking of power quantitatively, then the answer must be no. If we speak qualitatively, however, then the reply must be in the affirmative, for the United States apparently lacks a diversity of *types* of power. To use a military analogy, the United States has been unable to fight an immediately successful diplomatic bush war in Cuba. It is not that power is lost, but rather that no newly appropriate ways of employing power have been found. Again, to cite Professor Morgenthau:

> Our impotence in the fullness of our power is, then, in some measure the result of objective conditions over which we have no control and which restrict the power of other powerful nations as well. In good measure, however, the source of that impotence is in ourselves. We are paralyzed because our moral, intellectual, and political judgment has gone astray. Our judgment must be reformed before we can expect to recover the use of our power, and upon that recovery the improvement of our foreign policies must wait.[19]

The effect of Cuba on the hemisphere *qua* hemisphere has been like the salt in a stew: little has really been added, but all the tastes in the brew have been accented. The meat and potato problems remain the same. They are all the old ones: (1) how to promote responsible nationalism; (2) how to make for social development; (3) how to push economic development; (4) how to wrap those three questions in a political package acceptable to domestic politics in the United States and the several Latin American republics; (5) how to keep the Cold War out of the hemisphere while all those objectives are being accomplished; and (6) how to develop the administrative mechanism which will make the pursuit of the preceding goals possible in ways appropriate to each Latin American republic.

If we are to tot up a score, then it may be said that the United States

[18] *Ibid.*, p. 385.
[19] *Ibid.*, p. 386.

has so far succeeded in depressing Communist influence in the nineteen republics and in keeping Cuba demilitarized in the atomic and rocket sense; and the next credit must be chalked up for realistic innovation in linking social to economic development in an Alliance afflicted with the debilities already mentioned. In all other respects the United States has suffered a flat failure by default—a necessary failure because it did not even try. Only vague words have been occasionally sounded to assist the growth of Western ideologies of national identification in Latin America. Social development has been translated only into the materialistic terms of housing, literacy, and land reform instead of also into the meaty questions of status, identification, the finding of a new consciousness in the excitement of building a decent Latin-America. Economic development has been toyed with as a simple apolitical matter of market places and capital allocations—an exercise in dehumanized gamesmanship which, if successful, will see industries happily belching forth democratic people at the end of the process. Finally, it is obvious that good administrative practices cannot be established if the administrators do not know the policy they are supposed to follow.

Even below these grand levels, operational decisions have failed to imbue actions with consistency within the tested categories of a reasonably sophisticated typology. Military insurrections are then good in Guatemala and Ecuador, acceptable in Argentina, bad and then good in Peru, very bad and then perhaps all right in the Dominican Republic and Honduras. Austerity programs are a punishment to friendly nations who do not wish to argue with the United States; recalcitrant ones can get the funds anyway with a little dickering. Panama is made the site of training grounds for paramilitary activities and civil control, but a mixed mob of Panamanian students and adult nationalists must be amateurishly fired upon in order to control them.

Aside from the hopefully only temporary loss of Cuba to the Western world, then, Castroism worked no fundamental change in hemispheric relations. The fall of the island to Communism has exacerbated pre-existing problems and cast them in a new light. Democratic groups still have time to find proper solutions, however, and there is little reason to think that the ration of time is not fairly generous in most of the republics. If a relaxation in East-West tensions leads to a relaxed American attitude concerning the developmental problems of Latin America, then Latin American "neutralism" may become somewhat less warm to the United States if not to the West. If the United States is successful in infusing the hemisphere with political excitement and public hope, then the reward may well be an enlargement of the effective Western community providing increased basic security for all, a commonality of long-range policy, and the friendly converse of brothers in the dealings of the day.

The Design of Action. Many recent books of scandalized appraisal of the Latin American "case" march bravely along to close with sets of bold recommendations. There they fall to pieces. Either they retreat into international social work, or propose that the American government act in ways entirely antithetical to domestic policy considerations, or blandly announce that nothing can be done and that the United States should simply abdicate its position in the hemisphere. This author has no intention of entering into this game, for he is firmly in the anti-philosopher-king camp, convinced that academic expertise ends when the artistry of political choice begins. The opening paragraphs define the intent of this study as to "justify an addition to the literature by trying to use . . . [the] profession to help others make whatever may be their choices in a mood of more rationality and self-awareness." In pursuit of this end, these concluding paragraphs will be dedicated to suggesting appropriate levels of policy making so that the control of greater self-awareness and better technique may infuse the taking of action.

Most recommendations for the improvement of American foreign policy have been of "Ugly American" persuasion. That is, they have concerned themselves with the administration of day-to-day problems, with the instrumental part of the task alone, and even that in a narrow sense. Thus we are told that all will be well if our representatives in Latin America speak Spanish and Portuguese, if their personalities are warm and they get out and talk to the "people," if the "one-feathered Indians" will learn at once both to be responsible and not to subvert policy from above, and so forth. What it is that they will say in their Spanish and Portuguese to the "people" and how the yeoman in the foreign assignments can both god and slave are left unspoken. In any event, this portion of the problem is one for adequate administrative management. It is by no means an unimportant consideration, for the tone and style of daily affairs depend in good measure upon the routine activities of American representatives abroad and their counterparts at home. Insufficiencies here can cause small incidents to become serious ones or can cause bad reporting and information evaluation which impede rational direction from Washington. Recommendations for improvement at this level are numerous, and it is the subjective impression of this author that the quality of American representation abroad has risen sharply in the last few years. It might be added that greater inter-agency coordination seems patently desirable, a matter not only for administrative housekeeping experts but also for the weavers of guidelines in Washington.

At the opposite extreme from day-to-day problems lie the profound policy interests, where the cultural heart of the nation beats. To make any recommendations for action here would seem pointless not only because we are all agreed that man should be good and free and decent, but also because so little can be done to change matters at this level. Because it is this core of values which publicists like to project as an "image," however, a more explicit awareness of implicit attitudes can well be of operational significance. For example, it is hackneyed to point out that F. D. Roosevelt was beloved of the Latin Americans although his administrations did little materially for them, or that the great sadness evoked by the assassination of President Kennedy called forth a profound sense of identification from all peoples of the hemisphere. The United States, to take another example, has often been singled out as the most revolutionary factor in Latin America because of the stimuli for change, emulation, and aspiration with which it bombards other countries merely by existing. Many public-opinion polls taken in Latin America reflect this fundamental identification with what the United States symbolizes,[20] although the same persons who express this primary sympathy may also attack specific American foreign policy with great bitterness.

The filling of the psychological and ideological gap in the hemisphere, the generation of "magic," depends on some definition and projection of this area of basic value stance. The accomplishment of this task is not in the hands of bureaucrats, except in its relatively secondary technical aspects. The crystallization of "image" depends from the topmost levels of government, where style, conviction, and decision flow together. If the executive establishment itself does not choose to reflect from the profound well of the American value system those attitudes appealing to the deepest convictions of Latin America's modernizing nationalists, then hemispheric relations will have to struggle along at a reduced intensity of emotional warmth. Certainly it is clear that American presidential politics cannot be decided upon the basis of what will promote identification with the present or future leaders of the developing areas, Latin or otherwise.

The Latin American modernizing nationalist seeks sovereignty, international respect, economic advance, impersonality in administration and politics, and a full measure of the consensus and political legitimacy patterns of the nation-state. He is inevitably something of a pop-

[20] See, for example, Alain Girard and Raúl Samuel, *Situación y perspectivas de Chile en Septiembre de 1957,* Santiago de Chile: Ed. Universitaria, 1958, in which we find the United States the most favorably seen non-Latin American country by a third of the Chileans interviewed; West Germany is next with 20 per cent, and only 4 per cent chose Soviet Russia. About 85 per cent named democratic Western states.

ulist, for his views demand that all persons in his society should be included within the polity and the economy. Unless he establishes a functioning national community, he cannot have the markets needed for industrialization, the voters needed for his support, the initial popular enthusiasm required for him to brush away the moldy structure of Iberian neo-feudalism. He wants colleagueship from the United States in his endeavors. He has no choice but to perspire, to be fanatical, and to wave his arms in a struggle which sometimes costs him his life. When he speaks of freedom and dignity, he is certainly not thinking in the structural and administrative and procedural terms of the United States. But what he fears is that he is not speaking in our basic value terms, either. Once he is reassured in this respect, American policy will have gained the enormous freedom of broad latitudes at the applied policy level, and any number of gaffes in day-to-day relations will be dismissed in the glow of a deeper identification.

At this profound level of affairs, having to do with cultural integrity and security, the United States should have a deep interest in Latin America as a growingly active and contributing power in Western life. Berle is certainly correct in saying that economically the United States can "live" without Latin America. But is there here also an inference that we can live as well culturally if a potentially major group of Western nations chooses developmental paths which may leave the democracies of European orientation more conceptually and ideologically isolated than they need to be? Latin America is the largest readily available reservoir of recruits to Western modernism in the world. It would appear to the obvious benefit of the deepest values in American life that they become ever more creative parts of the Western social continuum for the mutual cultural enrichment of all concerned.

The most difficult intellectual task of the statesman is to "operationalize" his country's basic values, to recognize them and then transmute them into long-term policy statements. Even when such policy seems firm, the line between its formulation and its application in specific situations is open to attack by everyone from stevedores to oil-company executives. Whatever the political difficulties, however, effective policy need not always be consistent or entirely predictable, but it must at least be coherent and fitting to the conditions for which it has been designed. At this point Professor Morgenthau's lament about American policy must again concern us. The incoherence in our hemispheric actions may arise because sometimes we immediately and directly address a problem, successfully solve it, and pass on; or other times we become alarmed and swat furiously at the air; and on still other occasions we try to stop the tides. There are many more cases of power and policy well and skillfully applied than are well known, for failure makes

APPENDIX

TYPES OF SOCIAL STRATIFICATION IN LATIN AMERICA—c. 1950

COUNTRIES	PER CENT MIDDLE & UPPER STRATA	PER CENT IN PRIMARY ACTIVITIES	PER CENT IN CITIES OVER 20,000	PER CENT UR-BAN MIDDLE & UPPER STRATA	PER CENT LITERATE	UNIVERSITY STUDENTS PER 1000 POP.	ANNUAL RATE OF URBANIZA-TION	PER CENT EMPLOYED IN INDUSTRY
ARGENTINA ⎫ Predom-inantly	36	25	48	28	87	7.7	17	13.5
URUGUAY ⎬ urban	—	22	50	—	95	5.2	14	13.0
CHILE ⎭	22	35	43	21	80	3.9	16	9.1
COSTA RICA ⎰ Predom-inantly rural	22	57	18	14	80	3.9	16	4.8

a. Middle strata: 20 per cent and over; b. cultural, psychological, and political existence of a middle class; c. ethnic and cultural homogeneity; national identification and considerable level of participation among various social sectors; d. urban-rural differences and geographical discontinuity exist, but in lesser degree than in other Latin American countries.

COUNTRIES	PER CENT MIDDLE & UPPER STRATA	PER CENT IN PRIMARY ACTIVITIES	PER CENT IN CITIES OVER 20,000	PER CENT UR-BAN MIDDLE & UPPER STRATA	PER CENT LITERATE	UNIVERSITY STUDENTS PER 1000 POP.	ANNUAL RATE OF URBANIZA-TION	PER CENT EMPLOYED IN INDUSTRY
MEXICO — Lesser survival of traditionalism		56	24		59	0.9	17	6.7

a. Middle strata: between 15 and 20 per cent approximately; b. middle class emergent (but see d.); c. ethnic and cultural heterogeneity; pronounced imbalance in the level of participation in national society and other aspects of social life; d. strong regional imbalances with concentration of urbanization and industrialization in certain areas with rural ways of life predominating in the greater part of the country.

COUNTRIES	PER CENT MIDDLE & UPPER STRATA	PER CENT IN PRIMARY ACTIVITIES	PER CENT IN CITIES OVER 20,000	PER CENT UR-BAN MIDDLE & UPPER STRATA	PER CENT LITERATE	UNIVERSITY STUDENTS PER 1000 POP.	ANNUAL RATE OF URBANIZA-TION	PER CENT EMPLOYED IN INDUSTRY
BRAZIL — Greater survival of traditionalism	15	62	20	13	49	1.2	13	6.2

a. Middle strata: between 15 and 20 per cent approximately; b. middle class emergent (but the level of its self-identification is debatable); c. ethnic and cultural heterogeneity, pronounced imbalances in the degree of participation in national society and other aspects of social life; d. pronounced discontinuity between rural and urban areas and strong regional imbalances.

CUBA { Predominantly urban	22	44	37	3.9	21	78	9	8.0	
VENEZUELA	18	44	31	1.3	16	52	29	6.5	
COLOMBIA { Predominantly rural	22	58	22	1.0	12	63	17	4.3	
PANAMA	15	55	22	2.6	15	70	15	3.0	
PARAGUAY	14	54	15	1.3	12	66	12	3.3	
PERU	—	60	14	1.8	—	42	11	4.7	
ECUADOR	10	51	18	1.4	10	56	12	3.5	
EL SALVADOR	10	64	13	0.5	9	57	9	4.7	
BOLIVIA	8	68	20	2.0	7	32	9	2.8	
GUATEMALA	8	75	11	0.1	6	20	10	3.2	
NICARAGUA	—	71	15	0.7	—	38	8	2.0	
DOMINICAN REP.	—	70	11	1.2	—	43	10	3.0	
HONDURAS	4	76	7	0.7	4	35	10	1.6	
HAITI	3	77	5	—	2	11	5	1.4	

a. Middle strata: below 15 per cent; middle sectors emergent in some countries, but clear persistence in all in varying degrees of traditional patterns; b. ethnic and cultural heterogeneity in almost all; d. vast sectors of the population still marginal; d. rural predominance in general; regional imbalances.

Sources: For "middle and upper strata" and "urban middle and upper strata," elaboration by the author and estimates based on the Census of the Americas, approximately 1950; "employed population in primary occupations": CEPAL, "The Structure of Employment in Latin America," published in *Boletín Económico para América Latina*, Vol. II, No. 1, 1957; "per cent literate": Panamerican Union: *El analfabetismo en América*, Washington, 1958; "university students per 1000 population": *Anuario Internacional de Educación* and national censuses; "annual urbanization rate": CEPAL, *op. cit.*: this rate represents the annual increase of urban areas per 100 persons of the total population; "per cent employed in industry": CEPAL, *op. cit.*

Note: Reproduced from Gino Germani, *Política y sociedad en una época de transición: De la sociedad tradicional a la sociedad de masas*, Buenos Aires: Ed. Paidós, 1962, p. 169. Any errors of translation are the fault of K. H. Silvert.

news. But we have often beat at the air in our fear that all Latin Americans were being restrained from rushing into the embrace of Castro only through our own efforts. We have also tried to stop such tides as the Mexican Revolution and the growth of national politics in Venezuela, only to find later that in both cases stable, complex, and mutually beneficial accommodations could indeed be reached.

Effective policy making consists in equating basic values with available power and using the best operational means at hand in working within the set of possibilities delimiting whatever may be the given situation. The very reason for building typologies, of course, is to expose the range of possibilities within given Latin American situations. The reason for making foreign-service personnel of all agencies as effective as possible is that the loss of policy essence to the machinery of application should be as little as possible. The purpose of adequate long-term policy formulation is to breathe coherence and logic into a system of international relationships devised in such manner as constantly to test the validity of the basic goals assumed as measuring victory and of the power ratios realistically involved in each situation. The Latin American tide is modernization. This statement also implies that the tide is flowing toward industrialization, nationalism, and an opening of social structures. The process of development inevitably implies the growth of social areas of secularism, economic and political market places, impersonalism expressed in the rule of law and a merit bureaucracy, and of a value system supportive of these institutional structures. No country of the world should know these requirements of modernism better than the United States or know more intimately how important relative and pragmatic solutions to social problems are to the fabric of a democratic society of compromise. Policies which will channel power toward assisting in these profound transformations of Latin American life will be successful in assisting the nations of that area toward their basic goal of a modern existence, as well as toward our basic goals—of even greater human dignity and individual fulfillment. At heart the goals of democratic Americans are the same as those of modernizing Latin Americans. We should no more assist their enemies than we should our own, whether these inimical forces are of the Communist camp or from Latin America's own falangist traditionalism. An affirmative support of Latin America's modernizers with the insights gained from our own history of democratic development is the only effective bulwark against totalitarianism.

16

PEACE, FREEDOM, AND STABILITY IN
THE WESTERN HEMISPHERE

There will be no fruitful peace or stability in the Western Hemisphere without a growth of substantive freedom. The mark of our times is that this statement should emit a polemically hollow ring, instead of being heard as the reasonable inference from historical experience which it is. This reaffirmation of the philosophical views of many eighteenth- and nineteenth-century thinkers of France, England, and the United States serves to remind us that awareness of the relationship between development and freedom is not new, albeit neglected. Hypnotized by the apparent strength and efficiency of authoritarian rule, doubtful of our ability to arrive at ethical or moral decisions concerning public life, and simplistic in our thinking about the processes of development, many of us surrender easily to the crude generalization that by definition underdeveloped lands cannot be democratic and that therefore the direct fomenting of freedom is not a meaningful policy concern.[1] The blanket excuse of necessary authoritarianism may then be called on to rationalize political action whenever justification must be found for supporting policies of a repressive or extraordinarily partisan nature. But because such a simulated *Realpolitik* is distasteful to persons who espouse democratic beliefs, we tend to relax our terminological rigor to cover the implicit opportunism. Thus our lexicon has grown so gross that we

[1] I am very grateful to Dr. Bernard Rosenberg, Professor of Sociology at the City College of New York, who on a beach in Piriápolis, Uruguay, destroyed my own facile belief in this fallacy and pushed me into thinking about the functional relationship between freedom and development.

assume barracks revolts can remove countries from democracy to authoritarianism from one day to the next, or that a neatly placed assassin's bullet can manufacture a free polity. This easiness of thought prevents effective prediction; it is also intellectually undignified.

The original conceptual sin is to think democracy synonymous with freedom. The exercise of freedom involves the making of effective choice among meaningful alternatives; democracy is the formal political system which institutionalizes the practice of civic choice. The firmly rooted existence of the power to make ordered and periodic political selections among reasonably different alternatives which we call democracy naturally tends also to guarantee the continued ability to make free choices in some non-civic areas. But certain kinds of freedom can be practiced independent of full political freedom. Certainly there are many easily observable situations in which the political mechanism does not conform even to a loose definition of formal democracy, but in which a large and socially significant measure of other freedoms exists. The government of Mexico, to take Latin America's most notorious case, is not organized to permit an effective and periodic intervention into the policy affairs of the state by an electorate grouped in significantly differing political parties. Mexico's is a constitutional government but not a constitutional democracy. Even so, compared to many neighboring republics, there is certainly a large measure of genuine civil liberty in Mexico: speech is quite freely exercised; the press is perhaps too unfettered; religious beliefs may be expressed through a variety of disestablished churches. In a larger social sense, the freedom to move about, to seek personal advantage, to be socially mobile—all have been made more possible for more persons during the past fifty years. Surely no reasonably strict categorization could include Mexico within the ranks of the formal democracies; and conversely, certainly we contribute nothing to clarity by dismissing that country as simply another authoritarianism because of its party and electoral systems. In order to avoid lumping Mexico in with Paraguay, for example, most academic as well as lay observers prefer to group it with Great Britain and New Zealand, as though this categorical monstrosity is to be excused because we have at least not insulted Mexico. Plainly we are not meeting the facts with adequate theory and reasonably fine terminology.

The temptation is often great to shrug off the immediate effects of repressive politics on the grounds that certain dictatorial measures which favor economic development also will be conducive in the long run to the establishment of full-blown democracies.[2] This ricochet the-

---

[2] Authoritarian techniques of development have certain capabilities, of course, They can be used to build pyramids and factories, force savings and mobilize

ory of development is commonly held in Latin America. The implied unilineal act of faith runs somewhat as follows: a change in the "economic base" necessarily affects the occupational stratification system, which in turn must be reinforced by appropriate adjustments in the educational system; when persons find themselves in new occupations certified by formal educations, they feel themselves in a different class situation; the job plus the education plus the attitude create the middle class; persons in the middle class have a stake to defend in the community; they therefore organize special-interest groups and parties; these actions in themselves define a pluralistic society, which is the very essence of modern democracy. Conclusion: from industrialization all else flows automatically into ultimate human freedom and dignity.

The Latin American experience, however, particularly as it is exemplified by Uruguay, Argentina, and Chile, teaches us that this procession can—and probably must—break down into depression, stagnation, and even on occasion death and destruction. Development is neither unilineal nor automatic. The choices of men and their ability to translate those choices into action constitute one of the determinants of whether the process will be expeditious and immediately fruitful or nasty, brutish, savage, and corrupt, and perhaps even a total failure. In short, freedom of choice does not come at the end of the line; it must be exercised throughout in ways apposite to the situation and the types of change being wrought, and the responsibility for making such choices must grow and extend itself in some reasonable relationship to the increasing specialization, interdependence, and complication of modernism. Viewed in this fashion, freedom is at least as intrinsic to the development process as is occupational specialization, capital investment, or industrial urbanization.

Full development is not merely a state of existence; it is also a process, a means of organizing change so that further development can proceed without breakdowns. It is in this dynamic sense that stability is essential to development—a stability not of being, so to speak, but of becoming. The acceptance of the idea of process is thus also a recognition of the responsibility for making the choices which allow self-sustaining development to continue. These modern choices can only be made by modern men; any theory of development must obviously include a concept of developed persons.

The ability of Latin American countries to muster persons capable of making those decisions requisite for development cannot be measured by global questions concerning their over-all authoritarian or liber-

labor. Their fundamental limitation is that when the development is toward contemporary modernization, authoritarianism eventually breaks down as incompatible with fully self-sustaining societies. Authoritarianism does not generate the attitudes and values necessary for the chain reactions of the modern, empirical society.

tarian situations. We must start from recognition of the obvious, that all twenty Latin American republics lack democratic organization and substantive freedom in one or another fashion crucial to their further growth. That statement does not imply that they lack all significant areas of freedom, that there are not striking differences among them, or that persons able to exercise freedom are totally absent. A positive approach would seek to identify the persons in Latin America capable and desirous of acting as modern persons. We need to learn to what extent freedoms exist because the pre-national societies of Latin America cannot support governments strong enough to be effectively repressive. Is unfreedom practiced in such a manner as to hamper the general developmental process? Does whatever freedom is exercised tend to generate further freedom? Does the developed international community support the extension of rational and free choice in Latin America through its policy posture, its cultural stance, and its specific diplomatic and economic measures?

This search for the types and areas of freedom and unfreedom is not a pandering to a mere taste for romantic political thinking. It is rather a search for those persons and groups in Latin America most capable of recognizing and accepting the full and painful costs of political, social, and economic modernization. And make no mistake—the adoption of modernism implies the dolorous extirpation of the comforts of traditional privilege and the blindness of the equally traditional ignorance of the underprivileged. Aldous Huxley has put the matter thus:

> The advance from primitivism to civilization, from mere blood to mind and spirit, is a progress whose price is fixed; there are no discounts even for the most highly talented purchasers . . .
>
> Human Bondage, in the words of Spinoza, is the price of Human Freedom. The advantages of the first state (and Human Bondage has many and substantial advantages) are incompatible with those of the second. We must be content to pay, and indefinitely to go on paying, the irreducible price of the goods we have chosen.[3]

MODERNISM AND THE WORLD EXPERIENCE

The hallmarks of modernism can be found only by explicit historical reference to the already developed states. There need be no fear that such an exercise in drawing a cultural base line presumes the attempt in any narrow sense to recreate the world in the image of the modern West. The specifics of time and technological level as well as the point of departure of each of the developing lands preclude the possibility that the patterns of change or the results thereof will be the same everywhere at all times. We may also permit ourselves the hope that

[3] *Beyond the Mexique Bay*, Penguin Books Edition, 1955, pp. 219–20.

the ingenuity and generosity of man will be employed to "skip stages," to "telescope time," to make the advent of the modern society at least in part the product of rationality and reasoned choice, as we have implied before. Withal, there must be something similar running through all modern peoples—a statement which is no less than a definitional necessity, of course. Even at the risk of incurring an ingenuous charge of xenophobia, or of distressing our underdeveloped neighbors who want both absolute cultural integrity and sweeping change, I must insist that the only way to keep from thrashing about more than is necessary is clearly to recognize the minimum and universal cost of becoming modern, that irreducible price which all must pay for industrial civilization and its fruits, both bitter and sweet.

Relatively less attention has been paid to the political invariables of development than to the economic, social, and international factors. And yet it is precisely in the area of public organization that we can find certain imperatives which are no less universal than, for example, the economic truism that a higher level of occupational specialization is an inevitable concomitant of development. First, fully modern, self-sustaining economic development has thus far been found to occur only within the social scene of the nation-state. When technology and communications were more rudimentary, it was sufficient if the nation included only upper- and middle-class persons, as in the England of the last century. But mass production, mass communications, and the necessity for mass markets have bred the popular, total nation-state which bridges certain differences among all social levels. A state's ability to make a peaceful and regular transition from the restricted nation-state (nineteenth-century England) to a total nation-state (modern England) provides an important measure of the degree of its social and political development. The process of transformation into a total nation-state strains to the utmost the self-sustaining capabilities of a country and demonstrates whether it has succeeded in institutionalizing the ability to change.[4]

There is yet another clear imperative: every nation-state that has succeeded in reaching the highest levels of economic productivity and in enjoying self-sustaining social development has also had a political structure which has guaranteed public liberty to a degree that it has been possible to discover the alternatives of the period, debate their merits, and choose from among them. Every fully developed nation is a

---

[4] The crises of the thirties in the United States, for example, in part concerned the extension of full participation in the nation to lower socio-economic groups. The Southern race issue is cut from the same cloth. Postwar problems in the United Kingdom, and especially the matter of education, also concern the mitigation of class difference and a wider access for all to the possibilities of the total society.

political democracy.[5] There are no historical exceptions to these two rules.[6]

The addition of the political to the economic and social concepts of development suggests that a fundamental likeness among all developed lands is that they have found a way of synthesizing complexity, of creating and channeling public power, and of organizing individual participation in and access to society and its institutions. These syntheses sprang from new understandings and a new concept of community; similarly in today's underdeveloped world a new kind of man is needed for the creation of the new symbols and their continued comprehension. When man undertakes to remake himself, when he embarks for whatever the reasons on the modern experience, he becomes a different kind of human being.

Western man has something which neither the preliterate nor any of his ancestors did possess, something that imposes the privilege and complicating duty of intellectual integrity, self-criticism, and generalized disinterestedness. If there is such a thing as the white man's burden, this is it.[7]

The modern world depends for its continued existence upon persons

[5] The Soviet Union is usually classed as an intermediately developed country. A very strong case can be built for the argument that as development has proceeded, of necessity certain areas of liberty have opened within that country. The relative freedom allegedly given to Soviet scientists is some hint that developmental success and areas of liberty also go hand in hand in Soviet Russia. It will be remembered that the ethical justification advanced for the American policy of containment was precisely that of giving the Soviet Union a chance to work out its internal dynamics, at the same time attempting to minimize the risks of her expansion. The spectacle of a nation possessing thermonuclear weapons and advanced rocketry still suffering the pangs of political succession is a clear case of the dangers inherent in warped growth—and is a problem which must be solved if that country's general development is to proceed without internal institutional break or suicidal war.

Nazi Germany is another example of only partial development and points up for those addicted to naked economic and technical assistance the disastrous error of assuming that economic development alone is sufficient to guarantee continued general development.

By the terms of the argument (that full development involves the ability to make further change without breakdown), France, too, shows signs of insufficient maturity. The French crisis appears to be in the nature of the difficult adjustment to the complete national community and the mitigation of class conflict.

[6] What the social scientists of the future may write is another matter. The forms of public decision making may well change with increasingly complex technology and growing world interdependence which enlarges the needed political community. But if the fundamental thesis of this paper is correct, then the question of the exercise of effective and responsible judgment will of necessity extend itself.

[7] J. C. Furnas, *The Anatomy of Paradise,* New York: William Sloan Associates, 1937, p. 488, as quoted in Robert Redfield's valuable book, *The Primitive World and its Transformations,* Ithaca: Great Seal Books, 1953, p. 158.

who have these qualities of "intellectual integrity, self-criticism, and generalized disinterestedness." The elevated degree of mutual interdependence and the long-term nature of individual and collective commitments erect themselves upon a great working faith in other persons and in the social order as a whole. Modern man must predict over generations, or he cannot predict for the next moment, let alone educate his children or accumulate investment capital. He must have faith in persons at a far social remove, or he will have no confidence in an electric light switch. He must therefore also renounce a public absolutism which lessens the advantages of a high order of specialization and hinders the processes of that limited relativism to which modernism commits him in his public life.

In the civic sphere, then, modern man must be free to learn and inquire, he must be pragmatic, empirical, and secular, and practice a general loyalty of a most impersonal and extended nature. Anything less is inefficient and threatening to the entire system. The efficiency springs from the necessity to construct as unfettering a social order as possible in order to permit maximum harmony between innate individual ability and its full flowering. The mobilization of capital resources to which so much attention is paid is a trifling matter compared to the organization of human resources, on which the modern employment of capital depends. This relationship between freedom and efficiency is not a novel concept among philosophers of science; a slight substitution of terms in the following quotation makes it most apt for a theory of development and underscores the intimate relationship between science and the modern society:

> The existing practice of scientific life embodies the claim that freedom is an efficient form of organization . . .
>
> The co-ordinative principle of science . . . stands out in all its simple and obvious nature. It consists in the adjustment of each scientist's activities to the results hitherto achieved by others. In adjusting himself to the others each scientist acts independently, yet by virtue of these several adjustments scientists keep extending together with a maximum efficiency the achievements of science as a whole . . .[8]

But the scientific community, of course, is not society as a whole. The process of self-adjustment and the finding of mutual benefit within a homogeneous scientific community are not subject to the same inhibitions found in stratified societies. For people as a whole to benefit from the same freedoms and their related efficiencies, there must be a general recognition that social unfreedom lowers productivity and restricts

---

[8] Michael Polanyi, *The Logic of Liberty: Reflections and Rejoinders*, Chicago: The University of Chicago Press, 1951, pp. 34–35.

consumption. If class exclusions in semi-industrialized lands such as we find in Latin America are carried to the extremes of being castelike, for instance, they create a direct threat to the social order and to the entire set of complicated predictions upon which it is based. Partially developed lands unwilling to open the national community to all eligible participants must apply a politics of force, progressively violating what limited freedoms may exist and upon which the limited sector of modernism is rested.

Great personal risk is inherent in the kind of freedom implied by anticipatory self-adjustment and an extended impersonal reliance on others. In modern society the national state is employed as the regulating and sanctioning public institution to minimize the dangers inherent in such far-flung and impersonal commitments. Law is accepted as a secular substitute for religious sanction in public affairs, assumed as it is that a law will be obeyed as though absolute until it may be changed. More important, the rule of law itself is the central operational measure of the mitigation of class and other internecine conflict, and thus the rule of law permits the emergence of that general social interest within which the greater individual freedom and efficiency play. To the extent to which man is equal before the laws, he begins to escape the bondage of class and those other ascriptions which enslave him by limiting his power to act in ways that benefit both himself and his society. Liberty to be rational and to project oneself and an environment which opens to the individual opportunities for social confidence, equality before the laws, and the fraternity of the enlarged national community are still primary guides to the social and political requisites of development.

Pre-national peoples have not the capacity to see across the space, time, and social dimensions of modernism. The tribal man is caught in the trap of his face-to-face relationships and his intimate intermingling of the secular with the religious in his systematization of causation. The medieval traditional man with his roots in feudal universalism looks only up and down in his view of authority, assumes his status and that of all others to be ordained and unchangeable, and subscribes to the view that all acts are to be judged by the two swords of the formally religious and the narrowly secular. His views are much more complex and stylized than those of tribal man, but they are still too restricted, strikingly anti-pragmatic and anti-secular, too dedicated to stasis to contribute to a society that has been at least partially organized to institutionalize change.

In Latin America all these qualitatively different kinds of men and societies coexist. It is as though the course of human history were stood on end—hunting and fishing cultures, tribes, the feudal fief, mercantilistic states, and national enclaves all coexisting. Nevertheless, in every Latin American state there are persons who, in their attitudes, values, training, and desires, are equipped to pay the costs, assume the responsibilities, and enjoy the privileges of the modernization which is at least the avowed goal of all public spokesmen.

Just as hardly any Latin American statesman can protest that he is anything but a lover of democracy, so all must respect the ritual of the obeisance to development. The nature of Latin America's authoritarianisms, viewed from the angle of how they are equipped to give power to modern elements, may afford a clue as to the likely significance now and in the future of such protestations.

AUTHORITARIANISM AND MODERN MEN

A summary statement of the developed individual in his social functions will establish the complete definition here being advanced. In matters political modern men ideally accept the rule of law and a given operational sphere for government as the ultimate arbiter of secular dispute; in social affairs they can look far from their own class base, project themselves into the situation of the other person, and accept certain areas of social equality; in the economic order they are self-adjusting to the work of others, have sufficient confidence to be specialized and to predict, and recognize the essential logic of the cumulative, specialized, and coordinative nature of the modern, roundabout, mass-production economy. These characteristics, spelling out some ways in which such persons have the capacity to exercise freedom and to permit others to exercise it within a framework of process, add up to a difficult and admirable exercise in the extension of the human imagination for the sake of a continued expansion of human capacities. These abilities are not the restricted powers of the few. Most persons, at all levels, in modern societies act as though they have these capabilities, whether or not they are conscious of them.

Persons with these social abilities are not scattered at random in Latin America. They tend to cluster in occupations close to the areas of most dynamic development, and they can be found in large proportions in those intellectual pursuits most closely dependent on the scientific attitude. Their habitat is, by and large, the city.[9] The overt political ideologies they hold may vary widely: they may be classical Manchesterian Liberals, traditional Gallican-oriented Radicals, Chris-

---

[9] These statements appear clearly supported by empirical evidence gathered in K. H. Silvert and Frank Bonilla, *Education and the Social Meaning of Development: A Preliminary Statement*, New York: American Universities Field Staff, 1961, mimeo., a study supported by Carnegie Corporation of New York. Samples were taken from Brazil, Argentina, Chile, and Mexico of groups ranging from slum dwellers in Rio de Janeiro to members of the Mexican National Congress.

tian Democrats, Socialists, or Communists. They will almost never identify with the traditional scale of political ideology, from Latin American Conservatives on the right to Falangists imbued with Mediterranean syndicalism on the left. If modern persons rarely or never adopt a traditional ideology, it is not true that some marginally traditional persons do not adopt a seemingly modern ideology. Many persons allied with the spectrum running from Liberalism to Communism are either quite traditionalist in their values or else quite mixed. The quasi-modern party structure often splits between left and right precisely over the questions of the full acceptance of the implications of modern organization and the procedures with which the events of such an order must be, can be, or will be brought about.

The chances of finding modern or potentially modern individuals must vary, naturally, with the level of social advance already attained and with the amount of public freedom which may have accompanied economic and social elaboration. Insufficient research has been done in Latin America to permit an absolutely confident construction of typologies of authoritarianism and freedom, especially as they may be related to the social attitudes of the several citizenries. The following essay in this direction is somewhat speculative, then, but does no particular violence to conventional and reasonable views.

The simplest authoritarianisms in Latin America are the personalistic dictatorships—the *caciquismos* and *caudillismos*. They exist in such socially rudimentary and fragmented countries as Paraguay and Honduras. Only in the uppermost stratum of these countries can there readily be found persons of modern mentality. They are the products of acculturation, of foreign or foreign-style education, and cosmopolitan tastes. The *mercantilistic authoritarianisms*—Nicaragua and the Dominican Republic under Trujillo at the simpler end of the spectrum, emerging from the *caudillismos,* with such a country as Batista Cuba at the more complex end of this scale—are governments which, to put it baldly, are in business. Such states may support themselves upon relatively primitive social situations, or yet again on relatively advanced ones in terms of urbanization, but the common denominator is that the political leadership takes advantage of a sharp split between a strong international economic structure and a weak domestic one. The power derived from the former is used for the imposition of quasi-modern control techniques over the entire polity. The modern social sector sometimes can be quite extended in this form because of the international nature of the commitments of the leadership, their usual disdain for certain of the more traditional measures of social status, and the large numbers of persons who must be trained to run the enterprises owned by or ancillary to the ruling group. When such governments operate within the context of fairly developed cities, they often find themselves threatened with social revolution and at times descend to widespread and extreme brutality to remain in power.

The *Liberal-Conservative oligarchies* are a very traditional form, classically revealed in the recent histories of Argentina, Chile, and Uruguay, among others. They are extant today in such countries as El Salvador and even in Colombia. These trust governments often discharge fruitful transitional functions. Usually imbued with notions of French libertarianism and positivism, these oligarchies have sometimes provided the bridge between traditional class-bound *caudillismos* and the emergence of new middle-class groups into party politics and the seats of power. Where such oligarchies have in the past succeeded in exercising important modernizing functions, they still provide the core of those conservatives who hold modern attitudes.

The most developed countries are ruled either by *tutelary, quasi-national governments* based on a limited social nation embracing only the upper and middle classes, or else they combine the tutelary function with *syndicalism* in the specific effort to industrialize without modernizing public life in the secular mold. Chile, Uruguay, and Costa Rica are evident cases of as yet unfinished nation-building. Each has an area of interclass identification, loyalty, and freedom which thus far has permitted it to weather enormous crises of development— including stagnation—without fatal institutional rupture. Argentina, on the other hand, has spent the last thirty-five years in continued attempts to organize a local variant of a corporativist syndicalism in order to avoid the full price of modern organization. The resultant disaster is the clearest demonstration as yet in Latin America that a high level of economic development is no guarantee of automatic adjustments in the social and political realms. Mexico, for its part, may very well be at the point of a decisive national decision, teetering between a further determined advance into greater freedom for all within an extended national rubric, or an extension of the philosophy of its present corporate party structure in a dangerous attempt to maintain the present distribution of power and privilege.

The common journalistic complaint that all members of the Latin American élite are selfishly blind to the requirements of growth is untrue; they may know no more than we what are the procedures of non-violent modernization, but there are important élite groups of modern mentality in all Latin American countries engaged in an almost desperate search for solutions and ideas. But élites, of course, are not everywhere the only lonely hosts of a few marginal moderns. In the progression from the less developed to the more developed among Latin American countries, modern attitudes sweep down the social scale from the top to—in certain cases—the very bottom of the urban heap. If internal migration patterns are any clue, then in addition certain at least partially modern values are also held by rural groups, as has been clearly seen in Argentina and Uruguay, and is probably increasingly the case in given regions of Chile, Brazil, Colombia, Venezuela, and Mexico. The larger, more mature Latin American countries are all possessed of developed national sectors of great size and importance. But they have not won decisively their battle against traditional man anywhere; they have been offered no truly viable ideologies of modern development outside the Marxist persuasions; they have been too often led to think that their desire for freedom is to be used only as a device of the Cold War polemic and not as a tool vital for development itself; and they have by no means been given the unequivocal support of the international developed community. Dubious of their own premises, fighting for their survival, and feeling neglected, if not abandoned, by the Western democracies, many modern persons in Latin America have become apolitical, others seek refuge in espousing a "government of technicians," and still others, in their desperation, have become Marxist revolutionaries.

The example of Cuba provides the last item in the typology of authoritarianism: *the modern national, Socialist dictatorship,* whose advent has put the challenge of development to the West in its brightest, most uncompromising light. Spawned of a negligent father and a faithless mother, the Castro regime has turned to the rival school of development for its inspiration. There can be no denying that the present Cuban government has given a kind of freedom to some Cubans: it has provided access to the national society to the farm laborer, forged a national ideology for the urban dweller, and indeed, it has created a national society—the first relatively modern state in all of Latin America. The cost in terms of liberty, and thus in terms of the chances for continued crisis-free development, have been enormous. The liquidation of a large part of the professional middle class, economic rigidity, and Cuba's international captivity, added to the personalism of its leadership, all signal the certainty of profound difficulties. But let us be aware that these troubles are essentially of a modern and not a traditional nature. They concern rebuilding middle social groups, not opening the middle. The *fidelistas* also will suffer crises of succession within the context of a polity of truly national and not merely class responsibilities, so that their civil troubles will always be potentially bloodier than those of their less socially integrated neighbors. The consequences of economic maladroitness by the government will be more widespread than under previous administrations, and there will also be more room for error in a diversified economy whose agricultural sector is strongly influenced by literate farmers and not illiterate *guajiros*. Internal subversion will be much more bitter but more national in goals and thus less liable to influence from abroad than before. The Cubans, too, will have to learn the full price of the goods upon which they have made a down payment, and will either perish as an aborted revolution or will themselves prove once again that the strait jacket of a narrow determinism is incompatible with the fully human developmental experience.

It is rational, dignified, free human beings whose social works ultimately have survived history. Utterly convinced universalistic ideologues have merely written the bloody pages of history.

The United States is accepting its responsibility as a member of the democratic, developed community through its attempts to assist in a modernization process which will not exact the same human cost as the revolutionary Marxist solution. In this task it will not lack for persons in Latin America who would like to be allies; in turn, the United States must learn who its colleagues in spirit really are, how to recognize them, where they exist, and what it is they must be offered so they can best assist themselves.

THE BASIC POLICY COMMITMENT

I have been pleading the viewpoint that development is a total social phenomenon. The heavy accent on the factors of freedom and dictatorship is called for because these words have come to be used in hortatory and exhortative senses, while the conviction of action has flowed almost entirely through economic channels. But if the developmental process is truly a single package, then lopsided assistance may well be self-defeating, for there must be a reasonable degree of coherence among the components of the universal change of social life that spells modernization.

It is the utter completeness of the transformation to modern life which policy makers both in the United States and Latin America have been unable to comprehend. We hear much talk of social revolutions, both pacific and violent, but little or no spelling out of the profound changes in individuals and in societies which such revolutions involve. The economic part of the affair is the easiest with which to grapple: money can be somewhat neutralized, and material things can be supplied by foreign lands without bringing substantive questions of social and political organization immediately to the fore. But the development of impersonal social institutions, new classes, supraclass identifications, the rule of law, and the style of freedom inevitably involve social values and ideologies, and thus demand the most profound of policy decisions. Nevertheless, even when involved in this most intestinal turmoil, the developing lands need not stand alone. The Western world can assist, in the first instance, by providing a social-science lesson, the fruit of discovering more about its own growth processes to learn exactly what part freedom and social openness have played in general growth. If we are to be taken as honest in our protestations that libertarian development is not only more efficient than authoritarian development, but is indeed what the development process in itself is all about, then we must recognize that the practice *is* the promise, the promise determinant of the practice. This knowledge must impregnate our own assistance policies, and the reasoning must be made clear to all policy planners in recipient or petitioning nations. Let there be an end to a reliance on merely "technical planning" as a voodoo doll simulacrum of the entire metamorphosis.

When we know what it is we seek, we shall then know when we find it. I suspect we shall then discover many more allies than we had thought possible. We will know when compromises have to be made —and will thus recognize a compromise for what it is, instead of touting the best of the bad as the best of the best in our anxiety to defend policies based on vulgar economic guesswork and the cheap determinism which we substitute for hard thought in attempting to predict the outcome of economic assistance. By discarding patently false views of the automatic nature of social change, we should gain the ability to weigh the possible short-run advantages of a given economic policy against the possible political and social long-range disadvantages, for example, and take a decision which need not be defended by recourse to romanticism or easily satisfied "hard-boiled practicality." As an immediate consequence, we also will have the concepts needed to analyze in total context the so-called orthodoxies of the International Monetary Fund, the Export-Import Bank, and the International Bank, as well as the "softness" of the Inter-American Bank. And we shall know better when a dictatorship is more or less archaic, and to what extent moneys spent in given authoritarianisms will serve only the purpose of retarding development, for indeed there are situations in which capital investments can fortify social and political sectors which, thus bolstered, will more strongly inhibit further economic or any other kind of advance.

The United States must also decide that in choosing allies among the modernizers in Latin America, it also makes enemies among the traditionalists. The lowest level of interventionism—and the most effective, paradoxically—resides in giving all aid possible to the modern social sectors in the several Latin American republics, aside from those groups so fundamentally opposed ideologically to the Western democracies that there is no hope of rapport. The fortification of the democratic modernizing groups by pointed assistance can help tip the domestic political scales in their direction, saving the United States from its present confusion of the levels and types of assistance which should be offered. Moneys spent on the kind of education, for instance, which will attract persons of a modern mentality can be confidently expected to assist the general move toward development. Moneys spent in bettering or certifying the positions of students of a traditional cast will only make more robust the anti-developmental sectors. To take another example, extractive industries often have little multiplier effect and fortify tradition; modern industrial plants and commercial undertakings usually have great multiplier effect and give economic, political, and social power to individuals in the modern camp. This selective view of assistance also changes the nature of the problem of whether or not to be gentle with the harsher dictatorships: if help can be extended to the attitudinally developed in such countries, then it should be done. Otherwise assistance merely certifies non-development or invites unpredictable revolution.

To continue without such criteria in Latin America is to be most impractical. Tax funds are dissipated, hopes expended, and eventual crises deepened by loans and grants which serve only to make the anachronistic survive a little longer. The closer Latin American dictatorships manage to get to the twentieth century in their economic structures without introducing political democracy, the more likely that the attempt to even out the polity will be accomplished under the banner of a neo-Marxist or a Falangist populism.

The measure of the development of the developed world will be taken by whether or not it is able to use its reason, power, and freedom to write new "laws" of historical change for the developing lands. If riches, military might, great universities, and the ideologies of freedom evolved in the West are not employed to ease the throes of the growth of others, then we are refusing to pay the price of our inheritance. "The privilege and complicating duty of intellectual integrity, self-criticism, and generalized disinterestedness" are indeed the modern man's burden.

CONCLUSIONS

17

SOCIAL DEVELOPMENT AS

REVOLUTION

That all of Latin America is either going through profound change or preparing for it is obvious. Of course the accompanying events must attack the comfortable and challenge the accustomed. To oppose change, however, simply because it is inherently uncomfortable for some or favor it merely because it satisfies a yen for excitement is something less than rational. In order to reach those reasoned judgments necessary to our making a choice, we need first to spell out the nature of the changes, their possible range, and their likely costs. And in addition, we must query ourselves as to whether conscious control of social development is desirable and to what extent it is possible toward the ends of mitigating costs and maximizing benefits. Only when the facts of the matter and the possibilities inherent therein are known can the choices of personal taste be made with reason and foresight.

Contemporary modernization. The preceding chapters have sought to indicate where the various Latin American countries find themselves in their social development and to indicate the degree of complexity and sophistication to be found in such sectors as the economy, the university, the military, and even in some elements of daily life. Although the range of situations is wide, we are not dealing with wholly feudal or traditional societies of completely isolated, illiterate populations insensitive to the pressures of the world. On the contrary, there are in all the Latin American republics sufficient cosmopolitan persons, economic complexity, and political awareness to make every one of them in one or another degree susceptible to the effects of new technologies, consumption desires, and ideologies. If the range goes from Argentina, Brazil, Chile, Mexico, and Venezuela (which have already experienced or are attempting what W. W. Rostow calls "economic takeoff" [1]) to Honduras, Ecuador, Guatemala, and Paraguay with their large non-national populations, still the spread is not so wide as to include any land composed entirely of traditionalist groups.

In consequence the media of mass communications everywhere have some impact, and in some countries a very great influence indeed. Because functional literacy is not essential to an understanding of the message of radio, television, and jukebox, great areas of Latin America are developing desires and attitudes appropriate to highly developed (or what some commentators have perhaps facetiously called "overde-veloped") countries. These aspirations sometimes can grow even in the absence of any high degree of national integration, industrialization, or complexity of class structure. In order to satisfy the ideological and consumption goals of fully developed countries, must Latin America proceed to go painfully through all the "standard" stages of growth—must it crawl slowly out of feudalism to early capitalism and then on to whatever humane adjustments the industrial world has been making in the last half-century?

The Western countries have posited no direct answer to this question. The only implicit reply comes from the area of business and economic endeavor, in which the machinery and techniques transferred to Latin America often have been of the most advanced. No responsible person involved has ever proposed that exported plant and "know-how" should be based on the designs and practices of 1870 so that the importing countries could have the opportunity to develop small businesses and industries instead of jumping directly into what more often than not amounts to monopoly. Yet many of the same businessmen and economists (both Latin American and North American) subscribe to the notion that "Latin America is a hundred years behind the United States." Is it true that Latin America is directly "behind" the United States, or rather following a different road? Whether the destination is the same we are not for the moment discussing, but certainly the route taken must in any event be different. If this statement is self-evidently true for the economic happenings to which so much attention is paid, may it not also be true for other social events?

Another element simply not taken into account in studies of development has to do with the very speed of the changes involved. When a country moves in less than half a decade from being, for instance, a very minor steel producer to one possessing an export steel industry, is

[1] *The Stages of Economic Growth: A Non-Communist Manifesto*, Cambridge: University Press, 1960, Ch. 4, especially pp. 43–44.

there a substantive difference between such a happening and the same development spread over a fifty-year period? Although the very long-term result may be the same, chronological telescoping must perforce result in a process of adjustment and accommodation dissimilar from that of the relatively slow rearrangements within Western Europe, the United States, and the Commonwealth countries. The habits and values of traditional society must be commingled in the individual with the demands of the new occupational and income situations to which he submits himself. And the society itself must learn to live with a dangerous disharmony between the old and the new, at least for a time. The pattern of politics, then, must adjust itself to the clash between archaic and modern social structures, to the conflict between what can be produced and what the populace wishes to consume, and to the gap between what extant ideology and administrative technique can organize and what is expected of government. Politics within this setting cannot have the tranquillity and time for adjustment seen in the Great Britain of the last century. The phenomenon will respond in part to the rules of standard theory, but in other part demands new conceptions.

Modernization in the contemporary underdeveloped world is not then a mere repetition of European experience, not only because of the uniqueness of each cultural area involved, but also specifically because of the influence of (1) the present content of the ideologies of the industrialized nations; (2) the high level of technology immediately available; (3) the homogenizing effects of mass communications; and (4) the socially twisting results of high-velocity stimulus. This difference in process, however, is not matched by a parallel divergence in what the results must be, for to modernize means essentially the same thing everywhere in terms of at least certain basic characteristics. These common earmarks of modernism are obvious: industrial cities, high literacy rates, impersonalism, a complication of occupational structure, receptivity to the organs of mass communications, popular politics, a pull toward xenophobia, widespread desires for upward social mobility, "facelessness," and so on through the familiar list. Many suggestions for the theoretical organization of these characteristics are available for already complex societies, but few are at hand for the peoples in transition toward modernism except for some rather crude indices of economic and demographic data.

A recent social psychological study argues that a "characterological transformation" must accompany modernism, a change called "psychic mobility, with empathy as its mechanism."

We are interested in empathy as the inner mechanism which enables newly mobile persons to *operate efficiently* in a changing world. Empathy, to simplify the matter, is the capacity to see oneself in the other fellow's situation. This is an indispensable skill for people moving out of traditional settings . . .

. . . high empathic capacity is the predominant personal style only in modern society, which is distinctly industrial, urban, literate and *participant* . . .[2]

Modern society thus demands a very special identification of the individual with other individuals and with the society. Such an organizing concept at the level of a social value is needed if we are to order sensibly other institutional, individual, class, and group manifestations. Perhaps it is my disciplinary bias intruding itself, but I prefer to talk of Lerner's "empathy" as a subdivision of political science's "nationalism." Granted that nationalism is in common use an abused and bloated concept, there remains a core of very hard reality indeed to the notion.[3]

If we divorce the idea of "nationality" from nationalism in order to remove from our consideration simple patriotism, juridical notions of sovereignty, citizenship, and so forth, we make the concept somewhat more manageable. Then if we proceed to divide the remaining idea into two grand parts—nationalism as a loyalty value first, and then nationalism as it is expressed in ideology—we are left with a viable idea which includes a portion of Lerner's empathy and at the same time relates a "feeling" of loyalty to the power structure of government.

Modernism implies, then, the necessity for an ordering of loyalty concerning social institutions and individuals: it makes mandatory the existence of an institution supreme in the mediating of those conflicts which threaten the continuity of the interdependent condition of man in modern society. Because modernism depends on a high degree of specialization, the individual needs a guarantee against crisis which may undermine what he has been taught is fundamental to the good life itself.

National consciousness has been the public organizing idea *sine qua non* of modernism. One might as well try to raise living standards through industrialization and the training of specialists without employing the loyalty wrapped up in nationalism as to try to raise sheep without a ram. A recognition of the functional importance of nationalism is basic to effective dealings with the developing countries. Attempts to arrest its growth amount to a retardation of the process of social development, but how to channel the ideologies of nationalism into healthful and democratic avenues is quite a different matter. All

[2] Daniel Lerner, *The Passing of Traditional Society,* Glencoe: The Free Press, 1958, pp. 49–50.
[3] See Chapter 2 for a much fuller discussion of nationalism. The two preceding chapters apply the concept in more detail.

too often in Latin America ideology has become self-defeating, bogged down in xenophobia, exclusivism, inordinately romantic narcissism, and blind anti-imperialism. Unfortunately the ideological rigidity of the United States has also had something to do with fostering antagonism and hindering the very development both sides presumably desire.

Nationalistic Ideologies and the United States. The differing world views and short-run interests of the United States and Latin America have impeded cooperation and encouraged some of the more negativistic aspects of nationalism. The United States is a Protestant culture; Latin America is a Catholic culture. The United States speaks vociferously of free enterprise and practices a mixed economy; Latin America is not particularly attached ideologically to free-enterprise capitalism but yet affords many striking examples of unbridled profit making and monopoly, both on the land and in the city. The United States views the Cold War as a threat to its very survival; Latin America by and large does not feel deeply involved even yet in matters affecting Soviet Russia but does take internal Communist movements seriously indeed. The United States is emerging into a cautious and hesitant internationalism; Latin America is moving toward national integration and at the same time delicately playing with a few international economic arrangements without a full understanding of their implications. This list could be extended almost indefinitely.

Both sides also manage profoundly to misunderstand each other. As has often been noted, Americans tend to blur all of Latin America into one country, a composite of Mexico and a banana republic; Latin Americans still tend to see a frenetic, garish, cheap combination of Los Angeles, Miami Beach, and New York. Almost all Americans think Latin America is a boiling barrel of self-seeking revolutionaries; "progressive" Latin Americans think the United States has only bland, wishy-washy, self-interested, and incompetent political leaders. Certainly most North Americans think there is no middle class in Latin America, that everybody is either enormously wealthy or miserably poor; almost all Latin Americans continue to think of almost all Americans as being well-to-do. This list of stereotypes (which is also stereotyped in the mere telling, of course) could also go on and on.

The point I have been trying to make is that there are certain areas in which agreement is difficult of realization. The areas of common understanding will have to include concepts of a much more basic nature than those we have been writing of. Perhaps it is at the level of a common attachment to freedom that consonance can be found. If this most affirmative of commitments cannot be strengthened in terms of specific measures, then the present more negative alliance based on antagonism toward a mutual enemy will have to do. The latter alternative is a weak one, of course, for it offers a constant temptation to those political leaders who hate the United States more than they may fear a more distant symbol of menace. The danger of more *fidelismos* and Latin *nasserismos* is by no means past.

The all too obvious difficulty with the suggestion that common ground must be sought in massive objectives and not in narrower interest and procedural terms is that usually the former is defined in terms of the latter. That is, freedom is often explained as freedom to invest money, to make a profit, to be free of governmental restraint, and to sell whatever the market will bear. The identification of freedom solely with a particular manner of making a living hopelessly confuses the issues. What is really meant is usually merely free rein to individual desire to make a profit instead of a total and self-reinforcing political and economic system of liberty. Whether for good or ill, private economic activities in the United States are of course hedged in by governmental regulation and the activities of party and pressure groups. Such restraint cannot be imposed by most Latin American countries for a great variety of reasons: parties and governments are usually technically inept and often corrupt; trade unions are more often than not weak and ineffectual, or else arms of the government, and thus cannot exercise an independent power; and the general economic situation can allow little opportunity for real competition. If most of Latin America is still so socially underdeveloped that democratic forms cannot be as yet filled with democratic substance, then it cannot be expected either that any high level of economic sophistication exists. Private *ownership* thus does not bear the same relationship to private *enterprise* in Latin America as it does in the United States.

In answer to attacks by Latin American nationalists and protectionists, American businessmen often privately complain, "But all we wanna do is make a buck." The ineffectiveness of this reply is clear enough. But what the not directly participating American citizen suffering, say, the Cuban defeat to American prestige has a right to know is whether there is any connection between "just making a buck" and what we are now witnessing in the Caribbean. When the lines of the politics of national revolution and Communism came close in Guatemala and then blew apart in revolution, the United States viewed the collapse of the Arbenz government with understandable satisfaction, murmured a few polite words, and then forgot about the entire episode. Now that the menace to national security has recurred in much more virulent form even closer to our borders, most of us continue to refrain from asking to what degree American behavior may have contributed to the debacle.

The answer does not lie in a simple diatribe against American Business, which invariably evokes a defense listing the hospitals, schools, and churches which have been built by kind employers. The accusation and the riposte are both superficial. One of the fundamental facts is that Cuba (which I am discussing here merely as a surrogate for all of Latin America) is relatively underdeveloped and the United States is mightily developed—or, to put it in more operational terms, Cuba is weak and the United States is strong. Always between the weak and the strong an exploitative relationship grows up, and not entirely in one direction. The strong tends to exploit the weak materially, and the weak tends to exploit the strong emotionally, playing on pity and whatever degree of civilization may be restraining the hand of the strong. But in relations among nations the very devices used to exploit the weak tend also to make him stronger, and often the weak eventually grows up to power, hating his exploiter because he has given up so much to him on the one hand and owes him so much on the other. The story is now such an old one: Mexico, Iran, Egypt, China, Indonesia, Cuba, the Congo, and long before the United States itself.

Let us be brave enough not to quail before the word "exploit." Of course the United States exploits Latin America in the sense that our market does not pay prices for Latin American products sufficient to permit the producers to live at the level of Americans in similar occupations. Whether we *should* pay more is a matter of ethics; that we do *not* pay more is a matter of relative power in the market place. As the power of the Latin American producer rises indubitably so also will the price of coffee, for example, at least until such time as consumer resistance grows intense enough to force the introduction of machinery. In any case, our desire for sugar and coffee and oil and bananas as cheaply as they can be bought causes the introduction into Latin American countries of certain producing mechanisms which cannot be kept isolated from the rest of society. The dollars returned to Cuba for sugar—even with all the leakage for luxury and corruption subtracted—helped create modern cities which became populated with persons who wanted a market in their own national hinterland. The city which sugar helped create could not continue to grow with the internal market which sugar afforded. And all the while the country next door continued to bombard Cuba with advertising, tourists, university educations, and talk of freedom and progress. Seasonal sugar workers and striving middle-class nationalists and Havana and the United States mix up into a necessary explosion.

To have brought the mixture into being may be viewed simply as a historical accident. To have done nothing to damp the effect of the blowup is most inept political leadership. But not even to recognize the part one has played is more than ignorant—it is morally reprehensible, because of the lives involved. It is also self-destructive and anti-democratic, for our national strength and thus the freedom the United States demonstrates by its domestic polity are also at stake.

Remember that the thesis leading to the previous discussion was that "private ownership does not bear the same relationship to private enterprise in Latin America as it does in the United States." The reason, then, is to be found not only in weak governments, little competition, and cheap and disorganized labor, but also in that any large-scale foreign investment or any technologically advanced undertaking is necessarily a revolutionary—not evolutionary—element when introduced into pre-industrial lands. Can we really continue to afford highly rational economic procedures only to wallow in romanticism and wishful thinking about their impact? Those who argue that we can are not really thinking in *laissez-faire* terms but rather in the style of an ingenuous economic determinism.

The United States government, too, by means of its technical assistance programs, student and professional exchanges, inter-university agreements, book translations, and information services is performing a revolutionary function. All the cultural stimuli constantly pouring out of the United States also cause restiveness. These so oft-repeated statements are usually advanced to demonstrate that it is the United States, not the Soviet Union or Red China, which is really the major catalyzing agent for social change in Latin America and elsewhere. Polemics aside, and granted that the argument has much validity, is it logical to help prod countries into revolution by both witting and uncontrollable actions and then cross our fingers and hope that they will indulge in revolutions we will like?

We cannot lightly assume that the imposition of ideological purity in economic affairs will automatically bring desired political dividends. The opposite is all too often the case, for economic development often creates new power groups which hinder the growth of democratic institutions. For this reason the United States does not look like a democratic country to many Latin Americans, and especially to young ones. Where American democratic influence seems to be felt is below the level of ideology and economic assistance and rather in deeply felt cultural stimuli, historical past, confrontation with Soviet Russia, and general identification with the West. Our general stance serves to aid the growth of democracy in Latin America; our specific policies often retard it.

The political aspects of economic development are usually neglected by Western countries; nothing is given greater practical importance by the East. Some sophistication in this area is an utter necessity if the growth of a true nation-state system in Latin America is to be accomplished with the requisite speed and respect for human life and dignity. A few political propositions may be advanced which might be of some limited help:

1. The governments of economically retarded countries cannot be judged on the basis of whether or not they are authoritarian, but rather in accordance with certain criteria concerning the preparation of the groundwork for eventually open political systems. Their actions, then, including those involved in development, may be non-democratic for the non-national sectors of their societies, but not necessarily anti-democratic. There is no escape from the responsibility for tutelary government in underdeveloped areas—no escape for the domestic governments concerned or those foreign governments which presume to assist toward growth.

2. Speed is an essential, as pointed out earlier, because technology prods from one side and aspirations from the other. Fitful developmental policies are not only wasteful but invite to solutions of violence and force.

3. Private enterprise when operating within a system in which the checks and balances of government and other competing groups are impossible simply cannot be trusted to be moderate, unselfish, and far-seeing. To ask an angelic role of American direct investors abroad without control is not only to plead for the impossible but is also an unwarranted cession of the making of American foreign policy.

4. The Latin American countries have developed eclectically many different variations of attitude toward the proper distribution of private and governmental economic functions, but all are more or less dedicated to mixed economic notions, convinced of the equity of social-security systems and so forth. This complication of structure and desire to spread income aid in softening the blows of modernization. Democracy is better served by supporting such ideas than by viewing such devices with well-bred disdain.

5. The Western countries (not only the United States) can prevent political strain leading to harsh government by contributing substantially greater amounts of capital than in the past, at the same time insisting on rationalizing arrangements such as common-market agreements and customs unions, a planned order of priorities for governmental investments and guarantees of private sector investments, massive assistance to education, and encouragement of the growth of interest groups and of responsible trade-union movements.

6. Moderate ideologies of national identification can be encouraged to prevent insofar as possible extremist outbursts of pent-up frustration.

7. The ultimate measure of the worth of a Latin American government should not be whether or not it is a paradise for foreign capital,

but rather whether it is becoming always a firmer and more active member of a free international community. The criteria, in short, should be primarily political and only secondarily economic—instead of a shortsighted reverse.

What would help Latin America in non-material manners perhaps more than anything else would be the ability to draw upon fresh hope and elastic ideology from the West. This problem touches upon the very heart of the political process in the United States and Western Europe, however, as is demonstrated by the growing preoccupation with the question of orientation and objectives in the United States.

Let us continue to recognize that even in Catholic Latin America the opposition from the East is not an easy one. To many Latin American eyes there is joy and thrill in the revolutions of the Communist world and the promise of social involvement and grand goals always tasty to the new nationalist. It is the task of the West to demonstrate that growing freedoms and growing economies are not only compatible but mutually reinforcing, a demonstration made difficult in the degree to which we continue to insist on an ideological purity denying our own experience and our own pragmatism. A surer and deeper self-knowledge and a greater faithfulness to libertarian principle will assist us to more wholesome foreign relations.

> Times of crisis not only try man's soul but also challenge his accustomed ideas and interests. No wonder that it is exactly at these break-lines of time and of space that the social sciences flourish and the quest for comparison becomes the natural vista of seeking man.

> "To know thyself, compare thyself to others." The comparative approach is, above all, an eye-opener to a people's self-recognition and to its taking a stand. It is not accidental that great civilizations, like the Renaissance, were developed at the crossroads of mankind and articulated by the meeting of contrasting systems. This encounter alone made an awakening Europe fully aware of her own character and qualities.

> We are again living in such a period of open frontiers which will force us to recognize the values and concepts we live by and to test them anew against their challenge from abroad . . .[4]

We cheapen ourselves by insisting on justifying our actions in terms of narrow self-interest, by arguing that a helping hand to others should be extended only in expectation of immediate return. But in a larger sense the classical doctrine that we all rise or fall together is becoming every day more axiomatic. If we are to go up or down, to new Renaissance or to thundering Twilight of the Gods, let us at least comfort ourselves by knowing why and with whom.

[4] Sigmund Neumann, "The Comparative Study of Politics," *Comparative Studies in Society and History*, Vol. I, No. 2, January, 1959, p. 105.

INDEX

agrarian reform, in Guatemala, 69, 70
agriculture, in Cuba, 268–69
Alexander, Robert, 28
Alliance for Progress, 10–11, 29, 120, 233; Dominican revolt and, 147; Cuban policy and, 238–43
Alsogaray, Alvaro C., 103
Anti-Communist Unification party (Guatemala), 71
Aramburu, Pedro E., 87, 102, 120, 201n.
Arbenz Guzmán, Jacobo, 61, 62; overthrow of, 66–67, 230, 280; Indians and, 69; corruption, 76; opposition to, 80
Arévalo, Juan José, 62, 69, 79; corruption, 76
Argentina: class structure, 6, 14–15; politics, 6, 86–90, 101–104; regionalism, 20; riots, 22; army, 23, 120, 193–227; political parties, 26–27; history, 47; under Perón, 79; economic development, 83–86; Peronism, 90–101; education, 109, 110, 112–17; fascism, 111; students, 124; Uruguay and, 129; compared with Guatemala, 169–72; upper class, 182–90; meat and wheat, 189; reaction to Castro, 232–33, 236; neutralism, 242; oligarchy, 267–68
Ariel, 132–40
Armour & Co., 130, 131
army: role in revolutions, 19–20; in politics, 22–23, 159; in Argentina, 79, 83–84, 86–88, 91–92, 98–100, 120, 193–227; in Guatemala, 79; in Cuba, 234. *See also caciques; caudillos*
asylum, right of, 19, 230
authoritarianism: in Argentina, 85; Peronism as, 103–104; appeal of, 243; underdevelopment and, 257–59, 265–69. *See also* totalitarianism

Batista, Fulgencio, 20, 51, 266; students and, 124

Batlle y Ordóñez, José, 25
Belgrano, Manuel, 197–98n.
Berle, Adolf A., 158, 228, 253
Blancos (Uruguay), 26, 129
bogotazo, 21
Bolívar, Simón, 83, 213n., 228
Bolivia: tin, 189; reaction to Castro, 232, 236; social structure, 247
Brazil: class structure, 15; regionalism, 20; army, 22; political parties, 27; fascism, 92; education, 122–23; nationalism, 141; coffee, 189; Argentina and, 210n., 215n.; reaction to Castro, 232–33; neutralism, 241–42; income, 244; modernity, 246
Brazil, Federal Technical University of, 123
Brazil, University of, 123
British Honduras, 43
Buenos Aires, 97, 99; religious education, 122; students, 124; freedom, 165–68
Buenos Aires, National University of, 112
Buenos Aires, University of, 114–17; student federation (FUBA), 114, 117
Bunster, Alvaro, 146, 149

caciques, 12, 20, 266
Camelot project, 143–50, 153–55, 159–60
Campo de Mayo, 217–18
Capdevila, General, 222
Cárdenas, Lázaro, 64
Caribbean reaction to Castro, 232
Caseros, battle of, 200, 225
Castillo Armas, Carlos, 61–82
Castro, Fidel: students and, 124; influence of, 228–56
Castroism: in Argentina, 90n.; receptivity to, 243–56
Catholic Church, 31–32; in Guatemala, 68–69; in Argentina, 89, 203; universities, 117, 125, 149

285